Red Scotland!

To my grandfathers
William Kenefick and William O'Rourke
my grandchildren
Allie-Jo and Millar
and my wife
Pauline

Red Scotland!

The Rise and Fall of the Radical Left, c. 1872 to 1932

William Kenefick

Edinburgh University Press

Edinburgh University Press Ltd
22 George Square, Edinburgh

Typeset in 10.5/13 Sabon
by Servis Filmsetting Ltd, Manchester, and
printed and bound in Great Britain by
Biddles Ltd, King's Lynn, Norfolk

A CIP record for this book is available from the British Library

ISBN 978 0 7486 2517 8 (hardback)
ISBN 978 0 7486 2518 5 (paperback)

Contents

Acknowledgements

This book was written while I was on sabbatical leave funded by the Arts and Humanities Research Council (AHRC), and I would like to acknowledge their role in this publication. I would also like to thank Ian Hutchison, who as my academic referee played a crucial role in securing the AHRC Sabbatical Leave Award, and Hamish Fraser and Callum Brown for reading and evaluating significant sections of this book. Other colleagues and friends have provided help and assistance and include Helen Carmichael, Paul Dukes, Murray Frame, Neville Kirk, Arthur McIvor, Chalres McKean, Alan MacDonald, the late Neil Rafeek, Sara Reid, Chris Storrs and Murray Watson. I would like to thank the former members of the now sadly defunct Dundee Labour History Group, and in particular Michael Allardice, Andrew Brown, David McRae, and the late Neil Glen. I would like to acknowledge the help and patient assistance of John Davey, Roda Morrison and latterly Esmé Watson and Eddie Clark at Edinburgh University Press and copy editor Sarah Burnett. As ever the usual caveat and disclaimer apply, for although I was happy to draw on their advice and guidance they are in no way responsible for the analysis contained in this book.

Much of what appears in this book is based on original research largely supported and funded by grant awards from the Carnegie Trust for the Universities of Scotland; augmented by the History Research Fund, University of Dundee – for which I thank Research Committee. The Carnegie Trust funded a research trip to Moscow, which unearthed sources that considered the impact of the Russian Revolution in Scotland, and materials relating to William Leslie (one of Scotland's less well-known revolutionaries) and his view of communism and political developments in the city of Aberdeen. The Carnegie Trust also helped fund research trips to study the role of Scots and the South African Trade-Union and Labour Movement before 1914, and likewise, the Canadian Commission London (and Ottawa) funded research trips to study Scottish workers in Canada. This material does not figure prominently in this book, but it will form the next significant phase of this research. Indeed, some of the more important aspects of Scottish political radicalism are more clearly revealed in the context of how well radical ideas were received by the Imperial working class abroad, and from that perspective this material has already informed elements of this study of the radical left in Scotland. I would also like to thank Alan McKinlay for bringing to my attention an important 'life history' source on William McKie, held in the Nat Ganley Collection, Archive of Labor and Urban Affairs, Wayne State University, Detroit. Like William Leslie, William McKie is largely unknown in Scotland, yet for almost thirty-five years he was an important and leading figure in the Edinburgh trade union and socialist movement. I would also like to thank Ian Donnachire for materials he entrusted to me relating to the Independent Labour Party.

I would also thank staff involved with Historic Collections, University of Aberdeen; Ayrshire Local History, Ardrossan; Local History Centre, Central Library, Dundee; National Library, Edinburgh; the National Archives, Edinburgh; Moray Local Heritage Centre, Elgin; Special Collections, the Gallagher Memorial Library Caledonian University Archive, Glasgow; Mitchell Library, Glasgow; Brody Collection, in Special Collections, Glasgow University Library; the British Library Newspapers, Colindale, London; and the Russian Centre for the Preservation and Study of Documents of Recent History, Moscow, Russia.

Last, but not least, I would like to acknowledge the role of family and friends. They have sat on many occasions over the last year (often on the other end of the phone) listening to me recount the ups and downs of working on the book, and none more so than my daughters Susan and Alison and my dear wife Pauline. Pauline has the patience of a saint and without her love and support, notwithstanding her exceptional endurance and stamina, this book might never have been finished.

Tables

Abbreviations

ASE	Amalgamated Society of Engineers
ASLEF	Associated Society of Locomotive Engineers and Firemen
ASRS	Amalgamated Society of Railway Servants
BofT	Board of Trade
BSP	British Socialist Party
CPGB	Communist Party of Great Britain
CWC	Clyde Workers' Committee
FCL	Fife Communist League
FWC	Forth Workers' Committee
GHLU	Glasgow Harbour Labourers' Union
GLHW	Glasgow Labour History Workshop
GRWU	General Railway Workers' Union
ILP	Independent Labour Party
IWW	Industrial Workers of the World
LRC	Labour Representation Committee
MRC	Miners' Reform Committee
NASFU	National Amalgamated Sailors' and Firemen's Union
NCF	No-Conscription Fellowship
NSFU	National Sailors and Firemen's Union
NSHMA	North Scottish Horse and Motormen's Association
NTWF	National Transport Workers' Federation
NUDL	National Union of Dock Labourers
NUR	National Union of Railwaymen
NUS	National Union of Seamen
NUWM	National Unemployed Workers' Movement
PSS	Proletariat Sunday School
SDF	Social Democratic Federation
SDP	Social Democratic Party (1908 – formerly SDF)
SHMA	Scottish Horse and Motormen's Association
SL	Socialist League
SLC	Scottish Labour College
SLLL	Scottish Land and Labour League

SLP	Scottish Labour Party (1888–94)
SLP	Socialist Labour Party (1903–19)
SPF	Socialist Prohibition Fellowship
SPP	Scottish Prohibitionist Party
SRU	Scottish Railwaymen's Union
SSF	Scottish Socialist Federation
SSS	Socialist Sunday School
STGWU	Scottish Transport and General Workers Union
STUC	Scottish Trades Union Congress
SUDL	Scottish Union of Dock Labourers
TGWU	Transport and General Workers' Union
TUC	Trades Union Congress
WEA	Workers' Educational Association
YCL	Young Communist League

Introduction

This book explores the rise of the radical left in Scotland from the first tentative steps towards industrial political action during the 1870s, through its relative decline at the time of the Independent Labour Party's disaffiliation from the Labour Party in July 1932. As we journey through these turbulent and rapidly changing times we can observe how Scottish artisans responded to legal restrictions placed on trade activity in the 1870s; the impulse towards trade union formation among the unskilled during the 1880s and early 1890s, and the extent to which this was influenced by socialism; and over the closing decades of the nineteenth century the emergence of the Scottish socialist movement, the drive towards independent labour representation, the formation of the Scottish Labour Party in 1888, the Independent Labour Party (ILP) in 1893, and the enthusiasm for 'land reform' and Scottish 'home rule'. The story of the rise of industrial left radicalism, Labour politics and the impact of socialism takes us through the trials and tribulations of the first decade of the twentieth century, and the first stirrings of the 'labour unrest' in Scotland over the years 1910 to 1914.

These are some of the main topics covered over the first three chapters of this book as they relate specifically to the period c. 1872 to 1910 (the years 1910 to 1914 will also be considered briefly in this section). The main research component part of the study is presented in Chapter 2, which examines industrial radicalism and the new unionism; and Chapter 3, on political radicalism, and labour politics and socialism. But in order for the reader to come to a better understanding of the subject matter explored in each, this book opens with an introductory chapter on some important themes and issues in labour and social history in Scotland up to the years before the first World War. Chapter 1 will help familiarise the reader with the historiography in these subject areas, and the 'themes and contested issues' that emerge from the general discussion on the topics explored in greater detail over Chapters 2 and 3.

When comparing the structure of the Scottish and English trade-union movements, most labour historians would argued that the Scottish structure was by far the weaker of the two. The English trade unions, for example, were essentially industrial unions, organised along national lines, highly centralised and bureaucratic, and their membership controlled by a powerful national executive. Scottish trade unions, on the other hand, were much smaller in scale, and largely local and federal in structure and composition, and power and control rested at branch level rather than through one powerful national executive. The Scottish Trades Councils were crucial in coordinating national programmes among the rank-and-file-led Scottish trade unions, and in furthering the cause of trade unionism among the less skilled. Had the Scottish structure been similar to the English model before 1914, the unskilled may have been left largely unsupported. In attempting to explain the success of the new unionism in Scotland, it is essential that the reader is made aware of such factors and the critical role played by the Trades Councils in Scotland.

Likewise, ethnicity and sectarianism are important issues, for the social history of Scotland is intimately related to religion. The divisive issue of religion deeply affected trade-union formation in Scotland and none more so than within the ranks of the miners. If the miners could overcome such hurdles, then this would act as a blueprint for other workers to follow. Given the great number of Catholic Irish living and working in Scotland, it was crucial that they were encouraged to join trade unions, and once again the Trades Councils were central in this drive. But it was argued that the Irish were so committed to Home Rule for Ireland that they refused *en masse* to vote for any party other than the Liberals. Thus the Irish stood accused of depriving Scottish Labour of its potential working-class vote, and of holding back the development of the trade union and labour movement in Scotland before 1914. But recent research suggests that this view is no longer tenable, and given that many Scottish workers remained loyal to the Liberal Party, it would be harsh to blame all Labour's woes on the Irish. It is therefore necessary to become familiar with aspects of Irish political culture and social history, to better gauge the extent to which the Irish differed in their thoughts and actions when compared to other Scottish workers.

Chapter 1 also considers the role of the Irish and their relationship to the new unionism, in particular the influence of politics in the development of general dock unionism, and this also raises questions regarding the difference between old and new unionism in the 1880s and early 1890s. Many historians have come to view the 'militant and aggressive' form of new trade unionism as evidence of new directions in industrial relations, and because of the connections with socialism evidence of a new class consciousnesses. The theme of socialism and its impact is therefore important to any discussion of the new unionism, and this is further developed into a more wide-ranging debate concerning the relationship between socialism and the labour movement more generally before 1914.

Chapter 2 considers in much greater detail the rise of industrial radicalism and the impact of the new unionism on the Scottish trade union movement, by presenting two case studies. The first considers the dockers, carters and seamen who as a body of workers were generally looked upon as 'unskilled' and who only became organised in 1889 – the year commonly held to be the birth-date of the new unionism. The second case study looks at the Scottish railwaymen servants' union, who were formed in 1872, and were therefore an old union, but considered more skilled than the dockers, carters and seamen. By adopting a comparative approach, this chapter examines the origins and nature of the new unionism, the long-term impact of this movement, the relationship between 'old' and 'new' forms of trade unionism, and important landmarks in the history of the dockers and railwaymen through to 1910, and as a postscript briefly consider the 'labour unrest' period. This chapter will also examine the emergence of powerful and proactive employers' associations, the 'counter-attacking' role of such employers' federations, and press and public attitudes to developments taking place with the trade union and labour movement in Scotland.

The third chapter examines the early emergence of the socialist movement in Scotland, what influenced its development, the relationship with the broader trade union movement, and the growing importance of 'political action'. This chapter also incorporates a case study of the Broxburn miners' strike in 1887, in order to more closely consider how political action, in conjunction with an ongoing industrial dispute, encouraged closer ties between the trade unions and the labour movement, and how this helped the political cause of Independent Labour in Scotland. This chapter considers the formation and impact of the Scottish Labour Party between 1888 and 1894, the origin and development of Scottish socialism, and the political influence of the Marxist Social Democratic Federation and other socialist groups in Edinburgh and the east of Scotland before 1914. The final section considers the emergence of the ILP, its relations with more extremist left political parties, and the somewhat tentative advance of Scottish labour in the early twentieth century.

* * *

As dawn broke on the new century, a sharp economic downturn plunged industrial capital into crisis, and resulted in high unemployment, lower wages, deskilling and a considerable degree of poverty. From 1909 economic conditions improved, and over the next four years, and despite facing a formidable employer class, there was a rapid upsurge in unionism, and, fuelled by socialist and syndicalist ideas, a widespread and intensive period of industrial and social unrest. The First World War brought the unrest to an end, but the experience of war on the 'Home Front' played a critical role in further incubating workers' grievances, and re-awakening the pre-war spirit of rebellion that ushered in the era of Red Clydeside. The Scots responded gallantly to the call to arms, but a dedicated minority opposed the war, military and civil conscription, and in doing so established Scotland as the main centre of the anti-war movement in Britain. The events of the October Revolution in Russia in 1917 also fuelled the fires of class-consciousness, and further inspired a growing band of industrial radicals, socialist and revolutionaries to convert Glasgow into the Petrograd of the North – a revolutionary storm centre second to none!

There was a clear transformation in the Scottish working class, as more workers than ever before – and disproportionately so among the lesser skilled – flocked to join trade unions. There was a palpable and growing class-consciousness among Scottish workers and this drew them away from the politics of the Liberal Party towards the radical left in Scotland. Scottish Labour and the ILP were to be the main political beneficiaries, and between 1922 and 1929, the political map of Scotland was re-drawn. The period signalled the rise of Scottish Labour and the decline of Liberalism, and while the Communist Party had much less electoral impact, it was strong in the mining areas of Lanarkshire, Fife and Stirlingshire, and well represented in Aberdeen, Dundee, Greenock and the Vale of Leven.

The themes outlined above are focused mainly in the period c. 1910 to 1922, and the examination of the Red Scotland era begins with a second introduction to 'themes and contested issues' in labour and social history. Chapter 4 provides further guidance for the reader, and introduces him or her to a wide and varied historiography, the overlapping themes explored over Chapters 5, 6 and 7, and the main debates that emerge from the general discussion of this important period in Scottish labour and social history. The first theme considers the period of unparalleled labour unrest and widespread social discontent experienced between 1910 and 1914. Until recently it was argued that Scots were less involved in this 'display of rank-and-file temper' than workers in the industrial regions in England and Wales. Research conducted by the Glasgow Labour History Workshop (GLHW) on the unrest in the industrial west of Scotland demonstrates that this view is no longer tenable. The strike wave that convulsed the west of Scotland was at the very least comparable to other industrial regions of Britain. Chapter 5 adopts the GLHW method and approach in a comparative study of the industrial east of Scotland. Taken together, these studies demonstrate a consistently high incidence of strike activity across Scotland between 1910 and 1914. Moreover, and importantly, there was no sign of the labour unrest abating in the months before the war. Indeed, the statistical analysis suggests that the labour unrest was intensifying, as too was the influence of socialism and syndicalism.

The theme of labour unrest is also considered in George Dangerfield's classic treatise, *The Strange Death of Liberal England* (1935), and that part of his work which examines the 'labour war' in England (Britain). Dangerfield's treatment of the labour unrest is sympathetic to the needs and desires of workers, and at times highly critical of the employers and the 'vindictive manner' in which they treated their workers. Importantly, he considers the political dimension to the unrest, in particular syndicalism, and he looked forward to the industrial upheaval that was expected to take place in the autumn of 1914. But Britain went to war in August 1914, and 'the great General Strike of 1914, forestalled by some bullets at Sarajevo . . . slipped away into the limbo of unfinished argument'. Writing from the vantage of the mid-1930s, Dangerfield concluded 'that the spirit of the workers in 1914 had never since been equalled'.

The third and final theme relates to the 'Red Clyde' debate and the general impact of the First World War in Scotland. The issue of Red Clyde is a broad, wide-ranging and much contested topic of interest, and the literature on the subject is now fairly extensive. Some historians argue that the 'Red Clydeside' was essentially a myth, and its 'legendary status' came about in order to explain 'the revolution that never was', and to provide some solace to future generations on the left. Other historians assert that the Red Clyde was real, but that the radical industrial political movements that emerged during this period owed more to the organisation skills and propaganda activities of the ILP than the revolutionaries. The main concern of Chapter 6, however, is not Red Clydeside; rather, it considers the role of Scotland's war resisters and anti-militarists. While many of Scotland's war resisters were deeply involved with the troubles on the Clyde, other worked tirelessly in Dundee and Aberdeen to proclaim the anti-war message, and give the people of Scotland the opportunity to consider a critique of the war at a time when few dissenting voices were heard. International Socialism failed when war was declared in 1914, but the actions of Scottish war resisters *did* provide a stirring example for the radical left in Scotland.

Chapter 7 examines the other nerve centres of discontent that were forming beyond the west of Scotland in such places as Aberdeen, Dundee, Edinburgh and the mining districts of Fife. The example of Scottish war resisters clearly demonstrates that they were politically active across much of Scotland, and that the impact of the Russian Revolution only added an impetus and further momentum to the development of the radical left throughout the country. Dundee was to become the main centre of the anti-war activities of the No-Conscription Fellowship and the ILP during the war, and a stronghold of communism in the 1920s. There was a pacifist majority on the Aberdeen Trades Council's executive committee by 1918, and in relation to its size and population Aberdeen was considered 'more red than Glasgow' by the early 1920s. In Edinburgh, the 'Hands Off Russia' campaign united political radicals across the capital and drew the Trades Council into closer contact with left radicals. In January 1918, Willie Stewart, ILP activist and editor of the ILP propaganda organ *Forward*, argued that if a revolution were to occur in Scotland, it was as likely 'to start on Tayside or the North East Coast as on the banks of the Clyde'. Stewart clearly saw the bigger picture: it was not simply about the Clyde, it was about the country as a whole. It was about Red Scotland!

The 1920s would prove to be a difficult decade for Scottish workers, and the trade-union and labour movement in Scotland generally. The decade began in hopeful mood, but as the economy slipped into depression, and returning soldiers and sailors swelled the growing ranks of the unemployed, hope turned to desperation. Trade union membership swelled massively between 1910 and 1920, but thereafter declined rapidly. Levels of industrial militancy declined, and the failure of the Triple Industrial Alliance in April 1921, and the General Strike in May 1926, severely weakened the trade union movement and workers' confidence. The Communist Party of Great Britain was formed in 1920, and for a time they were close allies of the ILP. But from 1921 this relationship soured and continued to deteriorate thereafter. The ILP was also caught up in an ideological struggle with the Labour Party, and this came to a head after the fall of the Labour government in August 1931. Scottish Labour won half of Scotland's parliamentary seats in 1929, but the party was left with only seven seats in 1931. Chapter 8 is the closing chapter of this book, and concludes by considering the impact of the ILP's disaffiliation from the Labour Party in July 1932.

The 1930s would prove to be a difficult time for the Scottish working class, and the demise of the ILP, its brand of community-based activism, and its infectious enthusiasm for socialism, could not have come at a worse time. The ILP was to fall into political decline and, as its influence waned, grass-roots activism diminished, and membership of Scottish Labour fell away. Indeed, it presaged the decline of a radical left and socialist tradition in Scotland that could trace its roots to the closing decades of the nineteenth century.

*   *   *

The significance of this study lies not only in the original detail of some of the research, but its overall distinctiveness and some of the revisionist conclusions it makes. Existing literature on Scottish labour and indus-trial history tends to focus very heavily on the west of Scotland, thereby marginalising and often ignoring events taking place elsewhere in Scotland. This book considers the activities of the radical thinkers and industrial workers in Aberdeen, Dundee, Edinburgh and Leith, and the coalfields of Fife and the Lothians. Indeed, in the epilogue it looks beyond Scotland and briefly considers how the impact of the Scottish diaspora helped engender industrial and political radicalism abroad.

This study aims to demonstrate that these neglected areas made a much more significant contribution to the development of Scottish left radicalism than hitherto recognised. It does not neglect the important examples of Glasgow and the west of Scotland; it places them in a much broader comparative context, both temporal and geographical. Was Scotland ever Red? This is clearly a much contested historical issue, but in broadening the parameters, this study will help readers to come to a better understanding of this debate and judge for themselves the outcome of a process that was sixty years in the making.

1

Radical Scotland, c. 1872 to 1910: Themes and Issues

THE SCOTTISH TRADE UNION STRUCTURE

Before 1914 the structure of the Scottish trade union movement differed considerably from the rest of Britain. There was no development in the growth of large national trade unions in Scotland typical of the highly centralised and bureaucratic 'New Model Union' common in England and Wales by the second half of the nineteenth century. Indeed, Scots were generally suspicious of the growing impulse towards trade union amalgamation that was gathering pace from the 1890s onward if it meant joining English unions. Scottish trade unionism was much smaller scale, largely local and federal in structure and composition, and power and control was exercised at branch level rather than by one powerful national executive body. There were attempts made before and during the 1880s to forge national organisations among miners, printers and ironmoulders and to consolidate local societies along the lines of the English 'model unions' but this met with varying degrees of success.

Hamish Fraser suggests that this attachment to local self-government and federated self-rule was more or less a natural development and mirrored the regional structure of Scottish industry and economy. Workers generally defined their interests in terms of locality or region and were unwilling to surrender or abandon what was regarded as a cherished principle of trade union democracy in order to forge national industrial unions alliances with broad national agendas. The 'new unionism' of the 1880s and early 1890s saw the dockers and railwaymen develop an inter-regional and national industrial network of support. But as the early energy of the new unionism began to wane, the locally-led federal structure became firmly re-established and more or less remained in that form until after the First World War when the process of trade union amalgamation began in earnest. Despite Scottish objections to bureaucratic centralism, there was still clearly a need to form 'joint-trade' or

'joint-industrial' bodies to help co-ordinate activities locally and region-
ally across Scotland and this role was filled by the Scottish trades councils. According to Fraser:

> The formation of the trades councils in Scotland from the end of the 1850s
> was of vital importance for Scottish trade unionism. Trades councils played
> a more crucial role in Scotland than they did south of the Tweed, because of
> the structure and relative weakness of Scottish unions.

The Scottish Trades Councils achieved much in terms of making trade
unionists more politically and socially aware and in promoting trade
unionism among both skilled and unskilled workers. Federalism made
sense given the economic and industrial topography of Scotland, but
clearly Scottish trade unionism was regarded as relatively weak and
somewhat backward as a result.[1]

When comparing Scotland with other parts of Britain, trade union
density in the late nineteenth century was considerably lower that in
England and Wales. Estimates by Sydney and Beatrice Webb suggest that
there were 147,000 trade unionists in Scotland in 1892, or the equivalent
of 3.7 per cent of the total population compared to 4.9 per cent in
England and Wales. Overall trade union membership in Scotland was
thought to be 20 per cent lower than in England, and as percentage of the
employed population this was 'half that of South Wales and Humberside,
and only a quarter of the north east coast of England'.[2] Ever critical of
Scotland, the Webbs asserted that the Scots had to be 'thrashed into Trade
Unionism by severe depression or tempted into it by strikes'.[3] A recent
study by Gregor Gall (employing a comparative inter-regional quantitative historical approach) suggests an alternative view and that from the
mid 1890s (through to the 1970s), 'Workers in Scotland [had] recorded
traditionally high, although far from the highest, union density compared
to other regions of Britain'.[4] A close examination of affiliated trade union
membership to the Scottish Trades Councils shows a slow but sustained
growth in trade unionism from the mid-1890s to around 1910. Had the
Webbs paid more attention to these figures, they would most likely have
found it necessary to reappraise their measurement of union density in
Scotland at this time and their somewhat pessimistic view of Scottish attitudes to trade unionism.

THE ROLE OF THE TRADES COUNCILS

Unlike the miners, and perhaps to a limited extent the railwaymen and
port transport workers, by the end of the nineteenth century few other

groups of workers had come to recognise the value of industrial unity at national level when in dispute. Fraser suggests that 'strike movements in Scotland tended to be local movements embracing a number of local trades in a given area, rather than a national movement of one particular craft'. But he stresses that the trades councils were crucial in co-ordinating local initiatives across different locations and in time this encouraged a broader less localised perspective. The Edinburgh Trades Council was formed in 1853, and the Glasgow Trades Council five years later. The Glasgow council's mission proclaimed that it would 'examine, devise and execute the best means of improving the working classes, morally, socially and politically'. Trades Councils were formed at Greenock, Dundee and Aberdeen in 1860, 1864 and 1868 respectively and sought to follow the Glasgow council's lead. By the 1860s around two-thirds of all the organised trades in Glasgow had affiliated to the Trades Council and in the 1870s this included the Lanarkshire miners. Some trade societies were already unhappy with certain aspects of Trades Council operations and the Association of Carpenters and Joiners stopped a local branch from affiliating to the Edinburgh council because it embodied 'politics as part of their programme and politics were not strictly matters for trades councils'.

The 1870s saw a raft of legislation pass through parliament granting trade unions greater legal freedom, and in Edinburgh the Trades Council was to play a leading part in this campaign. Other forms of political action came in support for an 'Eight Hour Bill' which was presented to the Trades Union Congress (TUC) at Dundee in 1889, but ultimately defeated. By then both the Edinburgh and Glasgow councils had parliamentary committees to supervise any legislation that would affect labour and among other issues proposed was the municipalisation of public utilities. The Trades Councils encouraged a wide range of discussion on a host of civil, social and political matters and were involved in what were in effect political pressure-group activities.[5]

The new unionism is commonly held to have arrived with the greatest force in the year of 1889, and, as it heralded a new and more aggressively militant phase of trade unionism, marked a distinctive break with the past. But this distinction was often blurred, not least because old-style unionists were playing a vital role in organising new trade unions amongst unorganised workers.[6] The Edinburgh Trades Council organised a Labourers' Association in the 1860s; the Aberdeen Trades Council organised a Shore Labourers Union and a Scottish Farmers' Union in the 1880s; and the Glasgow Trades Council helped to organise unions among mariners, harbour labourers and carters in the 1880s. Indeed, the Scottish

Table 1.1 Trades Councils in Scotland and Total Affiliated Membership for Selected Years between 1894 and 1914; including STUC Affiliate Membership, 1898–1914.

Year	Number of Trades Councils	Affiliate Membership	STUC Membership[1]
1894	16	84,831	n/a
1898	16	107,297	100,000
1902	16	119,713	120,142
1906	19	124,101	74,470
1909	21	135,446	63,266[2]
1911	30	155,000	138,705
1912	33	187,000	99,875[2]
1913	35	230,000	196,217
1914	38	223,000	225,158

(1) Figures represent the membership of individual trade unions affiliated to the Scottish Trades Union Congress and do not include the affiliated membership figures of the Scottish Trades Councils (which are incomplete in any case).
(2) 1906, 1909 and 1912 do not include Scottish Miners Federation (in 1911, 1913 and 1914 they had a combined membership of 68,000, 75,000 and 75,000 respectively).
Source: A. Clinton, *The Trade Union Rank and File: Trade Union Councils in Britain 1990–1914*; STUC figures compiled from STUC Annual Reports, 1900–1914.

Trade Councils actively assisted English trade unions to form branches among gasworkers, seamen and brickworkers. The Scottish Trades Councils were committed to furthering the cause of trade unionism and, as Fraser suggests, 'their approach was distinctive and pioneering'.[7] It was a role that the English Trades Councils, who lacked the influence among national unions of their Scottish counterparts, were reluctant to assume. The Glasgow Trades Council played a pivotal role when assisting in the formation of the National Union of Dock Labourers (NUDL) at the port of Glasgow in February 1889, but when the NUDL moved its headquarters to Liverpool in 1891 it steadfastly refused to have anything to do with the Liverpool Trades Council until 1906, because the council had done nothing to help organise 'unskilled labour around the docks'.

The NUDL collapsed at Glasgow (and across much of Scotland) by 1910 but the Glasgow Trades Council was determined to reorganise the port and six months later the ten-man committee appointed to oversee the task announced the formation of the Scottish Union of Dock Labourers (SUDL). Within a few months the SUDL had a membership of over 5,000 dockers and far exceeded the best achievements of the NUDL at the height of its popularity in 1890.[8] This demonstrates an ongoing commitment to the cause of trade unionism and, in line with Gall's analysis, demonstrates a steady increase in affiliated membership from the mid-1890s through to the First World War. The Scottish Trades Councils clearly played a vital and distinctive role in progressing trade unionism and from the 1890s until 1914 they would come to play an increasing supportive role in relation to the development of labour politics in Scotland.

The small-scale and independent nature of Scottish unions arose naturally from the basic structure of the Scottish economy and it is for this reason that Fraser, Bill Knox and R. H. Campbell generally support the notion of an inherent weakness. It is also clear that the Scottish Trades Councils were vitally important in encouraging trade-union growth among the unskilled workers. Indeed, had the Scottish structure been similar to the English model, and more centralised as a result, the unskilled may have been largely ignored – an accusation levelled at 'old unions' by 'new union' leaders in England and Wales in the 1890s and early twentieth century. When compared to Scotland, the lack of organisation among English carters before 1914 is arguably a good example of this inertia. Given the regional development of the Scottish economy, the trade union structure that emerged admirably suited the peculiarities of industrial Scotland:

> The early and persistent concentration on small-scale and independent trade-union development in Scotland was a strength which led to a growing sense of solidarity and the formalisation of independent political strategies. Arguably, the nature and character of Scottish trade unionism [and Scottish trade unionists] should be defined in terms of their actions, leadership and their campaigns, rather than the notion of bureaucratic efficiency.[9]

A stronger reliance on a federal system of organisation in Scotland resulted in trade unions becoming collections of small autonomous societies and semi-autonomous branches with decisions made at the local level. When the carters, dockers and other transport workers left larger British trade union organisations in the years before the Great War it was again argued that this was a sign of weakness and backwardness. The strength of these bodies was not diminished by secession and in each case they went on to form larger organisations and increased their membership.

There was a significant drop in trade union membership in Scotland between the early and the mid-1890s, and the reason for this will discussed in Chapter 2. But thereafter it steadily increased and this was achieved within a fiercely independent, localised and federal trade union structure with the Trades Councils at its very core. The structure promoted a greater degree of interaction between skilled and lesser skilled workers and 'rather than a weakness . . . could be interpreted as a strength'.[10] Considered from this perspective and the quantitative analysis of affiliated membership levels to the Trades Councils it would seem clear that the long-held view of the weakness of Scottish trade unionism before 1914 is no longer tenable.

RELIGION AND SECTARIANISM

The social history of Scotland is intimately related to religion. It deeply affected trade union formation and particularly so within the ranks of the miners. The miners had for some time been organised into small local unions but attempting to amalgamate into broader national movements proved difficult. Campbell notes that Alexander McDonald made strenuous efforts in the 1850s to build a general association of miners in Scotland (the Coal and Iron Miners' Association) but that this foundered by 1862–3 'on the shifting sands of racial and religious jealousies'. The religious dimension was a feature of Scottish mining life and in the 1860s Lodges of Free Colliers appeared. Modelled on masonic lodges, they functioned as a type of social club and appealed to what Campbell termed 'an unusual mixture of nationalist sentiment and opposition to Irish Catholicism'.[11]

Racial and religious differences not only worked to exclude Irish Catholics but they also delayed trade union penetration within mining communities. Unionisation was successful around mines at Protestant Larkhall where there was a relatively stable population sharing the same religious background, and the traditions and culture of the 'independent collier', commonly associated with the Free Colliers Movement (FCM). In such areas local combinations of miners were easily sustained even against pressure from local mine owners. By contrast, in religiously-mixed communities such as in newer coalfields in Lanarkshire, unionisation was relatively weak and the employers could and did exert a greater degree of control. Ian MacDougall notes that the miners of Mid and East Lothian joined the FCM ('a revival of an old secret society') in quite considerable numbers in the mid-1860s, and that there had been frequent and violent clashes between Protestant and Catholic workers. But by the late 1870s, as levels of Irish immigration into the Lanarkshire and the Lothian coalfields began to tail off, widespread sectarian violence diminished significantly (although the introduction of the Lithuanians – commonly referred to as 'Poles' – into mine work from the 1890s created more ethnic and religious tension later).[12] The FCM gradually diminished as a force in mining by 1870 and this was accompanied by a revival of miners' unionism in Scotland, and once again Alexander McDonald would play a leading role.[13]

It was not only in mining that religion was to prove a problem: sectarianism was rife in the construction, metal and shipbuilding industries, and the net effect was that it raised barriers against trade-union penetration.[14] Where working men did not share the same religion or country of birth, sectarianism and racism, fired by a high degree of sectional mistrust, acted to inhibit further trade-union development and thus the growth of national and even regional and local organisations. This was a problem that was largely peculiar to the west of Scotland, and while sectarianism was evident among workers at Cardiff, Liverpool, London and Manchester – particularly between port and waterside workers – it was never of the same order of magnitude: even in sectarian divided Liverpool. As one Glaswegian noted in the 1880s, the Irish were different: 'their religion was not our religion . . . and their customs were different . . . as was their speech . . . the less we had to do with them the better.'[15]

Sectarianism rubbed both ways of course and Knox notes that Catholic Irish miners in Lanarkshire considered 'Protestantism . . . more obnoxious than low wages'.[16] Forming any trade union which would include Irish or Scottish Catholics mixing with Protestant workers was bound to be difficult given such entrenched views, but it would not prove insurmountable. Irish Catholics did join miners' unions and they formed the backbone of the NUDL at Glasgow where the second major group were Protestant Highlanders. Indeed, in forming the NUDL they were actively aided by the Glasgow Trades Council which was overwhelmingly – although not exclusively – a body of skilled Protestant workmen. Clearly, the deeply held religious conviction of many Protestants did not stand in the way of progressing trade unionism.[17]

Sectarianism was, nonetheless, still a problem that affected the coalfields perhaps more than any other industry. But the divisions were gradually overcome as larger organisations of miners began to take shape, and when miners across the country came into greater contact with each other through campaigns of political action. By the early 1870s the campaign for the 'Eight Hour Day' saw miners in Fife, Lanarkshire and the Lothians accept the authority of the Associated Confederation of Miners of Scotland. A sharp downturn in economic activity saw this organisation quickly disintegrate, hastened, it must be added, by inter-district squabbles and wild-cat strikes. But it demonstrated that some form of proto-national organisation was at least possible. The first step towards a truly united organisation finally came with the formation of the Scottish Miners' National Federation in 1886, with James Keir Hardie as secretary. This body became the Scottish Miners' Federation in 1894 coinciding with the first national strike of Scottish miners between June and October. It also affiliated to the Miners' Federation of Great Britain in that same year. By the end of the nineteenth century the miners were better organised than ever before at both local and regional level and across Scotland as a whole. By 1900 the Scottish Miners' Federation had 50,000 members and before 1914 between 75,000 and 87,000.[18]

Despite deep-rooted racial and sectarian tensions, and a degree of district and regional mistrust, it was from within the mining industry that there emerged the gradual recognition that workers could not hope to improve wages and conditions across an industry as a whole unless they accepted a greater degree of centralisation. This meant developing a national strategy for the industry leading to a plan for political action intended to further the miners' cause in parliament. The miners were among the first to recognise the need for a coordinated national organisation and they did overcome serious divisions in their ranks. This is not to suggest that sectarianism, sectionalism or regional and local jealousies were swept away, for it remained very much a part of the daily life of many Scottish workers. But, it was proof that such problems could be overcome in support of a common cause. Such an example supports William Marwick's assertions that the strength and initiative of the trade-union movement in Scotland owed much to the example set by the miners.[19] They arguably led the way for other industries in overcoming sectarianism.

THE IRISH AND THE TRADE UNION AND LABOUR MOVEMENT

The role of the Irish in the making of the Scottish trade union and labour movement has proved a somewhat contested issue. James Smyth notes, for example, that 'the orthodox analysis of the Irish' prior to the First World War 'is essentially a negative one', for the Irish 'held Labour back because their primary commitment was to Home Rule for Ireland' and in doing so deprived Labour of its 'potential working class vote'.[20] This was certainly the opinion of David Lowe, Dundee socialist and Labour activist, as noted in *Souvenirs of Scottish Labour* (1919). His book traced the history of the Scottish Labour Party (SLP) between 1888 and 1894 and in sections he spoke very highly of individual Irishmen and in particular John Leslie of the Edinburgh Social Democratic Federation (SDF) whom he described as 'a perfervid Irishman and true poet . . . early intimate with Irish agitation'. But in almost every other respect he was uniformly critical of the Irish. He clearly blamed them for not backing the three SLP and the four Scottish United Trades Council labour party candidates running for election in 1892 and stated that 'the necessities of

Irish politics' lost Robert Smillie his chance in Mid-Lanark in 1894.[21] By way of a contrast, J. D. Young, writing in the 1970s, argued that the march of socialism was actually held back in the coalfields of Fife and east Scotland 'because there were few Roman Catholic miners of Irish origins' settled there, whereas in the coalfields of the west of Scotland where Catholic miners were active in the Irish National League 'socialism spread like wildfire'.[22]

Smyth's examination of socialism and sectarianism in Glasgow presents a more complex and complicated narrative of Irish political involvement in the Scottish trade-union and labour movement than either of these perspectives allows. He notes that from the 1880s onward many ordinary Scottish working men were supportive of Irish Home Rule, and points to the leading and active role played by individual Irishmen and Irish organisations that worked alongside and within the labour movement around Glasgow.[23] He challenges the notion that the Irish had sufficient electoral clout to influence labour politics to any great extent or that they would always vote as an electoral block. There was a considerable cultural gap between the artisans and the unskilled and poorer classes in Glasgow and this was complicated further 'by the existence of a large Irish-Catholic community' concentrated in the low-paid occupations. Despite a clear racial and sectional division operating within the city, 'the strength of socialist and labour support for Irish Home Rule' helped blur ethnic and religious boundaries.[24]

Regarding Irish electoral practices, Smyth noted that in 1892 the Catholic *Glasgow Observer* 'fulminated against traitors who voted for Labour in Camlachie and Tradeston' and that from the 'virulence' of this report it was clear that a significant number of Irishmen 'had done just that'. Similarly, in 1895 the recently formed Independent Labour Party (ILP) had Smillie standing as the Labour candidate at Camlachie. Although he did not win, 'his relatively high poll' was likely to have been a reflection of the 'level of support' from the Irish Home Government Branch in that community. The ILP ran five candidates in 1895 but thereafter barely existed as a credible electoral force and did not repeat that challenge on the same scale until 1918. Clearly, many Scottish working men stood aloof from Labour Party politics during this period and it would be harsh in any case to blame all Labour's woes on the Irish. [25]

The Irish National League was crucial in bringing the Irish working class into the mainstream of Scottish and British politics. According to George Boyce, the formation of the 'League and its alliance with the Home Rule Party' created a 'mass movement' not only uniting rural Ireland but helping to consolidate Irish opinion across industrial

Britain.[26] The issue had a great impact in Scotland generally and across west central Scotland in particular where Irish and Highland industrial migrants lived and worked cheek by jowl. Following the example of the Irish Land Leaguers, Skye crofters seized control of land in 1881 only to be evicted by force of arms during the 'Battle of the Braes'. In opposing the 'might of British imperialism' and in response to reports of harsh treatment in prison, the crofters won the admiration of lowland workers and widespread support for land reform and land nationalisation.[27]

The Land Restoration Society was founded in both England and Scotland but it took root in Glasgow where 'the crofters question and the Irish land question . . . had been forced into prominence'. James Mavor wrote that 'Henry George's *Progress and Poverty* was a prime mover in that regard' and in Scotland the land question raised feelings of hostility against both political parties and 'contempt for their domestic policies'.[28] Printed in *The Glasgow Herald* in 1882, the following extract stressed how this issue affected the Irish:

> There can be little doubt that the Irishmen of Glasgow are today more united and more at one upon the political question concerning Ireland, than they have been for some time years past. This happy state of matters is in no doubt due in large measure to the beneficial influence of the Land League.

'And this was no bad thing', the writer asserted, for it was the duty of every Irishman 'to oppose by every means in his power those coercive Liberals'.[29]

But many Lowland middle-class Scots were resentful that the Irish had 'contrived to make the issue of Irish Home Rule a factor in Scottish politics'. The 'Land Question' may have been a common feature of politics in Ireland and the Highlands and Islands during between the 1880s and 1900s, but as Ewen Cameron suggests, this commonality only went so far, for some Highland land reformers were deeply anti-Catholic and anti-Irish nationalist.[30] T. M. Devine stressed that Irish nationalism posed a threat to the Union and the Empire and that for many in Protestant west Scotland, with its strong links with Ulster and the Orange Order, 'Home Rule' meant 'Rome Rule'.[31] There is evidence that some employers in Glasgow 'boycotted' Irish workers in response to the Irish tenant farmers' 'boycott' of landlords in Ireland. Over the early months of 1882 several letters to *The Glasgow Herald* indicate that some form of 'employment boycott' was in operation in Glasgow, although it was not widely supported.[32] For many Scots, however, the Irish were simply 'a race apart' and 'the unruly and turbulent ones' showed Scots what they might become 'if they did not keep to their own'.[33] That there was a palpable anti-Irish sentiment evident at this time is clear from a letter to the *North British Daily Mail* in March 1893:

> The Scottish Football Association was misrepresenting Scotland by allowing Irish, or Celtic players in a Scottish representative team. With all due deference to the Celtic men's ability, I hold an accident of birth don't make them Scotchmen. They, as a team, are banded together for Irish purposes.[34]

Signed by 'the Covenanter', it made it clear that second-generation Irish would struggle for acceptance within certain quarters of Scottish society.

Land Reform and Home Rule proved crucial to the formation of the NUDL at Glasgow in February 1889, and Edward McHugh and Richard McGhee, the Irish-born leaders of the NUDL, were supporters and colleagues of Henry George and of land reform, and were deeply committed to Irish nationalism.[35] Another leading figure in Glasgow was Irishman Hugh Johnston who was probably responsible for organising Bo'ness, Dundee and Leith, and Dublin, Belfast, Derry, Cork and Waterford in Ireland.[36] Another was Charles Kennedy who had established four branches of the NUDL at Liverpool and Birkenhead by June 1889. Kennedy was a member of the group who met at Glasgow in May 1888 to establish a Labour Party for Scotland, and who, with Keir Hardie and three others, made up the committee to organise the inaugural conference of the Scottish Labour Party in August that year. McGhee was also present at the inaugural conference, and Kennedy was also present in December 1894 when on a motion by Keir Hardie it was decided to merge the SLP with the ILP.[37] This is clear evidence of an active and positive role by 'individual Irishmen and Irish organisations' within the trade union and labour movement in Scotland and a tangible link with the nascent socialist movement. In essence the vexed question of religion and sectarianism had receded somewhat by the 1880s and continued to improve gradually from then until the issue of Irish Home Rule and the threat of civil war in Ulster before 1914 reopened an old and deep subterranean division. But it was only after the war, when the Scottish economy slipped into a serious and deep recession, that the fissure of racism and sectarianism all too glaringly opened up once again.

OLD UNIONS AND NEW UNIONISM

Sydney and Beatrice Webb first referred to the impulse towards the mass organisation of unskilled workers in the late 1880s and early 1890s as the 'new unionism'. Since then most historians have come to view this 'militant and aggressive' form of trade unionism as evidence of 'new directions in industrial relations' and, because of the connections with the early socialist movement, 'evidence of a new class consciousnesses'. It was commonly held that the impulse and origins were historically linked with the London dock strike of August 1889 or, at the very earliest, the match-girls' strike during the summer of the previous year.[38] Henry Pelling argued that this was 'usually regarded as the main phase of the new unionism' and it was only after the 'great spread of unionism' in London that 'enthusiasm' for trade unionism began to extend throughout the rest of England, Wales and Scotland.[39] Pelling also associates the emergence of the new unionism with socialism and the leading role played by London-based members of the Marxist Social Democratic Federation (SDF). One of the main features of the new unionism, therefore, is a close association with socialism, and this political impulse is commonly cited as one of the main causes behind the emergence of this phenomenon. This 'peculiarly myopic, London vision', suggests Fraser, 'although highly persistent . . . is a view that has long been untenable', and would point to the longer-term changes that were taking place in the 'industrial areas of the north' long before 'the middle class socialists of London had met their first trade unionist'.[40] Indeed, 'new unions were already appearing before socialist ideas had made much impact' and from that standpoint it would be prudent not to over-state the role of socialism.[41]

There is no denying the increase in union membership. According to *The Scotsman*, the TUC conference at Dundee in 1889 was expected to welcome 250 delegates representing an aggregate membership of 750,000 workers.[42] When the President of the TUC made his fraternal greeting at Liverpool the following year he welcomed 460 delegates representing a combined estimated membership of almost 1.5 million workers.[43] Most historians would agree with these figures, but Keith Laybourn argued that trade union growth was strong among a wide range of workers, and that the new unionists represented at best only 22 per cent of all trade unionists in 1890. Thus the influence of new unionism was 'fairly restricted' and its impact exaggerated:

> Instead of seeing it as moving the trade union movement towards socialism and political independence it is, perhaps, more sensible to see this phase of trade union development in a wider framework. Trade unions had always taken advantage of good economic conditions . . .[44]

In December 1890, Mr John Burnett of the Board of Trade (previously president of the ASE) submitted his report on 'Strikes and Lockouts for the year 1889', wherein he compared the labour movement and market condition of 1889 with an earlier period of trade-union growth in the early 1870s which involved skilled and unskilled workers. He concluded that 'under similar conditions of prosperity' there was little exceptional in the organisation of the unskilled 'which so many people asserted to be the chief characteristic of an era beginning in 1889'.[45] Burnett's report raised two important points. First, that in emphasising the economic dimension he was effectively dismissing political influence. Secondly, that there was a degree of continuity between the early 1870s and 1889 suggesting that the surge in trade union formation among the less skilled was not an entirely 'new' phenomenon.[46]

Another feature of the new unionism was that it followed a militant and aggressive industrial relations strategy and that this conflicted with the 'old and careful methods' espoused by leaders of the skilled unions.[47] While many 'new unions' were deeply indebted to 'old unionists' for their very existence, there was nonetheless clear blue water between the 'old' and the 'new' forms of unionism. The great majority of 'old unionists' were Liberal in orientation and openly and publicly denounced self-proclaimed socialists such as John Burns, Tom Mann, James Keir Hardie and R. B. Cunninghame Graham as 'scurrilous agitators'. Indeed, they confirmed their dislike of 'socialistic programmes' and schemes to encourage greater state intervention by robustly and enthusiastically ensuring the defeat of the 'Eight Hour Day' and the formation of an Independent British Labour Party at the Dundee TUC in 1889.[48] Because of that decision Keir Hardie castigated the leading representatives of labour for 'working hand in glove with the Capitalists'.[49]

Given such controversies, the press felt sure that the Liverpool congress in the following year would be the arena where 'old' and 'new' would vie for supremacy. In this battle the ASE would represent the 'old' and the dockers the 'new' trade unionists. But it was not as simple as 'old' versus 'new', and over the coming years each would learn from the other. Some 'old' and well-established unions such as the railwaymen and the engineers quickly recognised that industrial militancy resulted in substantial improvements in wages and conditions and increased membership. The dockers also found other methods of dealing with industrial relations problems without resorting to strike action.

The spirit of militant unionism among the unskilled was more or less broken during the early 1890s. But as far as the press was concerned 'the new unionists' simply regrouped and began to focus on the 'richer and more powerful old unions' such as the railwaymen, the miners and the engineers in order to push their 'socialistic programmes' of state intervention. The press applauded the triumphs of the Shipping Federation in

1890 and more decisively 1893, and the Engineering Federation's conquest of the ASE during the strikes and lock-outs of 1897 and 1898. According to *The Times*, it was only with the defeat of the ASE in 1898 that the tyranny of the new unionism was finally brought to an end.[50] It is perhaps no accident that the years between 1898 and 1907 were to prove the quietest for trade unionism in Britain since the late 1880s.[51] Given the two severe economic downturns during the first decade of the twentieth century, it was quieter still for the unskilled trade unions trying to maintain a foothold in Scotland. However, the labour unrest of 1910–14 sparked a fresh upsurge in unionism and militancy that far outstripped anything achieved at the time of the new unionism. But the link with the new unionism was crucial for, in essence, the labour unrest brought to a close a process in trade union formation that had begun twenty or more years before. But this time the gains made by the trade union and labour movement would not be lost and the impact of the First World War would only enhance their strength and standing.

SOCIALISM AND THE LABOUR MOVEMENT

An analysis of the structure of the trade union movement in Scotland, when compared to the process of trade unionism and industrial relations in England and Wales shows that there were clear and discernable paths of divergence and that part of the explanation for this lies in the quite distinctive structure of the Scottish economy. Would it be the case therefore that Scottish political institutions would mirror this divergence? Gregor Gall argued that from the 1920s there were strong similarities between the Scottish labour movement and the rest of Britain, but historically the Scots had something that was missing elsewhere: 'a strong sense of national identity enriched by social democratic tradition'.[52]

In focusing on 'national identity' as the main difference between Scots and other British workers there are clear echoes of the work of Scottish historian James Young. In his book *The Rousing of the Scottish Working Class,* Young argues, among other things, that the issue of 'national identity' and the growth of socialism were unavoidably connected and this resulted in the 'coalescence of Scottish socialism and nationalism'.[53] Viewed from Young's perspective, the Scottish workers were facing up to realities of industrial and economic life 'and the conditions of savage poverty and authoritarianism' they confronted daily. This struggle against poverty was nothing new but it was intensifying and this forced the Scottish labour movement 'to transcend primary concerns with economic issues that dominated labour movements in other countries where trade union movements were better organised'. It was a 'struggle for democracy and a Scottish Parliament' and a crucial element in this burgeoning resurgence of 'national identity' was that it created cohesion among the ethnically-diverse working class 'composed of Lowland Scots, Irish immigrants and Highland peasants'. In conditions of 'savage poverty' and facing an authoritarian and autocratic capitalist class, 'people of diverse ethnic origins began to develop an authentic sense of national identity in the process of class struggle and solidarity on the picket lines'.[54]

According to Bill Knox, one major drawback in Young's work is the manner in which he presents Scottish workers as more or less one homogeneous class caught in a 'constant struggle for emancipation', and he would point to T. C. Smout's *Century of the Scottish People, 1830 to 1930*, wherein is presented 'a more subtle account' of a Scottish working class and how they 'accommodated themselves to the main institutions of power and authority' in both Scotland and Britain.[55] Indeed, it is clear from his own work that Knox sees a much more subdued role for left radicals and socialists in shaping or indeed influencing the political attitudes of Scottish workers. If labour politics and socialism were to play as an important role in the lives of ordinary workers as Young suggests, then why did so many remain loyal to the Liberal-Labour alliance in Scotland before 1914? He does point out, however, that, because of economic concerns, Scottish workers were becoming disenchanted with Liberalism and 'the problem of starving in the midst of plenty . . . a prominent feature of Scottish working life'. Workers were thus 'encouraged the search for alternative ideologies',[56] although he has no time for the type of 'vanguardism' that is perhaps suggestive of Young's view of Scottish workers in the 1880s and 1890s.

Poverty was 'endemic throughout Scotland' in the late nineteenth and early twentieth centuries and as Scots also spent a proportionally higher proportion of their earnings on food and drink they were left then with considerably less disposable income than many English workers.[57] Bad housing, lower wages and limited social segregation between the skilled and unskilled heightened the sense of class consciousness among Scottish workers. As Bob Morris argued,

> Here was a culture composed of poverty, skill and insecurity and this not only promoted industrial and social solidarity and a keener sense of 'class identity' it also aided the development of class politics.[58]

Scotland's industrial development lagged behind that of England and the second phase of economic change was more intensely concentrated within a much shorter period of time. According to Young, this produced a different set of responses from capital and labour and led to an industrial relations' strategy based on 'conflict and coercion' rather than the more conciliatory approach adopted in England.[59] This 'harsh' and 'authoritarian' relationship between Scottish capital and labour sharpened the growing social tensions between the 'possessing classes and the working class',[60] particularly on the picket line. A great many Scottish employers simply wanted no truck with organised trade unionism and this is evident in the actions of the port and shipping employers of Glasgow. The example of the carters, dockers and seamen from the late 1880s onward shows that effective trade union organisation among the unskilled in Scotland was not impossible, but the ferocity of the employers' counterattack in the 1890s made life difficult. Indeed, that port transport trade unionism survived into the twentieth century is all the more remarkable given the Clydeside employers' fierce anti-union reputation which, as Arthur McIvor demonstrates, was reflected in the extensive network of employer organisations that had developed across Clydeside and west Scotland between 1900 and 1914.[61] In such circumstances, as the Aberdeen dockers and seamen asserted when engaged in their titanic struggle with the Shipping Federation in 1891, they would have to engage in a political struggle if industrial action proved ineffective.[62]

But given the diverse ethnic origins of the Scottish working class, and the continual ebb and flow of emigration and immigration streams, the emergence of class politics in Scotland could hardly be expected to be a linear development. Indeed, in many respects, its progress was unavoidably convoluted, reflecting as it did the regional and economic diversity of the Scottish economy. Catriona Macdonald's work on political change in Scotland, as seen through the prism of Paisley politics, clearly demonstrated that the 'transition towards class politics was a fragmented one', for the simple reason that social and industrial change did not affect 'all regions simultaneously'. In such circumstances political change could only take place when the older 'cultural and political foundations' were shaken and this would mean dislodging a powerful working-class attachment to radical Liberalism. Indeed, Labour had failed to fundamentally challenge the Liberal hegemony at Paisley even by 1914.[63]

The social and economic struggle against poverty and Labours confrontation with industrial capital helped to unite an ethnically-diverse working class and in so doing created the right conditions for the emergence of socialism to take root as an alternative ideology to Liberalism. Why then did not more workers embrace socialism, and was this a problem of the socialism movement itself? Perhaps the key question would be 'How socialist was Scottish socialism'? If defined in terms of its observance to a strict Marxist policy, then Bill Knox would suggest that it fell well short of the mark. English socialists did adhere to a distinctive Marxist doctrine, but Scots socialists had a closer attachment to the ethical socialism of Burns, Shelley, Ruskin and Carlyle. It was Henry George, and not Karl Marx, who was a 'key intellectual influence' on the nascent socialist movement in Scotland. Scottish socialists also failed to connect with trade unionists because their political programme was perceived as 'too wide and revolutionary in nature' and 'the avant-garde life style and dress of the more middle-class element alienated the working classes'. Edinburgh socialist John L. Mahon, for example, thought J. Bruce Glasier to be 'poetic and cranky' in his adoption of William Morris's 'fads and queer ways'.[64] Indeed, he made similar comments on Keir Hardie.

The denunciation of religion by many of the early socialists and their close association with atheism was also widely regarded as holding back greater working-class involvement in Scotland, and this was perhaps why initially 'few working men' in Edinburgh and Glasgow were members of socialist organisations.[65] On the other hand, Knox also identifies a strong Christian socialist tendency within the ranks of the socialist pioneers. Dundee-based socialist David Lowe noted how at socialist meetings 'those present in force applauded any allusion to Christ as a social reformer'.[66] Likewise, in John Gilray's account of the early days of the socialist movement in Edinburgh he noted an observation by French socialist Leo Melliet that 'believers in Socialism partook far too much of the nature of a church'.[67] Young noted that another Edinburgh socialist, A. K. Donald, repudiated elements of an English socialist secular manifesto arguing that it would 'create unnecessary bitterness against us in religious Scotland'. Thereafter, Donald attempted to make 'socialist propaganda "popular" by organising Sunday meetings' in Edinburgh[68] in a similar manner to Lowe in Dundee and James Leatham in Aberdeen. There is clearly some uncertainty about the impact and role of religion on the nascent socialist movement for it is clear that the Rev. John Glasse of Edinburgh and the Rev. Alexander Webster in Aberdeen played crucial roles 'in the emergence of socialism' in these cities'.[69]

Early Scottish socialists may have developed 'a critique of the social relations of capitalist society', argued Knox, but they were ill equipped to take that message to the ordinary workers. Moreover, unlike their English counterparts, they were largely devoid of 'political theory' and had little 'theoretical appreciation of the role of the state'.[70] When all the socialist parties came together to form the Independent Labour Party

(ILP) in 1893, Keir Hardie stated that he considered it a strength of the ILP that 'they had no worked out theory'.[71] All in all, taking into consideration Knox's view of the early socialists and their relationship with the broader mass of the working classes (which at times bordered on almost complete antagonism and aversion *vis-à-vis* their poverty and their affection for 'intoxicating liquor'), not discounting the respectable organised working man's deep political affinity with the Liberal Party, it would seem that the early socialist movement could not have had a more inauspicious start. Much of the thrust of historical writing on the subject would suggest socialism had little overall impact on the Scottish working-class mind before 1914 and this becomes abundantly clear in relation to the perceived lack of success in the arena of electoral politics. David Lowe asserted that 'to grow in numbers is not necessarily an increase in power' and was perhaps suggesting that a better indicator of success would be Labour's growing propaganda role within the broader trade-union and labour movement. Political action helped to radicalise the labour movement in Scotland from the 1870s onward, and as the socialist and labour movement developed they encouraged more workers into political action in Scotland from the 1880s onward. Indeed, political action was the very life-blood of Scottish Labour from its very beginnings and it is in this political arena that success or failure should be gauged.

NOTES

1. Fraser, 'Trade Councils in the Labour Movement in Nineteenth Century Scotland', pp. 1–2.
2. Knox, 'The Politics and Workplace Culture of The Scottish Working Class, 1832–1914', p. 149; Campbell, *Scotland Since 1707: The Rise of an Industrial Society*, pp. 237–8.
3. Knox, *Industrial Nation: Work, Culture and Society in Scotland, 1800–Present*, p. 156.
4. Gall, *The Political Economy of Scotland: Red Scotland? Radical Scotland?*, p 44.
5. Fraser, 'Trade Councils', pp. 2–4, 12–17.
6. Fraser, *A History of British Trade Unionism*, pp. 76–7.
7. Fraser, 'Trade Councils', pp. 6–9.
8. Taplin, *The Dockers Union: A Study of the National Union of Dock Labourers*, pp. 33–4; Kenefick, *Rebellious and Contrary: The Glasgow Dockers, 1853–1932*, pp. 23–4, 119–20.
9. Kenefick and McIvor, *Roots of Red Clydeside 1910–1914: Labour Unrest and Industrial Relations in West Scotland*, pp. 19–20.

10. Ibid. p. 21.
11. Campbell, *Scotland Since 1707*, p. 167.
12. MacDougall, *Mid and East Lothian Miners' Association Minutes, 1894–1918*, pp. 4–5; Brown, *The People and the Pew: Religion and Society in Scotland since 1780*, pp. 36–7.
13. Rodgers, 'The Lanarkshire Lithuanians', pp. 19–26; MacDougall, *Mid and East Lothian Miners'*, pp. 21, 101, 148.
14. Knox, 'Politics and Workplace Culture', pp. 149–50; Knox *Industrial Nation*, p. 116.
15. Kenefick, 'Irish Dockers and Trade Unionism on Clydeside', p. 24; Gallagher, 'The Catholic Irish in Scotland', p. 23.
16. Knox, *Industrial Nation*, p. 159.
17. Kenefick, 'Irish Dockers', pp. 24–8; Kenefick, *Rebellious and Contrary*, pp. 112–16.
18. Affiliated membership to the STUC in 1914 notes a figure of 75,000; Campbell, *Scotland Since 1707*, pp. 236–38, suggests a figure in excess of 87,000; while MacDougall, *Mid and East Lothian Miners'*, p. 31, no. 154 – citing the *Annual Report of the Miners Federation of Great Britain* for January 1914 – states that total membership of the Scottish Miners Federation was 82,000: Lanarkshire 40,000; Fife and Kinross 20,000; Ayrshire 12,500; and Mid and East Lothian 9,500.
19. Marwick, *A Short History of Trade Unionism in Scotland*.
20. Smyth, *Labour in Glasgow 1896–1936: Socialism, Suffrage, Sectarianism*, p. 125.
21. Lowe, *Souvenirs of Scottish Labour*, p. 168; *The Scotsman*, 6 April 1894; Smyth, *Labour in Glasgow*, pp. 126, 132.
22. Young, *The Rousing of the Scottish Working Class*, p. 152.
23. Smyth, *Labour in Glasgow*, p. 133.
24. Ibid. p. 21.
25. Ibid. pp. 134–6, 145.
26. Bull, *Land, Politics and Nationalism: A Study of the Irish Land Question*, p. 7.
27. Young, *Rousing*, p. 144.
28. Mavor, *My Window on the Street of the World*, vol. 1, pp. 174–5.
29. *The Glasgow Herald*, 21 February 1882. The reference to coercion was the liberal government's response to rural violence associated with the Irish National Land League's campaign and tenant evictions in Ireland and the powers given to the Royal Irish Police and British armed forces to enforce the law. The Land League was proclaimed a 'treasonable body' by the Lord Lieutenant of Ireland in October 1881. This move had been expected and was variously report throughout the British press on Friday, 21 October 1881. The proclamation was made on the previous Thursday evening, 20 October 1881.
30. Cameron, *Land Fit for People?: The British Government and the Scottish Highlands c. 1880–1914*, p. 199; Dewey on 'Celtic' perspectives on land

holding in 'Celtic Agrarian Legislation and the Celtic Revival: Historicist Implications of Gladstone's Irish and Scottish Land Acts, 1870–1886', pp. 56–68.

31. Devine, *The Scottish Nation 1700 to 2000*, pp. 301, 304.
32. Kenefick, 'Jewish and Catholic Irish Relations: The Glasgow Waterfront c. 1880–1914', p. 244, n. 58.
33. Kenefick, 'Irish Dockers', p. 24; Gallagher, 'The Catholic Irish in Scotland: In Search of identity', pp. 23–4.
34. *North British Daily Mail*, 7 March 1893: Kenefick, 'Irish Dockers', p. 25.
35. Ibid. pp. 22–9.
36. *The Glasgow Herald*, 6 February 1889.
37. Lowe, *Souvenirs*, p. 2, for references to Kennedy and McGhee; and Taplin, *The Dockers' Union: A Study of the National Union of Dock Labourers, 1889–192*, pp. 28–9, 151, 199. For general references to association with Land Reform and Irish Nationalism, see Kenefick, *Rebellious and Contrary*, pp. 112–18; Kenefick, 'Irish Dockers', pp. 25–6.
38. Webb, *Industrial Democracy*.
39. Pelling, *A History of British Trade Unionism*, pp. 86–90: Quelch, *Trade Unionism, Co-operation and Social Democracy*.
40. Fraser, *British Trade Unionism*, pp. 71–2.
41. Ibid. p. 74.
42. *The Scotsman*, 2 September 1889.
43. *Times*, 2 September, 1890.
44. Laybourn, *A History of British Trade Unionism*, p. 76; Fraser, *British Trade Unionism*, p. 73.
45. *The Times, The Glasgow Herald* and *The Scotsman*, 11 December 1890.
46. Charlesworth, *An Atlas of Industrial Protest*: Section B. 1850 to 1900, by H. Southall, pp. 59–121.
47. Kenefick, *Rebellious and Contrary*, pp. 184–6.
48. *The Scotsman*, 6, 7, 9 September 1889.
49. *The Scotsman*, 4, 6 September 1989.
50. *The Times*, 27 December 1898.
51. Gilbert, 'Industrial protest: 1900–39', in Charlesworth, *An Atlas of Industrial Protest*, pp. 122–3.
52. Gall, *Political Economy*, pp. 6–15, and chapter 6.
53. Young, *Rousing*, p. 134.
54. Ibid. pp. 135–6, 144.
55. Knox, *Industrial Nation*, p. 22.
56. Ibid, pp. 19–20, 126.
57. Treble, 'Unemployment in Glasgow: Anatomy of a Crisis': Rodgers, 'Crisis and Confrontation in Scottish Housing, 1880–1914'.
58. McKinlay and Morris, *The ILP on Clydeside*, pp. 8–9.
59. Young, *Rousing*, pp. 104–6.
60. Ibid. p. 168.

61. McIvor, 'Were Clydeside employers more autocratic?: Labour management and the "labour unrest", c. 1910–1914', pp. 44–7.
62. *The Scotsman*, 9 March 1891.
63. Macdonald, *The Radical Thread: Political Change in Scotland. Paisley Politics, 1885–1924*, pp. 125–6, 145–8, 178–83.
64. Knox, *Industrial Nation*, pp. 163–9 (quoted from *Morris and the Early Days*).
65. Ibid. p. 164.
66. Lowe, *Souvenirs*, pp. 77.
67. Gilray, *Early Days*, p. 14.
68. Young, *Rousing*, p. 146; Lowe, *Souvenirs*, p. 98; for James Leatham Buckley, *Trade Unionism in Aberdeen, 1878–1900*; Duncan, *James Leatham, 1865–1945: Portrait of a Socialist Pioneer* (1978).
69. Knox, *Industrial Nation*, p. 172.
70. Ibid. p. 165.
71. Thomas, 'How the Labour Party was Formed', pp. 2, 5.

2

Industrial Radicalism and the New Unionism

INTRODUCTION

There are major problems associated with any research into trade unionism in Scotland, not least in relation to the organisation of 'unskilled'
workers. This may explain why until recently there was no history of
dock workers in Scotland[1] and perhaps why the Scottish railwaymen
have had no historian of their own. There is a dearth of early trade
unions records, and those that do exist are so fragmentary that any in-
depth study of certain groups of workers would be extremely difficult
without recourse to the establishment press.[2] While this is not ideal, there
is much useful and detailed information contained in articles and press
reports, and while the editorial line is undoubtedly sympathetic to the
outlook of employers and the middle classes, there is much that can be
learned of these turbulent and exciting times when examined from this
perspective.

Fraser argues that the press played an important role in promoting a
wider public acceptance of legitimate trade union activity 'perceptibly
changing from unremitting and violent hostility in the early 1850s' to a
'grudging approval' by the 1880s. There was considerable press sympathy shown towards the unskilled agricultural labourers' strikes, the engineers' 'nine-hours movement' in the early 1870s and the Scottish shale
miners' strike of the late 1880s. For a time even the London dockers gar-
nered considerable press and public sympathy during the 1889 strike.[3]
By the 1890s, however, the establishment press recoiled significantly
from this position and became antagonistic to trade unionism. New
unionism in particular was seen as violent and aggressive and it was for
this reason that press and public opinion supported the equally aggressive response of the employers during the counter-attacks on the seamen,
dockers and railwaymen in the early 1890s, the Scottish miners in 1894,
and the engineers and shipbuilders in the late 1890s. Indeed, Fraser notes

that the increase in militant and aggressive strike activity encouraged the courts once again to take 'a new look at the position of trade unions'.[4] The press is therefore important in gauging public opinion if not shaping it and it is an important source for historical inquiry.

The historiography of the 'new unionism', like that of the later 'labour unrest', largely reflects the experience of English workers and with a few exceptions tends to marginalise the importance of this narrative in the Scottish context. In order to help fill that gap in our knowledge, this chapter will examine the impact of new unionism through two 'case studies'. The first considers the dockers, carters and seamen who as a body of workers were generally looked upon as 'unskilled'. The second looks at the Scottish railway workers, who barely figure in British historiography, and examines as a starting point the historic importance of the 1890–91 Scottish railway dispute. This case study specifically focuses on the Amalgamated Society of Railway Servants (ASRS) which was formed in Scotland in 1872 and was therefore not a 'new union'. The members of the ASRS were considered more skilled than the dockers or seamen but it was the example set by the latter which spurred the railwaymen into action during 1890 and 1891.

For those seeking to demonstrate that the new unionism was evidence of a new direction in industrial relations, and perhaps even confirmation of a new class consciousness, studying the emergence of powerful employers' federations may prove a good starting point. Indeed, no clear understanding of the growth and containment of the port transport, shipping and kindred trades' unions would be possible if the role and development of the Shipping Federation were not considered. This federation was arguably the most monolithic and effective of all the employers' federations to emerge during that period.[5] When the federation defeated the dockers and seamen in the early 1890s the press proclaimed this 'a great victory' for the forces of capital and for society as a whole. But this was merely the beginning, for it was only after the defeat of the engineers by the Engineering Employers' Federation in 1898 that the progress of aggressive and militant trade new unionism was finally halted.

CASE STUDY ONE: PIONEERS OF THE NEW UNIONISM – THE DOCKERS AND THE SEAMEN

Engels argued at the time of the London dock strike that if the dockers could organise, other sections of workers would follow. Harry Quelch, of the London South Side Labour Protection League, wrote how this dispute created 'the impetus and enthusiasm for combination' among large numbers of workers hitherto unorganised'.[6] In Scotland, however, local societies of dockers as well as seamen, carters and porters had been evident some time before the advent of the London strike. Indeed, the formation of the National Union of Dock Labourer (NUDL) in Glasgow in February 1889 marked the origins of mass dock unionism in Britain. Port and maritime trade unionism was thus not new to Scotland. The Aberdeen Shore Labourers Society was formed with the help of the Aberdeen Trades Council in July 1883; the Clyde Associated Mariners' Society was formed in 1886 with the help of the Glasgow Trades Council, as was the Glasgow Harbour Mineral Workers' Union in 1887 and the NUDL in 1889; Greenock Dock Labourers Union was formed in 1887, and for a brief time the American Knights of Labour organised dock workers at the port of Ardrossan on the Clyde in the late 1880s.[7] The Aberdeen Shore Labourers Society and the Aberdeen Trades Council together organised the seamen and financed Havelock Wilson's visit to speak to the seamen of Aberdeen. At a meeting held at the Shore Labourers' Hall in Aberdeen, a branch of the Seamen's Union was formed in January 1887.[8]

The Seamen's Union and the Trades Councils in Aberdeen, Dundee, Glasgow and Edinburgh were pivotal to developments in modern port and maritime unionism in Scotland. With the support of the Glasgow Trades Council, the seamen went on strike at the port during January and February 1889 and it was during the course of this dispute that the great mass of quayworkers became organised into the NUDL. The Edinburgh Trades Council similarly assisted the seamen in organising a branch at Leith during February of that year – as the dispute spread eastward across Scotland – and, in June, the Leith branch of the NUDL was formed, representing half the dockers of the port.[9]

The seamen at Glasgow were in dispute again in June 1889 and, when the dockers came out in sympathy, the strike spread to Leith, Bo'ness, Montrose, and Aberdeen and included carters and maritime workers in the kindred trades. The NUDL was making considerable headway, and a series of articles in the *North British Daily Mail* between June and early July charted the union's 'aggressive campaign' against the use of non-union and imported labour (commonly referred to as 'replacement' or more usually as 'scab' labour brought in during a strike). The strike was largely unsuccessful, but the end result was not unfavourable, for dock unionism had spread across Scotland from Glasgow and the Clyde ports on the western seaboard to Aberdeen, Bo'ness, Burntisland, Dundee, Grangemouth and Leith and on the east seaboard, as well as to Derry and Liverpool. By July 1889 the NUDL set up branches in all these ports (with the exception of Aberdeen and Greenock where dockers' societies already existed).[10]

But perhaps one of the most important aspects of the dispute emerged from the conditions imposed by the employers after the strike. The 'scab' labourers who were brought into Glasgow during the strike (mainly unemployed farm labourers) were kept on by the employers. It was widely reported, as the NUDL claimed, that it took thirty 'scabs' to do the work of ten dockers, and even the port authorities were on record as stating that in some cases it took the 'free labourers' three to four times as long to turn round a vessel. Despite all the evidence to the contrary, however, the employers declared themselves 'satisfied' with the replacement labour. Edward McHugh and Richard McGhee, the Irish-born leaders of the NUDL, seized upon this and advised all returning NUDL members to 'work like the farm workers worked'. This became known as 'Ca' canny' (also known as a 'go-slow' or a 'go-easy') and soon after this strategy was initiated McHugh was approached by the shipowners who promised wage increases if the men would work normally.[11] McHugh and McGhee also made wide use of the boycott by which they would target a particular employer, shipping line, or groups of small employers, usually over the issue of non-union labour or through sympathetic action with the carters and seamen. The boycott was not a strike but a course of action intended to cut off an employer's labour supply, and it was referred to as an Irish weapon of revolt: the principal method of civil disobedience exercised during the Irish 'Land War'. Thereafter, the 'boycott' and 'Ca' canny' became major planks in the industrial relations strategies of the NUDL, and the success of this policy enhanced the reputations of McHugh and McGhee within the trade-union world.[12] The NUDL's 'novel and daring' industrial strategies clearly paid dividends and this was recognised in the *Annual Report* of the Glasgow Trades Council in 1889 where it was noted that the NUDL represented 4,000 dockers at Glasgow, and that nationally the NUDL and the Seamen's Union had memberships of over 5,000 and 7,000 respectively.[13]

Indeed, the roots of Scottish dock unionism stretched back further to 1853 when the Glasgow Harbour Labourers' Union (GHLU or the 'Old Society') was formed. It was composed entirely of shipworkers, was highly exclusive and sectional, and was chiefly concerned with defending its 'artisanal' status in the face of growing competition from incoming Irish and Highland quayside workers. Like similar societies in London and Liverpool, the GHLU proved an obstruction to the early growth of dock unionism at the port and only attempted to organise the 'lesser-skilled' quayworkers during a dispute at Glasgow in 1872.[14] The strike ended in defeat after the employers brought in 'replacement' shipworkers from another port, and for a time the GHLU went into isolation.[15] Clearly, skilled and unskilled workmen were standing shoulder-to-shoulder in a 'new spirit' of solidarity and Scottish trade unionism manifested this 'new spirit' in abundance well before the shockwave of the London dock strike was felt.[16]

Port transport and maritime industrial relations were changing as the influence of the large steamship owners increased and they would not tolerate any combination of workers interfering. With ever-increasing numbers of steamship companies located and operating out of the Clyde ports the employers became more anti-union than was generally the case at other British ports.[17] The Glasgow port and shipping employers systematically smashed the Clyde Associated Mariners' Society in 1887 and the Mineral Workers' Union in 1888, and they inflicted sufficient damage on the GHLU that by the 1880s membership levels fell precipitously.[18] The GHLU also suffered at the hands of the NUDL and had grown distrustful of its 'arrogant and aggressive' tactics after it burst on to the scene in February 1889. Indeed, for a time the GHLU acted as 'scab labour union' during a series of disputes that took place at Glasgow, Belfast, Birkenhead, Liverpool and elsewhere between 1890 and 1892 in what was often reported as an 'old' versus 'new' union tussle for control. Some employers saw the GHLU as a Glasgow's 'Free Labour' movement and they engaged its members and 'boycotted' the 'mostly Irish' NUDL members who handled 'the rougher sorts of cargo'. This employment practice was similar to the operation of the 'Shipping Federation Ticket' which was presented to seamen and dockers who agreed to work on 'federated' vessels alongside non-union or 'free labour' men. The GHLU was expelled from the TUC which met at Glasgow in 1892 but was readmitted two years after it was shown that it no longer operated as a 'scab labour society'.

The Emergence of the Shipping Federation

The Shipping Federation was formed in September 1890 'in an age of hostility between employers and workman' and as 'a permanent battle-axe against oppression and abuse'. These were the days, noted L. H. Powel, 'when obdurate resistance was countered by ugly violence and when federation "ticket" crews were smuggled on board at dead of night to avoid pickets' and a time when 'officials were stoned on sight'.[19] By

the early months of 1891, however, the Federation emerged victorious
from a prolonged period of counter-attack against trade union gains and
thereafter asserted its dominance across much of the port transport
industry. First in its sights were the seamen, but in order to undermine
their union they would have to break the strong bond of solidarity
between them and other waterfront workers – most notably the carters
and dockers.

Shipping employers had formed associations in the past – such as in the
1870s when Sunderland shipping employers formed an association to
fight against Sunderland Seafarers' Society. In 1885 a 'Central Association
of Shipowners' was set up in Glasgow, Sunderland and Newcastle, and it
made the first serious attempt to organise a permanent country-wide body
to represent shipping interests across Britain. But it was not until the 'stirring and turbulent times' of the 1880s and early 1890s that serious consideration was given to the formation of a national 'fully incorporated'
Shipowners' Society.[20] Although the Shipping Federation was reputed to
have emerged from an organisation at Tynemouth, the industrial relations
methods the Federation was later to advocate and adopt were already
common practice at the port of Glasgow.

Ironically, Glasgow was one of the few ports not to join with the
Federation in 1890, although, according to evidence presented to the
Royal Commission on Labour in 1892, 'a very large number of Glasgow
shipowners' were in fact members. The Federation did not operate a
closed-shop or issue the 'federation ticket' at Glasgow as it did at other
ports, but the Clyde District of the Federation heavily influenced industrial relation strategies at Glasgow.[21] When it came to breaking the cycle
of sympathetic action and boycott by the carters, dockers and seamen,
the Glasgow port and shipping employers welcomed the assistance of the
Shipping Federation. But they would not be directed by the Federation
and this was evident at the time of the Shipping Federation's national
struggle with the Seamen's Union, led by Havelock Wilson, during 1890.
This was, nevertheless, to prove a defining moment in the history of
labour relation in the port transport industry and industrial relations in
Britain.

The 'Shipping Crisis' and the Struggle for Control

The great shipping struggle began in August 1890 when Wilson and his
Seamen's Union made public their demands that *all* seamen on board
British ships were to be members of the Seamen's Union (NASFU), and
that *all* seamen were to be engaged at the shipping offices and not on

board ship. The first stipulation meant the exclusion of all 'non-unionists' and a trade union monopoly in favour of the Seamen's Union, which was by no means the only union representing maritime workers. The second stipulation was intended to further enforce the first because once a seamen was on board his ship, there were 'no facilities for detecting' whether he was 'a union man or not' and little or no opportunity to compel him to join the union once at sea. But if sailors were engaged through the shipping offices, they could be identified and if not already in the union they could be persuaded into joining.[22]

The seamen were clearly preparing the ground for the next phase of industrial confrontation with the employers, but the real turning point came when Wilson publicly boasted that he intended to compel every 'shipmaster, officer and seaman' to join the union. Until this aim was achieved, however, he would instruct his members not to work any ship unless the master and officers were members of a sympathetic society known as the 'National Certificated Shipmasters and Officers' Union of Great Britain and Ireland'. Whether Wilson could have made good this promise is debatable, but, in making the threat, he precipitated a potential crisis in shipping, and it led directly to the formation of the Shipping Federation in September 1890 as a 'fighting machine to counter the strike weapon'.[23]

The Shipping Federation quickly secured the sympathy of the press after it demonstrated active and international trade union links between striking port transport workers in Australia and Britain, when seamen, dockers and other labourers working on the same shipping lines in Britain struck in sympathy with their Australian counterparts. The Australian dispute largely concerned the issue of the employment of non-union labour, but crucially the *cause célèbre* was the Australian unions' central demand that the shipping employers recognised the Marine Officers' Association's affiliation to the Australian Federation of Labour. This was more or less what the Seamen's Union was advocating in Britain and the Shipping Federation would have none of it:

> They would not willingly permit their trusted masters and officers to become the bondsmen of trade union officials, whose present and threatened actions [were] subversive of discipline, and fraught with danger to security of life and property at sea.[24]

The Federation backed up this promise with massive financial support and a levy of one penny per ton on members. The seamen and their allies now faced a powerful adversary and an 'organisation of shipowners representing capital of £100,000,000 invested in 6,500,000 gross registered tonnage'.[25] The Shipping Federation united almost the whole of the shipping interests across the Britain, and asserted that in the longer term,

> It would be open to all the colonial bodies ... not merely the United Kingdom, but the British Empire ... and the result, if necessary, being not only a bond of sympathy, but a common purse and combined action.[26]

'In the history of trade unionism', noted *The Scotsman*, 'it has seldom occurred that the combination of the workers has been met by such an organisation' as then confronted the Seamen's Union any where in the industrial world.[27]

The scene was now set for the struggle that was to take place over the early months of 1891. The dockers also became embroiled in the dispute at all the major ports in Scotland including Glasgow, Leith and Aberdeen. But there was a growing recognition in Scotland that the seamen's struggle was more or less a contest between the Federation and workers in England and Wales and, principally, port transport workers at Cardiff and London.[28] As a result Aberdeen was the only port in Scotland to become seriously involved in the dispute, and the Aberdeen Shore Labourers was the only dockers' union to come out in sympathy with the seamen in Scotland.[29] Leith became embroiled for a time over the issue of the introduction of the 'federation ticket' but reluctantly agreed to accept this situation when it became clear that the Federation had sufficient supplies of free labour to operate the port had they gone on strike. The dispute at Aberdeen, however, was of an entirely different order of magnitude, and, fighting more or less on one front, the Federation were able to double its efforts and increase supplies of replacement labour into the port in order to break the strike. Each new arrival of the 'Federation men' was met by a welcome committee comprising hundreds of strikers and the result was widespread violence and police baton charges, and on several occasions the Riot Act was read. In the meantime workers were coming before the courts for their part in strike activities and the meagre funds of the Shore Labourers Union, amounting to £700, were arrested.[30]

Meanwhile, Wilson issued a further warning to the Federation that if it persisted in pursuing the policy of issuing the 'federation ticket' he would call out the entire membership of the union across every port in the country. But this was generally seen as an empty threat, and in Scotland the employers knew there was little support for this action. A meeting of seamen at Glasgow, for example, unanimously passed a res-olution 'that the present relations with the Clyde shipowners did not warrant the members of the Glasgow branch taking any action' and the Leith seamen also refused to take any further action.[31] The shipowners did not impose the 'federation ticket' on workers at Glasgow and by mutual agreement had ceased the practice at Leith. As a result the seamen and dockers at these ports had little reason to become embroiled in Wilson's dispute, and, likewise, the employers felt no need to employ the services of the Federation.

At Aberdeen both sides of the dispute were reported as showing 'unflinching support' for their respective cause, and the seamen publicly acknowledged the important role played by the shore labourers. At one meeting it was argued that the imposition of the 'federation ticket' was the cause of the 'labour problem' and if the employers would not listen to reason they (the strikers) 'would adopt other methods – and these were political'. 'They would have to make use of the political machinery and return men to Parliament' to force the Federation to remove 'this abominable ticket'. It was also noted that 'two speakers gave expression to their socialistic views of the League with which they were associated' (a reference to the Scottish Land and Labour League).[32] It was clear from all the reports that the Shipping Federation was simply 'too strong' at Aberdeen, and by mid-March the strike came to an end.[33] *The Scotsman* asserted that 'the very basis of New Unionism [was] official despotism' and anticipated that the Federation's victory would encourage other capitalists to follow their example but added:

> The strength of the capitalist federation must, on the other hand, be the vindication of individual liberty . . . not only for the good of the capitalists concerned, but it is for the interests of society and for the benefit of the individual workman.

It may be hoped, the report continued, 'that society in general will have the wisdom to see that its most enduring interests are bound up with the maintenance of free labour'. But there would be no 'benefit' to those workmen who had taken part in the dispute for the Federation declined to have anything further to do with any striker 'vainly soliciting re-employment' after the dispute had ended.[34]

The Aftermath

It was only after the emergence of the Seamen's Union and the NUDL that there was any serious challenge to port and shipping employers' authority on the Clyde in particular and Scotland in general. Throughout the years 1889–90 they waged a formidable campaign against the

employers for trade union recognition and improved wages and conditions. But, in the final analysis, they met with more failure than success,
and by 1891 the high level of inter-union solidarity and militancy indicative of the early years was already beginning to break down. This coincided with the emergence of the Shipping Federation as the main
powerbroker in port transport and shipping affairs and, in its first serous
dispute, it won an emphatic victory. Scotland was less affected than the
rest of Britain because workers there did not support what was essentially seen as an English dispute. But workers stood firm in Aberdeen and,
as a result, the Federation set about the systematic destruction of both
the seamen's and the shore labourers' trade unions, and it finally achieved
it goal after a fresh wave of counter-attacks virtually wiped out port
transport and maritime trade unionism across much of the eastern
seaboard by 1894.

It was clear that waterfront industrial relations were changing as the
influence of the large steamship owners increased. The shipping and port
employers in Scotland – like the railway and later the engineering
employers – would not tolerate any combination of workers interfering
with their business. They particularly resented the attempts to unionise
foremen in the dock and engineering industries[35] or shipmasters and officers within the shipping industry. During the 1880s the employers at
Glasgow demonstrated that they were adept at 'union smashing' and
during the 1890s took it to another level of sophistication. They failed
to deliver a fatal blow at Glasgow – perhaps expecting the union to self-
destruct as occurred elsewhere – but their actions severely weakened the
NUDL.[36] At the start of the 1890s the NUDL at Glasgow had a membership of around 4,000, but by 1892 it had fallen to just under around
1,900, and in 1895 numbered only 1,400.[37] But the union survived and
when it affiliated to the Scottish Trades Union Congress in 1897 it
recorded a membership of 2,850. The GHLU also survived and amalgamated with the NUDL in 1889, taking the membership at Glasgow up
to 3,500. The NUDL maintained a foothold in Burntisland and Bo'ness
and hung on tenaciously at Leith and Port Glasgow. But membership was
low and as an organisation the NUDL was largely ineffective. It did reorganise Aberdeen in 1906 but lost the fight in Dundee which became a free
labour port in 1904.[38] Glasgow still had the highest trade membership
in Scotland throughout the 1890s and the early 1900s, but Liverpool
became the NUDL's principal stronghold and the union moved its headquarters there in 1891. Across the country, the NUDL survived the
employers' counter-attack in 1893, but was severely weakened, and from
a membership of 35,000 in 1890 (some estimates suggest 50,000)

numbers fell dramatically to around 10,000 by 1894 and more or less remained at that level until the labour unrest of 1910–14. [39]

CASE STUDY TWO: THE AMALGAMATED SOCIETY OF RAILWAY SERVANTS (ASRS)

After the defeat of the seaman and dockers, the press began to attack the leaders of artisan unions who, it would seem, were adopting new unionist tactics in flexing their industrial muscles. A prime example was the ASRS and the event that attracted attention was the Scottish railway dispute of 1890–1. It was an exclusively Scottish strike and thus generated more interest than the seamen's dispute. But as *The Times* reported in February 1891, the end result was the same: 'a complete defeat of the New Unionism by a tacit combination among the large employers of labour in Scotland'.[40] The press was of the opinion that there was a need for employer combinations in the industrial relations arena. Moreover, they clearly saw no distinction between 'old' and 'new'.

Despite the many hundreds of books written on the railway companies, only a few examine the lives and working conditions of railwaymen in Britain. The best known was George Alcock's history of railway trade unionism, first published in 1922, and Philip Bagwell's seminal work, *Railwaymen: The History of the National Union of Railwaymen*, first published in 1963.[41] Both books consider the role of the Scottish railwaymen but despite the long, if somewhat chequered, history of railway trade unionism in Scotland, the Scottish railwaymen have no definitive history of their own. James Mavor's *The Scottish Railway Strike 1891, A History and Criticism* (1891) is an exception and as the title implies is dedicated to one significant and celebrated strike in the history of the Scottish railwaymen.[42] The strike was conducted by the Scottish ASRS but it had major implications for all railwaymen and would prove something of a watershed in the history of railway trade unionism in Britain.

While the story of railway trade unionism forms part of a continuum stretching back to the first half of the nineteenth century, the modern history of the railway unions began in the 1870s. There were several societies for railwaymen and associated staff formed in Scotland from the 1870s onward but the first and most influential was the ASRS of Scotland. It was founded in 1872 with a membership of between 1,000 and 3,000 and, like the ASRS in England, Ireland and Wales, the Scottish ASRS was highly exclusive. Its main aim was to reduce hours and improve wages without recourse to strike. Its 'no strike' mission statement reveals much about the roots of the organisation and its formation in England in 1871, which Fraser noted, 'was largely due to the efforts of middle-class philanthropists'. Indeed, for twenty years it 'had middle-class presidents'.[43] The ASRS membership was confined mainly to the better-paid grades, and many other railway workers remained unorganised. In time other organisations did emerge – such as the Associated Society of Locomotive Engineers and Firemen (ASLEF) which was founded sometime later in 1880, and the General Railway Workers' Union (GRWU) founded in 1890 – made up of the poorest-paid railwaymen including porters and platelayers. [44]

Prior to the formation of the GRWU, there was a concerted campaign to encourage the ASRS to reduce the weekly contribution and open up its ranks to the lower-paid workers. This was first raised during the initial amalgamation discussions between the Scottish and the English societies at Leeds in July 1888. The Scottish and English weekly contribution was 3 pence and 5 pence respectively and the Scottish delegates wanted the upper level reduced, but the English body would not agree to any reduction. The debate regarding the level of weekly contribution was taken up again by Scottish delegates at the next Congress in July 1889, where it was argued that, if current scales were reduced, lower-paid workers would join the society in their thousands. If denied that opportunity, however, they would form 'opposition societies'. The 'cautiously minded' English delegates doubted that such action would 'add a single member to the Society' and would prove an unnecessary expense. The proposal was defeated. Within two months the GRWU was formed and, as the Scottish ASRS delegates had predicated, by 1890 it had recruited 10,827 members in support of a policy of 'militant trade unionism'.[45]

It is clear that there was a 'new mood' evident among certain sections of the ASRS in Scotland, and in attempting to recruit lower-paid railway workers they were manifesting early signs of what would later underpin a strong attachment to the principles of industrial unionism. Pragmatism fused with a growing sense of militancy seemed to be shaping ASRS industrial policy at this time. Bagwell notes, for example, that at the society's Annual General Meeting in October 1888, it agreed a motion by Edinburgh members to reword Clause 8 of Rule 15 in order 'to permit a specially summoned E.C. (Executive Council) both to authorise the withdrawal of labour and to expend money in support of strikers'.[46] This would better prepare the railwaymen for any forthcoming industrial struggle. John Burns, an SDF socialist and supporter of the new unionism, described the Scottish ASRS as 'a blend of the pioneers of old unionism with the newer, ethical, social and political tendencies of the time'.[47] The ASRS benefited considerably from an upsurge in membership and had gained much by following the example of dockers:

> If the dockers, who were even worse paid than the poorest paid railwaymen, could gain substantial improvements by aggressive unionism, why should not the porters, guards, signalmen and other enter the fight for more tolerable conditions of employment?

Throughout much of the 1880s, the ASRS had been wallowing in apathy and disillusionment, as was clearly reflected in poor membership figures. When the Scottish ASRS was formed in 1872, it had a membership of about 1,000, rising to 3,000 in January 1883 at the time of the first major railway workers' dispute, and this increased only slightly to 3,350 by the late 1880s. According to evidence presented to the 'Select Committee on Labour' at the time of the Scottish railway strike of 1890–1, membership levels in Scotland had increased to just over 7,000.[48]

John Holford's study of work and politics in Edinburgh makes some mention of the railwaymen and their contribution to the changing political culture of the city, but he also gives some sense of what all railway workers would face by taking on the employers. The North British and the Caledonian Railways operated out of Edinburgh and 'by a very substantial margin were the largest industrial companies in Scotland'. They were simply 'vast employers of labour'. But in order to coordinate this extensive and complex organisation the industry was structured along 'military lines':

> A process very similar to mobilising an army . . . Not just the structural, but the moral, elements of the military model were taken over: company uniform and livery, the language of going on 'duty', 'absence without leave', being put on a 'charge', 'loss of rank'; unquestioning obedience to 'officers' and 'superior officers'.

It was little wonder, he argued, that the railwaymen rebelled against this system and 'all the petty tyranny' that went with it.[49]

In the aftermath of the Scottish railway strike, James Mavor published his 'History and Criticism' of the dispute wherein he outlined the events that occurred over those six turbulent weeks. It is a painstakingly detailed piece of research which, in 'a dispassionate and scientific spirit' attempted to place the railwaymen's dispute 'in the general labour problem' of the time. The strike was called in order to force the employers to reduce the working week but in his 'narrative of the transactions prior to the strike' Mavor demonstrated that the roots of this 'agitation' stretched back to an earlier strike in 1883 and concerned the same issue: the demand for the ten-hour day.[50] It was well documented that the Scottish railwaymen men worked very long hours and that in Scotland a twelve-hour day was fairly normal. This was due to a system of payment and employment known as the 'Trip system' whereby a driver's wages were calculated on the basis of how long the trip took to complete, but took no account of excessive delays, hold-ups or congestion. The average trip was calculated at ten hours per day for six days – a weekly average of sixty hours. The total hours worked were often much higher and regularly reached fifteen hours per day, depending on the route. This meant the driver could work a ninety-hour week but was only paid for sixty hours, with no payment for the extra hours worked.[51] This was the basis for the railwaymen's demands for a ten-hour day and overtime payments for all extra hours worked.

Mavor gathered evidence that demonstrated that a fifteen-hour day was not so unusual and could often be higher. An Edinburgh driver on the North British Railway Line during March 1890 endured daily runs for the month that averaged seventeen hours: with a maximum number of hours on duty of twenty-one hours and a minimum for that month of twelve hours: hence the determination of the men not to concede their demand for the ten-hour day.[52] After six long weeks, however, the dispute ended in defeat for the railwaymen, and the employers refused to concede the ten-hour day or formal recognition of the ASRS. So what was the immediate impact of the strike? With no actual reduction in hours, the strike was ultimately deemed a failure. But Mavor noted that a broad agreement had been reached among unionists on the policy of 'state ownership of the railways' and he rather perceptively concluded 'that in the future this might become irresistible, should the evils associated with railway rates and railway labour continue to thrust themselves into the eye of the public'.[53]

The Scottish railwaymen's strike captured the attention of the trade-union movement, and, despite the negative pronouncements of the press, public opinion was not entirely unsympathetic to the railwaymen, particularly when the railway employers threatened to evict strikers from company houses. Some workers at Hamilton returned to work after the Caledonian Railway Company applied for eviction orders, but at Motherwell, 'the most intensely picketed place in Scotland', only two men out of sixty capitulated under threat of eviction. A sum of £6,000 'hard cash' from England and sympathetic action by Hamilton and Blantyre miners helped to steady the Scottish strikers' nerves. There was, however, no sympathy from *The Times* newspaper's Glasgow labour correspondent, who labelled the dispute 'the most abjectly stupid strike of modern times'. He did note that the threat of eviction scheduled for New Year's morning 'shocked Scottish feelings' and no matter how foolish or obstinate the men might be, to evict men in such a manner at a time of a Scottish holiday 'would have left a painful impression upon the public mind'.[54] But it was the riot at Motherwell in the wake of the eventual evictions that left a lasting impression on *The Times* correspondent. He arrived 'by cab' in plenty of time to witness 'the most violent and unreasonable riot' he had ever come across. The sheriff's officers, backed up with hussars and 150 Lancashire policemen (who replaced men from Glasgow), faced a crowd of 1,000 comprising the strikers, their supporters, and a large contingent of striking miners from Hamilton and Blantyre. The Caledonian Railway Company eventually won the day and the strikers were evicted, but not without much damage and destruction of property and a 'disgraceful disregard for the law' that had characterised the strike 'from beginning to end'. [55]

John Burns was regularly reported at this time for his 'perambulations across Scotland' and his travels took him from Dundee to Fife, the Borders, Edinburgh and Glasgow and finally to Motherwell in support of the striking railwaymen. In addressing a large meeting later in London, organised solely in support of the Scottish strike, he reported on his experience during the evictions at Motherwell and the excessive use of force by the military and the police. Letters and telegrams of support from all over the country were read out in what was a quite outstanding show of solidarity – not least in terms of financial support. Ben Tillett was in Scotland when the strike broke out, and noted that he was predictably blamed for starting it, and asserted that he 'had never seen a pluckier set of men than the Scotsmen he addressed on that day'. He hoped that 'London would help them fight for victory' and in this he was seconded by Fred Hammill of the London Trades Council and Will Thorne of the Gasworkers' Union.[56]

The press corps had reported from late December 1890 that the strike was on its last legs, but it was not until 2 February 1891 that the dispute came to 'an absolute end' and the remaining 3,000 strikers returned to work. *The Times* proclaimed 'a complete defeat of the New Unionism by a tacit combination among the large employers of labour in Scotland', although it failed to mention that they were ably assisted by the courts, the police and the military. The ASRS's National Congress, held in Liverpool in November that year, recognised that the strike was to an extent a failure, in so far as the men returned defeated, however,

> Its moral results were enormous in their importance. The public were educated by the revelations then made . . . since it was shown that the men in whose care the lives of the public are placed were worked abnormally long hours, the question has been elevated into a great national question . . . The public opinion so created had resulted in a marked degree of benefit of railway servants generally.[57]

The argument for nationalisation of the railways was now firmly on the political agenda and became a central demand of the railway trade unions thereafter, and after the strike the issue of state intervention was raised in parliament. There was a proposal, which was ultimately rejected, put to parliament that the Board of Trade should be given the power to fix the hours of railway labour. In the course of that debate it was agreed to set up a Select Committee to 'investigate the extent of overwork on the railways and to examine possible remedies'. According to Bagwell, 'the Scottish railwaymen had performed a valuable service to railwaymen all over the United Kingdom in focusing the attention of Parliament to this long-standing abuse'.[58]

To commemorate the strike, special medallions were struck in bronze, silver and gold (purchasable at nine pence, three shillings and twenty-one shillings respectively) for those qualified to wear them. On one side of the medallion was inscribed 'Scotch Railway Strike 1890–91' and on the other 'A.S.R.S. for Scotland'. How many were in a position to purchase these items is unclear, for membership of the Scottish ASRS fell sharply after the dispute. But it did hasten talks of a merger with the English ASRS. The month before the strike took place the two societies had met with ASLEF and the GRWU to consider federation and, although this ended with no firm agreement, when the strike broke out all three non-Scottish bodies pledged all possible help. By February 1892 it was decided by a very large majority of the Scottish members that their society should join with the English society, and by the end of August both had formally amalgamated. At what was the first Annual Congress of the ASRS of England, Ireland, Scotland and Wales in October that year, when the question of amalgamation with the GRWU was once again discussed, 'the Scottish society died an honourable death almost exactly twenty years from the date of its foundation'.[59]

What Bagwell's account does not make clear is that there was a significant degree of dissatisfaction regarding the amalgamation and some of the old Scottish ASRS members broke away to form an independent

Scottish Railwaymen's Union (SRU). The following press 'circular' gives some sense of their concerns:

> The scheme as it stands is too one-sided and unsatisfactory . . . It does not provide sufficiently for dealing with Scottish affairs . . . makes no provision for the democratic expression of opinion . . . [or the] collective voice as the society in the choice of permanent officials. We object to centralisation . . . [as it] militates against the effectiveness of railway unionism in Scotland . . . Hence the formation of the Scottish Railwaymen's Union! [60]

In response, the ASRS argued that Scottish members would not be treated any differently, and, under the new rules, there was actually 'more local control in the branches than was provided for under the old Scottish Society'. The history of railway disputes showed 'the necessity for centralisation' and amalgamation was the 'only means of securing the complete protection of Scottish railwaymen'.[61] All the available evidence related to the strike does seem to validate this conclusion, for, as Bagwell rightly suggests, had it not been for the financial support of the three non-Scottish societies 'the struggle would have been much shorter and less effective'.[62] Indeed, there was also considerable and significant support from the Edinburgh Trades Council and London trade unionists in January 1891.

It was this example of solidarity that provided the last push towards amalgamation and the great majority of Scottish railwaymen accepted this. A meeting in Dunfermline held under the auspices of local trades councils agreed that the ballot on the arrangements of amalgamation had been conducted correctly and that only thirty-eight men in Scotland actually voted against amalgamation. The railwaymen of Dunfermline believed amalgamation 'was the best means of promoting the interests of our class throughout the United Kingdom'. At a meeting at Bathgate with delegates from Glasgow and Edinburgh it was likewise agreed, and the meeting called upon 'all railwaymen to affiliate themselves to the Union'. At the same time Mr James Paisley was addressing a 'fairly attended' meeting of the newly formed SRU in Edinburgh.[63]

Despite the broad agreement on amalgamation, there was some considerable support for the SRU, and in February 1893 it organised 'a largely-attended meeting' in Glasgow.[64] Later in October the ASRS met for its annual congress at the same venue, and although there were 150 delegates in attendance the meeting was reported as 'rather small' when compared to the SRU congress eight months before. The October congress noted that despite the 'gigantic struggle' of 1890–1 the promise made then by the railway employers, 'meagre though they were', had been 'flagrantly abused' and as a result 'they had injustices existing on the Scottish railways that did not exist in any other part of the United Kingdom' (referring to a longer working week and lower wages). But the meeting agreed that the problems faced by the Scottish railwaymen were best served within an amalgamated union.[65] In the final analysis the ASRS was ultimately proved correct, for early in 1895 the SRU became defunct in Scotland. But in examining the SRU's short history, it is evident that there were real tensions in some quarters between Scottish and English notions of trade unionism.

After the collapse of the SRU there was a period of relative calm until the fairly widespread 'agitations' across Scotland between December 1896 and January 1897. These related to the ASRS demands for an 'eight' and 'ten' hour working week for 'signalmen' and 'shunters' respectively employed by the North British Railway Company. The epicentre of this movement was Edinburgh and the dispute concerned the hours of labour of workers primarily at Portobello and Leith docks, but this action later spread to Aberdeen, Dundee, Dunfermline, Perth and finally to Glasgow. By mid-January 1897 the Board of Trade had informed the ASRS that the company had agreed 'to reduce the hours of work for servants in question' and that it would include porters and ticket collectors in this arrangement.[66] The employers were in effect forced to comply with such demands under the conditions of the Railways Regulation Act 1893, which gave the men the right to appeal to the Board of Trade and Conciliation.

This was a sign of progress, for at the Annual Congress at Plymouth in October 1897 the ASRS confidently asserted that its members worked under more favourable conditions then than at any time in its history.[67] Indeed, this was to some extent borne out at the half-yearly North British Railway Company shareholders meeting at Glasgow just days later where it was noted that the railway servants now enjoyed 'many [more] privileges' than they had hitherto. Although the general reduction in hours had increased the wages bill significantly, it also enhanced the image of the industry, and the 'attractive nature of the service' resulted in a 'large number applicants for admission which had to be refused'.[68]

The year 1897 was something of a turning point for the railway workers, employers and the labour movement generally. The engineers' strike was the main focus of attention throughout that year, but the railwaymen's agitation to implement the 'National Programme' (an 'all-grades' campaign to regulate hours and wages of all railwaymen across Britain by joint negotiation) forced the railway companies to contemplate 'the formation of an association similar to that of the engineering employers' to act as a 'standing menace to the success of a forward policy among trade unionists'.[69] The railway employer faced the threat of widespread strike action in support of the ASRS campaign, but, in similar fashion to the seamen's dispute six years before, the mood in Scotland was somewhat different. According to *The Scotsman*, the Scottish railwaymen fully supported the 'National Programme' but 'recollections of the disastrous results of the last railway strike [were] still vivid'. In addition, its membership was not as large as it was before the strike. All three Scottish railway companies correctly assessed that the Scottish railway servants were not prepared to strike. If proved wrong, however, they would immediately combine to defeat the railwaymen as they had done in 1890–1.[70]

By December 1897 *The Times* was confidently reporting that the threat of a general strike of railwaymen had passed and it noted too the advice offered by John Burns (then an MP and with his militancy fast disappearing), that such an action was 'ill-advised' and that 'a thrashing awaited them' if they took on the railway companies at that juncture. The railwaymen had many new members but, unlike the Scottish members, had no experience of a 'bitter industrial war'. Burns believed the railway companies were attempting to lure the railwaymen into dispute because they fully expected to inflict a 'crushing defeat' on them.[71] Indeed, if a leading editorial in *The Scotsman* is anything to go by, the railwaymen were right to heed Burns' warnings, for the engineering dispute had shown that the employers were in no mood for compromise and were seemingly spoiling for a fight. The year 1897 would prove memorable in the history of the labour relations in Britain. There were other years in which strikes and other labour troubles were more numerous, but the example of the engineering strikes demonstrated that 'trade union aggression [had] been met and discomfited by the use of its own methods'. According to *The Scotsman,* the triumph of the Engineering Employers' Federation had 'undoubtedly given a check to the aggressive policy of the new unionist movement which first came to be heard in connection with London Dock strike 'nine years before'.[72]

The Early Twentieth Century

In its overall assessment of the year 1898 on relations between capital and labour, *The Times* reported 'that if 1897 closed amidst storm-clouds; 1898 ended in a very sunny and tranquil fashion'.[73] When in 1899 the newly-formed Shipbuilding Employers' Federation used its 'bargaining strength in the depression to curb the power of the Boilermakers'

Society', it seemed that organised aggressive and militant labour had at last been tamed. Indeed, by the early twentieth century, as Fraser suggests, the employers had it in their power to rid themselves of trade unionism, particularly during the depression years of 1902–5, but there were very few instances of organised employers taking advantage of this situation while industrial relations remained tranquil.[74] And so it remained in most cases until after 1907 when across England and Wales industrial unrest was once again on the increase.

The period between 1898 and 1907 was one of 'relative peace in British industrial relations'.[75] This was particularly true in regards to the railways for it was not until the resurgence of the 'all-grades movement' in 1906 that industrial relations in this sector became animated once more. But the railwaymen's union was at the centre of new political moves. It is clear that the Scottish railwaymen favoured and supported moves towards the formation of a single industrial union of railway workers and the nationalisation of the railway industry.[76] The ASRS was one of three trade unions – the others being the London Dockers and the NUDL – to propose the formation of an independent representative labour organisation in Parliament to fight for working-class interests in 1899. This resulted in the formation of the Labour Representation Committee (LRC) who put up fifteen candidates in the 1900 election, winning two seats. One seat was won by James Keir Hardie, and the other by Richard Bell who was general secretary of the ASRS. In Scotland, the political situation was a little different but the desire and drive for independent forms of labour representation were just as strong and often more vocal. Indeed, it was Scotland that led the way in its demands for independent labour representation when in 1899 – before the formation of the Labour Representation Committee (LRC) to represent England and Wales – the Scottish Trades Union Congress with its affiliated unions, the Scottish Independent Labour Party and other socialist societies, formed the Scottish Workers' Parliamentary Election Committee to nominate and provide support for labour candidates in Scotland. One of the members of the Parliamentary Committee of the STUC in 1899 was James Innes of the ASRS.

Not all trade unions were convinced of the need for independent labour representation and in both Scotland and England many railwaymen still supported the Liberal Party. But after the Taff Vale judgement in 1901 – a court judgment which resulted in the ASRS paying £23,000 in compensation plus costs to the Taff Vale Railway Company for a strike conducted the previous year – many more unions affiliated to the LRC.[77] Unlike the dockers and seamen, the Scottish railwaymen were functioning quite efficiently by the early twentieth century. By 1908, as the economy was just pulling out of general recession, the ASRS boasted an STUC-affiliated membership of over 7,000. The increase in ASRS membership also occurred in the aftermath of a series of disputes during 1907 connected to the 'All Grades Movement' and the campaign for employer recognition. The railway employers were steadfastly anti-trade union and consistently rejected calls for joint collective bargaining, not only in Scotland but across Britain. By 1908 the railwaymen had met with some success but the response of the employers was partial and somewhat patchy, and while the principle of establishing conciliation boards, to adjudicate on issues such as wages and conditions, had been broadly agreed (and these had been on the increase within other industrial sectors), there was a great deal of confusion surrounding this issue.[78]

The railwaymen still had their problems and another major legal battle came with the Osborne Case when Walter Victor Osborne, secretary of the ASRS Walthamstow branch, took the union to court 'on the basis that a trade union had no right to spend money on political activity, including financing the Labour Party'. Although a High Court judge dismissed the case in 1908, Osborne appealed, and both the Appeal Court and later the House of Lords gave judgment in his favour. This decision threatened the very existence of the Labour Party as its revenue was largely derived from the trade union movement. The Trade Union Act of 1913 finally reversed the decision, but once again the ASRS found itself centre stage at pivotal moments in the history of the British trade unionism.[79] Nevertheless, the railwaymen were in buoyant mood and when compared to other bodies of workers before 1910 – particularly the carters, dockers and seamen – their union was in relatively good shape, and during the labour unrest of 1910–14 would consolidate its position significantly.[80]

POSTSCRIPT: THE LABOUR UNREST OF 1910–14

The years 1910–14 saw a significant increase in industrial conflict and an upsurge in unionism that outstripped the advances made at the height of the new unionism twenty years before. The detail of the labour unrest in Scotland is considered in much greater detail in Chapter 4 of this book, but it is necessary to say something about the port transport workers and the railwaymen at this time in order to round off these two case studies. After almost forty years of trying, the railwaymen finally won a degree of union recognition in 1911 because of the general strike in August that year which in Scotland involved 16,000 workers. Indeed, this led to the government directly intervening in the dispute, forcing the employers to negotiate with the railway unions, and to accept a degree of joint-collective bargaining within the industry. This remarkable achievement paved the way for the next big step which came with the formation of the National Union of Railwaymen (NUR) in 1913, when the ASRS, the GRWU and the United Pointsmen and Signalmen's Society amalgamated (ASLEF remaining aloof). With the formation of the NUR, the railwaymen moved a step closer to attaining the goal of creating a mass industrial union.[81] Indeed, the experience of labour unrest in Scotland brought the railwaymen in Edinburgh into a close association with the Socialist Labour Party (SLP, a revolutionary Marxist organisation) and coincided with the NUR's general 'flirtation with syndicalism and industrial unionism' before the war. Put simply, syndicalism asserted that workers could change society through industrial or 'direct action' rather than political action and constitutional reform. But this is a highly contested issue, and rank-and-file opinion of the syndicalist industrial strategy varied from location to location. Whatever the facts of the matter, by 1914 the Scottish section of the NUR had a membership of 17,900 affiliated to the STUC.[82]

In August 1911 over 6,000 dockers and 7,000 seamen across Scotland took part in a national strike. This was another remarkable achievement because by late December 1910 the NUDL had collapsed across the west of Scotland, and nationally its membership was just over 1,700 – more or less representing Aberdeen, Burntisland and Montrose and a rump at Glasgow and Leith. More worrying still, representation among the Seamen's Union (the National Seamen's and Firemen's Union (NSFU) formed in 1894 after the old seamen's union collapsed) was by then virtually non-existent. But with the formation of the Scottish Union of Dock Labour (SUDL) in Glasgow in July 1911, there was a renaissance for dock unionism on the Clyde. The resurgent seamen's union (NSFU) worked energetically with both the SUDL and the NUDL on the east coast and, although less successful, together they reorganised in Aberdeen, Burntisland, Leith, Grangemouth and Methil.[83] The SUDL reorganised Bo'ness and Dundee in time for the dockers there to take part in the great carters' strike during December 1911. The strike only involved 600 carters and 700 dockers but together they brought Dundee to a halt, and 30,000 workers were unable to work as a result.[84] In the ILP's *Forward* newspaper the local organiser of the Dundee ILP was reported as saying that the strike was 'a glorious lesson in solidarity' because the broad swathe of Dundee workers actively supported the dispute.[85] Indeed, according to Alan Bell, leaning heavily on

E. P. Thompson, the working community of Dundee formed such a bond of solidarity at that juncture that they 'ceased to be a class in itself' and became 'a class for itself'.[86] It is perhaps somewhat ironic that at the beginning of August 1911, *The Scotsman* reported that Scottish workers did not get 'unduly excited' in industrial matters. But looking back over events some four months later, the tone was entirely different:

> The Labour Unrest has been recruited from a vague Syndicalism of the French Socialists, who suggest that the universal strike is the best means of bringing 'capitalism' to its knees.

The carters and dockers' strike at Dundee was considered an example of such syndicalism at work.[87]

The Seamen's Union and the NUDL were re-established at Aberdeen by 1906 but were thereafter fairly inactive even during the labour unrest. The Aberdeen branch of the Seamen's Union was alone in Scotland in not supporting a general strike call issued by the union's executive in June 1912.[88] This was a reversal of its position over twenty years before when it was the only branch of the Seamen's Union to take part in a British-wide strike against the Shipping Federation and, indeed, perhaps the memory of defeat was still fresh in their minds. With the help of the seamen and the Edinburgh Trades Council, the NUDL was reorganised at Leith and took part in a major and well-publicised dispute there in 1913. Eric Hobsbawm viewed the role of the seamen as crucial, for they were an enduring link between the new unionism and the labour unrest and 'main force of unity in both cases'.[89] In all, by 1914, the NSFU and other seafarers' unions had a total membership of around 7,000, the NUDL 3,500, the SUDL 7,000, and the carters of the Scottish Horse and Motormen's Association (SHMA) over 10,000 (Gillespie's North East Scottish Horse and Motormen breakaway was not affiliated to the STUC).[90] The National Transport Workers Federation (NTWF) was formed in 1910 to unite the carters, dockers and seamen, and, on the eve of war, the transport unions could claim the highest level of unionisation in the country.[91] It was truly a dramatic turn-around of events.

The Shipping Federation attempted a counter-attack, but only in Scotland and only at two ports – Ardrossan and Leith between 1912 and 1913 – and it was unsuccessful in both counts. In the NTWF the trans-port workers had an organisation that was in theory able to match the Federation, and when it joined with the NUR and the Mining Federation of Great Britain to form the Triple Industrial Alliance in 1913, it was con-ceived as a great achievement for the political proponents of industrial unionism. George Dangerfield considered this as one of the most potent weapons developed by the labour movement before 1914, and it was the direct result of agitation among the rank-and-file miners, railwaymen and transport workers.[92] The labour unrest of 1910–14 was to precipitate a period of intense industrial, social and political discontent. The industrial conflict abated when Britain went to war in August 1914, but within a year the Clyde was in revolt and across Scotland workers began to openly express their anger over rising prices, the curtailment of individual liberties, and the threat of military and industrial conscription. The First World War thus 'played a critical role' in incubating workers' grievances, 'raising class awareness, and drawing workers away from liberalism towards the left'.[93] This radicalising impulse continued beyond the war, and together the events taking place between 1910 and 1922 form an important and distinctive period in the history of the Scottish trade union and labour movement.

NOTES

1. Kenefick, *Rebellious and Contrary*.
2. Marwick, 'Early Trade Unionism in Scotland', p. 87, on labour history Kenefick, ibid. pp. 14–22.
3. Fraser, *Trade Unions and Society: The Struggle for Acceptance, 1850–1880*), pp. 198–207; Charlesworth, *An Atlas of Industrial Protest*.
4. Fraser, *British Trade Unionism*.
5. *The Times*, 18 March 1891.
6. Quelch, *Trade Unionism*, pp. 3–4.
7. Fraser, *British Trade Unionism*, pp. 74–5: Kenefick, *Rebellious and Contrary*; for The Mineral Workers' Union, pp. 93, 188, 192; for the Aberdeen Shore Workers, pp. 119, 185–6, also p. 186, n. 11; and for the Greenock Dock Labourers, pp. 87, 94. For the American Knights of Labour, see Kenefick, *The Key To the Clyde*.
8. Buckley, *Trade Unionism in Aberdeen*, pp. 36–7.
9. *The Scotsman*, 7, 14 March and 7 June 1889; there were about 1,000 dockers at Leith.
10. *North British Daily Mail* and *The Glasgow Herald* reported extensively on the dockers and seamen's dispute throughout June and early July of 1889 – specifically 13, 17, 19, 21 June and 1 to 6 July.
11. Kenefick, *Rebellious and Contrary*, pp. 190–1.
12. Taplin, The *Dockers' Union*, p. 30.
13. Glasgow Trades Council, *Annual Report*, 1888–9, p. 8.
14. Kenefick, *Rebellious and Contrary*, pp. 168, 189; Lovell, 'Sail, Steam and Emergent Dockers Unionism', p. 232.
15. *RC on Labour, 2nd Report, 1892*: Q. 13,417.

16. Fraser, *British Trade Unionism*, p. 77.
17. Lovell, *Stevedores and Dockers*, p. 85.
18. Kenefick, *Rebellious and Contrary* , p. 171.
19. Powel, *The Shipping Federation*, p. 1.
20. Ibid. p. 2.
21. *RC on Labour, 2nd Report, 1892*: Q. 13,417; Kenefick, *Rebellious and Contrary*, p. 178.
22. *The Times* Editorial Leader, 13 December 1890.
23. Powel, *The Shipping Federation*, pp. 4–7.
24. *The Scotsman,* 12 September 1890.
25. *The Scotsman,* 9 October 1890.
26. *The Times,* 10 September 1890.
27. *The Scotsman,* 9 October 1890.
28. *The Scotsman,* 12 February 1891.
29. *The Scotsman,* 27 February 1891.
30. *The Scotsman,* 5 March 1891.
31. Noted in a later report in the *The Scotsman,* 11 March 1890.
32. *The Scotsman,* 9 March 1891.
33. *The Scotsman,* 16 March 1891.
34. *The Scotsman,* 17 March 1891.
35. Fraser, *British Trade Unions*, pp. 111–12. The engineering employers deliberately set out to detach foremen from the ASE by forming a Foremen's Mutual Benefit Society after 1897, in the same manner as the Shipping Federation had done during 1890 by converting the existing Shipmasters and officers Society into a virtual company union.
36. Kenefick, *Rebellious and Contrary* , pp. 183–9, 197.
37. Glasgow Trades Council, *Annual Report, 1889–1890,* p. 8; for 1891 NUDL figures, see Taplin, *Dockers' Unions, Appendix,* p. 169.
38. Kenefick, *Rebellious and Contrary,* pp. 198–200.
39. Board of Trade, *Report on Trade Unions in 1899*; see Coates and Topham, *The Making of the Transport and General Workers' Union,* Table 4.1: Figures for Membership of New Unions, p. 95.
40. *The Times,* 2 February 1891.
41. Alcock, *Fifty Years of Railway Trade Unionism*; and P. S. Bagwell, *Railwaymen.*
42. Mavor, *The Scottish Railway Strike 1891*: James Mavor was at that time Professor of political economy and statistics at Glasgow University, and a founder member of the Glasgow Branch of the SDF in 1884 – 'The first Socialist organisation formed in Glasgow'; see Lowe, *Souvenirs,* p. 121.
43. Fraser, *British Trade Unions*, pp. 64–5.
44. MacDougall, *A Catalogue of some Labour Records in Scotland*, p. 360(b).
45. Bagwell, *Railwaymen,* p. 132.
46. Ibid. pp. 130–1.
47. *The Scotsman,* 22 September 1890.

48. Railway Servants Hours of labour: Report from the Select Committee; Proceedings, minutes of evidence, appendix and index, 1891 (1890–91), vol. xiv–xvi, p. 681 [Sessional Papers no. 342]; evidence of Henry Tait, Secretary of the Amalgamated Society of Railway Servants of Scotland, pp. 20–54; Bagwell, *Railwaymen*, p. 141. He suggests a Scottish membership of 6,703 by December 1890.

49. Holford, *Reshaping Labour*, pp. 80–1.

50. Mavor, *The Scottish Railway Strike*, 'Preface', p. 7.

51. *The Glasgow Herald, The Scotsman* and *The Times* regularly reported on the excessive hours worked in Scotland, and that Scottish railwaymen worked longer and for less pay than their English and Welsh counterparts: reported periodically from the 1870s onward. See also Mavor, *The Scottish Railway Strike*, pp. 25–32; Bagwell, *Railwaymen*, pp. 140–1, n. 24, and p. 151; and *The Engineer* (SRSA Trade Journal), 30 January 1890.

52. Mavor, *The Scottish Railway Strike*, pp. 25–6; and Table II, p. 66.

53. Mavor, *The Scottish Railway Strike*, p. 56.

54. *The Times*, 29, 30 December 1890, and 2, 3 January 1891.

55. *The Times, The Scotsman* and *The Glasgow Herald*, 6–10 January 1891.

56. *The Scotsman*, 12 January 1891.

57. *The Scotsman*, 17 November 1891.

58. Bagwell, *Railwaymen*, p. 148.

59. *The Scotsman*, 5 October 1892; Bagwell, *Railwaymen*, p. 149: also MacDougall, *Labour Records*, p. 361(a). Little is known of the SRU and very limited records exist at the National Archives of Scotland [previously listed in MacDougall as the Scottish Records Office (SRO) for 1889: see FS.7/88].

60. 'The Scottish Railwaymen Split', *The Scotsman*, 22 September 1892.

61. 'To the Railwaymen of Scotland': an official response of the Executive of the ASRS of England, Ireland, Scotland and Wales, *The Scotsman*, 26 September 1892.

62. Bagwell, *Railwaymen*, p. 149.

63. 'Railwaymen of Dunfermline and Bathgate for Amalgamation', *The Scotsman*, 26 September 1892.

64. *The Scotsman*, 6 February 1893.

65. *The Scotsman*, 9 October 1893.

66. *The Scotsman*, 28 December 1896 and 16 January 1897

67. *The Scotsman*, 7 October 1897.

68. *The Scotsman*, 11 October 1897.

69. *The Scotsman*, 8 November 1897.

70. *The Scotsman*, 4 December 1897.

71. *The Times*, 6 December 1897.

72. *The Scotsman*, 3 January 1898

73. *The Times*, 27 December 1989.

74. Fraser, *British Trade Unions*, pp. 108–9.

75. Charlesworth, *An Atlas of Industrial Protest*, p. 123.
76. Bagwell, *Railwaymen*, pp. 147–9.
77. There is an extensive literature on this and other developments such as the Osborne Case of 1909: see Bagwell, *Railwaymen*, chapters viii, ix, and pp. 199–261; Wallace, *Single or Return: the History of the Transport Salaried Staff Association*.
78. Fraser, *British Trade Unions*, pp. 111–12, 117.
79. Wallace, *Single or Return*; see chapter 3.
80. STUC, *Annual Report of Proceedings*; delegates list, societies and numbers represented, 1900–1910.
81. Bagwell, *The Railwaymen*, pp. 309–44.
82. STUC, *Annual Report* 1914, p. 9; Holford, *Reshaping Labour*, pp. 149–51.
83. Kenefick, *Rebellious and Contrary*, pp. 212–16.
84. Dundee *Courier*, 20, 21 December 1911.
85. Bell, 'A Glorious Lesson in Solidarity?'; also Bell 'New Sources in Labour History', pp. 173–89.
86. Thompson, 'Eighteenth Century English Society'.
87. *The Scotsman*, 26 December 1911.
88. *The Scotsman*, 13 June 1913.
89. Hobsbawm, *Labouring Men*, p. 217; Kenefick, 'Ardrossan Dock Strike, 1912–1913'.
90. Gillespie's union was not listed as affiliated members to the STUC between 1911 and 1914; see *Annual Report*, 1912 to 1914.
91. STUC, *Annual Report*, 1914, pp. 7–8; Fraser, *British Trade Unionism*, p. 116.
92. Dangerfield, *The Strange Death of Liberal England*, p. 318.
93. McIvor, 'Red Dawn Fades', pp. 8–11.

3

Left Radicalism, Labour and Socialism

INTRODUCTION

It is clear that there are pitfalls and dangers for the historian in attempting to make too close a connection between the upsurge in trade unions from the 1870s and the impact of political radicalism or socialism. But the absence of socialism did not preclude the influence of other forms of political action on trade-union formation. That is to say that 'radicalism' – whether this relates to industrial or political ideas and actions – 'does not merely equate with socialist leanings, however broadly defined': it is also associated with 'left wing social democracy [and] a willingness to campaign on wider political issues rather than just economic ones'.[1] The radical campaign to overturn elements of the Criminal Law Amendment Act – introduced in tandem with the 1871 Trade Union Act (which made picketing illegal; rendering a strike almost impossible to enforce) – politicised many trade unionists across Britain, and in Scotland drew workers and their unions into closer contact with local trades councils that gradually became the main focus for industrial and political debate on this issue. For example, opposition to the Criminal Law Amendment Act, and a growing 'distrust of middle-class Liberal politics' brought the Glasgow Trades Council into 'the field of politics' in setting up the Glasgow Liberal Working Men's Electoral Union, and the Edinburgh Trades Council became even more politically animated over this issue.[2]

This political impulse clearly derived from radical liberalism and emerged from within the ranks of the skilled artisans or 'labour aristocracy'. Moreover, this Scottish labour movement was small and somewhat isolated from the majority of working men and women during the 1870s. By the following decade, however, it broke free from this isolation 'just as a renaissance of international socialism was developing'. Socialism had taken take root in France and many other areas in Europe from the

1860s and 1870s onward, but only emerged in England in the early 1880s with the formation of the Marxist Social Democratic Federation (SDF). The appearance of socialism in Scotland had a similar provenance, but its influences were rather less Marxist than in England. It was derived mainly from 'ethical socialism' and in particular the theories of American 'land reformer' Henry George. George published *Poverty and Progress* in Britain in the early 1880s and widely toured Scotland lecturing on the issue of land reform. He argued that the gap between rich and poor could only be reduced by substituting the 'whole range of taxes' levied on capital and labour with 'one single tax' based on property valuation. At a simple level, it was a tax on the rich and property ownership, and this financial and fiscal burden could only be reduced through the redistributing of property. In Scotland Land Reform became closely associated with the issue of 'Home Rule' and together they had 'an explosive impact on Scottish politics' in the 1880s. Indeed, they pushed the Scots 'into the vanguard of the international socialist movement'.[3]

Thus it was Henry George, who was not a socialist, who became a 'key intellectual influence' on the nascent socialist movement in Scotland, and his theories helped to re-establish an older historic link with an radical 'anti-landlord' tradition that stretched back to the days of Chartism.[4] Thoughts of socialism may rarely have troubled the average working man in Scotland, but support for land reform and home rule was popular and widespread, and through the agitations of the labour movement 'nationalist and internationalist sentiments developed hand-in-hand'. These were, indeed, exciting times, but by the first decade of the twentieth century, argued James Young, this early promise had turned to 'defeatism, introspection and sectarianism'. The labour movement lost its nationalistic drive and its radical edge, and became 'culturally dependent' on England.[5]

Chris Harvie presents a somewhat less jaundiced perspective, however, and argues that by the twentieth century, because of Scotland's 'social, and even geographical position', the Scottish radical left, far from being 'culturally dependent' on England, 'was open to a wide variety of cosmopolitan influences'. This explains the split from the SDF and the formation of the Scottish-led and Edinburgh-based Socialist Labour Party (SLP) in 1903, and its rejection of 'political action' in favour of 'industrial action' as advocated by American Marxist Daniel De Leon. Scottish members of the SDF were involved in gun-running in support of Russian revolutionaries between 1905 and 1906, and their contacts with class-conscious Russian, Lithuanian and Irish workers in Scotland maintained close links between the Scottish and the internationalist socialist movement.[6] Such examples clearly challenge Young's gloomy prognosis of 'ca' canny Scotland' in the early twentieth century.

There is clearly some confusion regarding Scottish political movements during this period and this chapter aims to clarify the narrative of events by first considering the early emergence of the socialist movement in Scotland and what influenced its development. The chapter will also examine the relationship with the trade union movement and the growing importance of 'political action' and, through a case study of the Broxburn miners' strike in 1887, demonstrate how political action helped to generate closer ties between the trade union and the labour movements. This includes an examination of the Scottish Labour Party between 1888 and 1894, the political influence of the SDF in Edinburgh and the east of Scotland, the provision for 'workers' education' and briefly the events surrounding SDF 'gun-running' in support of the Russian Revolution of 1905. The final section considers the emergence of the Independent Labour Party, its relation with more extremist political parties such as the SDF and the SLP, and the somewhat tentative and muted advance of Scottish Labour between 1894 and 1914.

EARLY SOCIALISM AND EARLY SOCIALISTS

E. Belfort Bax stated that 1884 was to be regarded as the birth year of Socialism in England,[7] and for the same reasons 1884 was to be the pivotal year in the foundation of modern socialism in Scotland. The Social Democratic Federation (SDF) was formed in 1884 (from an earlier organisation, the Democratic Federation, established in 1881) and was a Marxist party willing to work towards social reform through parliamentary and political action. Others within the SDF leaned more towards the European revolutionary socialist model and non-parliamentary action as the means by which the prevailing social order would be changed. Chief among this group was William Morris and toward the end of 1884 he led a breakaway which resulted in the formation of the Socialist League (SL). Around the same time another group of socialists who favoured the 'gradualist' or 'evolutionary route to socialism' split from their parent organisation The Fellowship of the New Life (founded in 1883 by Scottish ethical socialist Thomas Davidson) to form the Fabian Society.[8]

The SDF became firmly established in Scotland in 1884 when branches were set up in Edinburgh and Glasgow and other locations around the country. According to John Gilray; in *Early Days of the Socialist Movement in Edinburgh* (1909), the first indoor meeting 'for the preaching of Modern Socialism' was held by Edinburgh University Socialist Society on 19 March 1884, at which William Morris – then a member of the SDF – was the main speaker.[9] The earliest record of 'open air propaganda of Modern Socialism in Edinburgh' took place on 22 June 1884 on the East Meadows where an address was delivered by Edinburgh iron moulder and socialist John Mahon. Gilray states that Mahon and Robert Banner (a bookbinder who was converted to socialism after hearing the Austrian socialist Andreas Scheu 'preach socialism' in Edinburgh in 1882) had already formed 'a Republican Society' towards the end of 1883 and sometime in early 1884 they affiliated to the Democratic Federation (the forerunner of the SDF).[10]

William Morris broke from the SDF in 1884 and established the Socialist League (SL). According to Young most Scottish socialists 'identified with the more authentic socialism and anti-imperialism of Morris' and joined the league. This was also to create something of an east-west split as more of the Glasgow socialists stayed within the SDF. There were also disagreements between Scottish and English socialists 'over the question of policy and party autonomy' and in particular the role and function of the Scottish Land and Labour League (SLLL) which was formed independently in 1884. According to Gilray, it was a combination of 'narrow patriotism' and the influence of 'a considerable number of Henry Georgites' which led to the formation of the SLLL:

> It was a consciousness of such facts doubtless which prompted certain spirits (*a certain spirit perhaps I should say, for the leading spirit in the movement in Edinburgh at that time was an Austrian called Andreas Scheu*) to think it advisable to hit on a name for a Scottish Society 'more homely, concrete, alluring, less abstract and foreign looking than the one which had been adopted.' Such a name was thought to be found in the Scottish Land and Labour League.[11]

Most historical accounts suggest that the SLLL (hereafter the Scottish League) functioned from the start as the Scottish section of the Socialist League. Gilray asserts that these changes 'took place in August 1884', a full five months before the Socialist League was officially constituted. Sometime in January 1885 the Scottish League affiliated to the Socialist League, but sent a clear message to the London leadership of the Socialist League that it would function as a fully autonomous and independent section of the SL and not merely a branch.[12] The Scottish League was clearly a distinctly Scottish body and under its auspices there began 'a vigorous propaganda of Socialism', mainly in Edinburgh and the east of Scotland.

From Gilray's observations, therefore, 1884 was the year when 'Modern Socialism' came to Scotland. It would seem certain that another pioneer of Scottish socialism, David Lowe, writing in *Souvenirs of Scottish Labour* (1919) some ten years after Gilray, argued that, in terms of overall political impact, the socialist 'morn of a new era' did not finally dawn until the formation of the Scottish Labour Party (SLP) in 1888.[13] Gilray would no doubt have some sympathy with Lowe in so far as he saw the early socialist movement in Edinburgh more as 'propagandist and educative' until the Scottish League became involved in 'political action' during the Broxburn miners' strike in 1887. Thereafter, the Scottish League came into closer contact with the Edinburgh Trades Council, and in forging closer links with the SDF and Edinburgh Christian Socialists, came together on 2 December 1888 at the first conference of Scottish Socialist Societies in Edinburgh.[14] Lowe considered this event in some detail and in particular the resolution noting the less than complementary role of the London leadership:

> 'Whereas it is necessary that a more systematic method of propaganda should be inaugurated in Scotland,' and 'Whereas London has shown itself to be unable to organise Scotland'; Therefore be it resolved: – 'That a Scottish Organisation be formed for propagandistic purposes;' [and] 'That a Central Committee, consisting of one delegate from each branch of the Organisation to be formed for the purpose of thoroughly organising the propaganda in Scotland' [*sic*].

The result 'was the severance of connection with London' and the formation of a separate organisation called the 'Scottish Socialist Federation' (SSF).[15] The hope was that the formation of the SSF would encourage all the branches across the country 'to form one Scottish Socialist Society'. But as Gilray noted, 'amalgamation on a wide scale, though not yet embracing all Socialist Societies in Scotland, came about in another way and from another point in the compass', when an SLP branch was formed in Edinburgh in November 1892.[16]

Gilray also noted the roles of Andreas Scheu and ex-Paris communard Leo Melliet in spreading the socialist message in Scotland, and of the Rev. John Glasse of Edinburgh.[17] Lowe also noted how Glasse 'gathered around him many ardent idealists, to whom he administered doses of Proudon and Marx', and that when visiting the manse in Tantallon Place 'the faithful were favoured with the words of wisdom from the lips of Morris, Kropotkin, Stepniak, and other distinguished visitors'.[18] Glasse was deeply involved with the SDF and latterly organised the SLLL in Scotland, and along with J. Bruce Glasier, helped establish the ILP in

Glasgow. He was a fairly unusual figure, not only because he was a rep-
utable and well-known Church of Scotland minister at Old Greyfriars
Kirk but became he was 'politically committed to the labour movement
in a way shared by few of his colleagues before the First World War'.[19]

Socialists nevertheless upset religious bodies in Scotland because they
tended to hold their regular political and propaganda meetings on the
Sabbath – none more so than when the Edinburgh socialists held a special
Sunday afternoon meeting to honour a delegation of sixteen socialist
workmen from Paris during September 1888. *The Scotsman* stated that
'as strangers' the Frenchmen 'ought to have respected the sanctity of
[Sunday] in Scotland', reporting that the Edinburgh Trades Council was
censured 'from various quarters' for arranging a banquet that evening.[20]
Gilray wrote of the event:

> The usual revolutionary toasts were drunk with great enthusiasm, and a
> number of speeches were made, in French, German and English. The
> *Carmagnole* was sung by our guests in splendid style. This was the first time
> that there had been an international gathering of workers in Edinburgh who
> pledged themselves to do all in their power to sweep away the frontiers of all
> countries, and to unite the workers of every nationality for the overthrow of
> their common enemy, Capitalism![21]

The French workmen had previously visited Glasgow where, much to
chagrin of *The Glasgow Herald*, they earned a degree of 'notoriety'
chiefly because they refused to toast the Queen at a banquet given in their
honour.[22] They were cheered away enthusiastically by 'a considerable
crowd' at Glasgow accompanied by a farewell speech in French from
R. B. Cunninghame Graham, and when met off the train at Edinburgh
were welcomed by the cry '*Vive la révolution sociale*'. The refusal to toast
the Queen was raised 'by one of the workmen' at Edinburgh who personally thanked the delegation 'for their conduct at Glasgow in *not
drinking* the health of that very fortunate old lady . . . who was the apex
upon which all this rotten system revolved'.[23]

The press reported on the French workmen's visit at some length, but
some detail is worthy of inclusion here. John Leslie of the SDF (who was
the uncle of James Connolly) chaired the meeting, which was jointly
hosted by the SDF and the Scottish League, and in proposing a toast to
'the working men of Paris' pledged to uphold 'the red flag' and assist 'in
the coming struggle'. Through an interpreter, Monsieur E. Bestetti stated
'that he had twice been deported for taking part in the republican movement' and that the main aim of 'social revolutionists' was to form
one single class, 'the class of the producer and the consumer'. Several

others spoke before Monsieur Auge sung the French Republican *La Carmagnole,* which was considered more in accord with the sentiments of the meeting than the *La Marseillaise.* The enthusiastic meeting closed amid great cheers and a toast to the 'The Solidarity of Labour'.[24] The following year, encouraged by Leo Melliet and another French comrade 'who fought for the Commune', the Edinburgh socialist held the first celebration in honour of the Paris commune and thereafter this celebration became an annual event.[25] The celebrations in December 1893 were to mark the last gatherings of the Scottish Land and Labour League. The following year the 'revolutionaries of the League', which Lowe asserted 'did much for socialism in Scotland', joined the ILP.[26]

Certain aspects of Gilray's account of developments of the early socialist movement in Edinburgh 'subsequent to the foundation of the ILP' will be familiar but not all. It is clear, for example, that the influence of European socialists within the Edinburgh socialist group was considerable. William Morris may have argued that few socialists in Scotland were familiar with Marx but Gilray would point to the halls and meeting places that 'often resounded to excited expositions of Socialist doctrine'. Kropotkin, Stepniak and Morris himself may have congregated around John Glasse and Greyfriars Manse, but they also lectured widely 'in Edinburgh, Fife, in the Borders, and in other towns'. Edward Carpenter was the first to have 'an indoor public lecture on Socialism at Leith' in 1887, and the Scottish League also 'held its own little meetings for the study of *Das Kapital*' in Edinburgh.[27] Gilray discussed the role of socialists in the Broxburn strike of 1887 and noted the involvement of the Scottish Socialist Federation in the railway strike of 1890–1, and how this enhanced the political profile of the socialists within the Edinburgh Trades Council. But the SSF had not merely fraternised with the trades councillors:

> Having taken active part in political action, it naturally come into very close contact with that branch of the labour movement – I refer to the Scottish Labour Party, founded in the West – to whom political action was the very life-blood.

That organisation 'by the very nature of its being', argued Gilray, was 'bound to try and extend its borders' and did so in forming a branch at Edinburgh in 1892. When the ILP was formed in 1893, however, it ultimately signalled the SLP's demise the following year. I will consider the brief history of the SLP later in this chapter but as the Edinburgh socialists experienced their first taste of political action during the Broxburn miners' strike in 1887 it is necessary to briefly consider this important event and the manner in which it encouraged closer union between the trade union and labour movement around Edinburgh.

'INTERMINGLING IN THE STRIFE' – THE BROXBURN DISPUTE AND POLITICAL ACTION

The Broxburn shale miners' strike of 1887 was a potent example of employer anti-unionism in Scotland. It started on 25 July 1887 as a wages dispute but quickly developed into a political *cause célèbre* in the struggle for workers' rights and trade union recognition. The Broxburn Oil Company 'had been firm and determined' in its efforts to persuade the men to submit to a reduction in wages, but stressed that the interference of the West and Midlothian Miners' Association, and its attempt 'to fix the working day at eight hours', had changed the nature of the dispute. In league with other producers, it formed the Scottish Shale Employers Association and instituted an industry-wide lock-out. 'Rather than be dictated to by agitators', the Association declared its intention to evict between 100 and 140 strikers from company homes.

The strike caused considerable distress, and in early August two Protestant ministers and a Roman Catholic clergyman formed a delegation to speak to the company in an attempt to resolve a worsening situation and alleviate the distress caused by the strike. The meeting was to no avail, but the presence of a Catholic clergyman clearly meant that Catholic miners were involved in pressing their demands as trade unionists alongside their Protestant co-workers.[28] *The Scotsman* reported that donations from the wider community and from the Edinburgh Trades Council assisted miners' families, and they also helped set up a soup kitchen. It was also reported that a wooden structure had been erected to accommodate the first thirty families who had been evicted (a similar structure was erected later during a second phase of eviction). Many well-known names came to offer their support, including the young radical Liberal campaigner R. B. Haldane MP, who met with the company manager to present the miners' proposals, but as their demands included the shorter working week and trade-union recognition the offer was rejected.[29]

The Edinburgh Trades Council became heavily involved in the dispute and in September organised a demonstration where it was agreed that the workmen of Edinburgh would 'provide material support to assist the miners in resisting the attempts of the companies to reduce their wages and destroy their union'. John Wilson, the Broxburn miners' leader, addressed the meeting, as did Mr Leitch, a miner from West Calder (and likely a member of the SDF), who asked 'if the employers themselves combined' why should miners 'not to do the same'? Neil Mclean of the Amalgamated Tailors' Society (and a member of the SDF) argued that the issue was about 'the annihilation of the union' and they needed to support the miners in their fight against 'this syndicate of capitalists'. Mr Haldane MP declared that Broxburn was not just a local question: 'It was a national question!' Towards the end, 'several Socialist orators' spoke, and it was reported in *The Scotsman* that they 'attracted some of the audience towards them'.[30] In October R. B. Cunninghame Graham organised a peaceful demonstration against scab labour and at one evening meeting discussed the public's perception of the strike:

> Wherever there were working men – wherever there was a reading public – they would read [about these] proceedings [and] understand that they in Broxburn had shown the spirit of men [who] were going to set their faces against that coercion which is now disgracing England in Ireland ever coming across and rooting itself in here in Scotland. (Cheers.)

They had the attention of the press and every trade union in England and Scotland, and he exhorted them 'as a friend very earnestly to stick to their Union whatever they did'.[31]

During the second week in October the National Conference of Miners of England, Scotland and Wales was held in Edinburgh and took time to discuss the Broxburn strike. By then between sixty and seventy miners and their families had been evicted, and up to 1,000 miners were locked out in the employers' attempt to 'abolish the Trade Union'. William Small of the Lanarkshire Miners spoke in support, and Keir Hardie proclaimed:

> [That] these men were fighting a battle such as not had been known in Scotland for many years past . . . Are the men to be allowed to maintain an organisation or not? The Broxburn Oil Company said 'No,' the men said 'Yes,' and that was the real point to the dispute.

The chairman, the Morpeth MP, Thomas Burt, deplored reports of men fighting against eviction while battling for their union. He had hoped that the 'system of eviction was dead' as far as the mining districts were concerned, and noted that throughout a recent seventeen-week struggle in Northumberland that not one miner had been evicted.[32]

The strike was to carry on until late November when it was finally resolved, but throughout the miners received the moral and financial support of the Edinburgh Trades Council and other trades bodies. There is, however, no evidence of support from any miners' county union outside Scotland. Despite the use of scab labour and the use of police and soldiers during the evictions, there were no arrests at Broxburn until mid-November when two miners appeared before Linlithgow Sheriff Court: 'the first case of violence resulting from the strike'. Sometime later the company conceded to five of the Miners' Association's six demands, but still insisted on the wage reduction. The miners returned to work having secured trade-union recognition and a shorter working week and, in January 1888, they fully recovered the cut in wages imposed the previous July.[33] By 'intermingling in the strife' at Broxburn in 1887 and three years later in the railway strike, Edinburgh's socialists were coming into ever greater contact with trade unionists, and in turn brought the previously aloof members of the Edinburgh Trades Council into closer contact with the politics of 'socialism'.

Indeed, in supporting the striking railwaymen, 'socialists and trade unionists stood on, and spoke from, the same platform', and at that time, noted Gilray, 'the Trades Councillors heard more socialism preached in an hour than they had possibly heard in all their life before'. As a result, in the general election of 1892, the SSF and the Trades Council agreed to run the Broxburn miners' leader, John Wilson, as the labour candidate for Edinburgh Central. During the municipal elections the following year, the Trades Council ran 'labour representatives' alongside the Independent Labour candidate, Fred Hamilton, 'a socialist compositor ... who had made a sortie among the miners of Midlothian'.[34] Hamilton was chosen to stand against Councillor Steel because Steel was on the board of directors of the Broxburn Oil Company at the time of the 1887 strike when the evictions had been carried out, and later became the chairman.[35] Hamilton also connected the Broxburn struggle with that of the Irish struggle where employers who 'with the aid of dragoons' evicted striking workers 'just as the Irish Landlord [did with] his tenants'.[36]

Because of such activities, Lowe made special mention of 'first-rank pioneers' including Gilray, the Rev. John Glasse, Irishman John Leslie, Frenchman and ex-Communard Leo Melliet, and the redoubtable Scot Alexander Dickinson, who was the first Edinburgh socialist to be elected to the Edinburgh School Board. Dickinson was also deeply involved with the SSF and in October 1894 launched (and thereafter edited) the socialist monthly and SSF organ the *Labour Chronicle,* which ran to fifteen editions until the time of Dickinson's death.[37] Lowe argued 'that the capital of Scotland was early infected with Socialistic ideas' but that there 'no strong Socialist element organised' until the SLP arrived on the scene in 1892.[38] But it is clear from Gilray's account that there was considerable socialist activity before then, and would no doubt remind Lowe in any case 'that the cause of socialism [was] not a mere city affair' and that as an Edinburgh socialist 'We look beyond ourselves'.[39]

THE SCOTTISH LABOUR PARTY, 1888 TO 1894

In the preface of his book on Scottish Labour, Lowe wrote that, 'To grow in numbers [was] not necessarily an increase in power'. Lowe was musing over the past thirty years of Labour party politics in Scotland, and from his vantage point in 1919 could with some pride note the considerable expansion in the ILP throughout the country since the war years. It was also a party that was no closer to a significant electoral breakthrough in post-war Scotland. Indeed, Knox suggests that the party struggled to convince voters that it was not merely a reconfigured Liberal Party when in terms of a political agenda there was little to distinguish between the two before the war.[40] However, Christine Thomas is mindful that the SLP was 'pledged to support independent working class candidates in elections' and, while this endeavour largely failed, the party's formation still 'marked an important step on the road to a mass independent workers' party'.[41] But such matters did not worry Lowe for his main aim was to go back to the very beginnings of that movement and the foundation of the Scottish Labour Party in 1888.

The material contained in Lowe's book is based on 'autobiography, extracts from correspondence, selection from speeches, and cuttings from memory intended to provide both atmosphere and action'.[42] Quantitative material such as membership figures is difficult to find but when describing the events that led to the formation of the SSF in 1888, for example, Lowe lists all the participant branches: seven SDF branches, Crieff, Edinburgh, Dundee (no. 1 and Central), Glasgow (Central and South) and Parkhead; the SLLL had six, Arbroath, Carnoustie, Edinburgh, Glasgow, Kilmarnock and West Calder. The Parkhead branch of the SDF and the Carnoustie and Arbroath branches of the Scottish League were not represented, but indicated that they would be 'guided by the decision of conference'. The Glasgow and Edinburgh Christian Socialist Societies were also in attendance.[43] He is rather hard on the Irish and the Home Rule issue for damaging the SLP's electoral chances in 1892 and 1895.[44] He refers to the influence of Irishmen in Scottish politics, including John Ferguson, and James Connolly and John Leslie in Edinburgh. Indeed, he praised Leslie's role in the socialist movement in the east of Scotland, describing him as 'a perfervid Irishman and a true poet, he was eloquent to a high degree [and] was early intimate with the Irish agitation'. But mainly, Irish workers in Scotland were blamed for holding back the SLP and similarly the ILP after 1894.[45]

Lowe was based in Dundee and, while Edinburgh and Glasgow invariably loom large, he notes many links and connections with socialists from across the country and the east of Scotland, although he is surprisingly rather quiet on the vibrant socialist scene in Aberdeen. Knox noted that early socialism in Edinburgh and Glasgow was largely artisan and middle class in orientation, but that in Aberdeen working-class socialists were to the fore. Rob Duncan notes that the first avowedly socialist newspaper in Scotland, *The Workers' Herald*, appeared in Aberdeen in December 1891, and was produced by James Leatham of the Aberdeen Socialist Society and the SSF. Leatham had also been responsible for the earlier *Socialist Leaflet* in 1887. The SSF was also actively connected with the seamen and dockers' struggle with the Shipping Federation during 1890, and in 1892 formed the Revolutionary Socialist Federation. In 1892 the Aberdeen Trades Council formed the Scottish Trades Councils' Labour party, and the following year Scottish Labour Party published its own organ, *The Aberdeen Labour Elector*, which included a call for an 'Eight Hour Day' by the Ploughman's Union. Leatham played a leading role in all these developments and, through publishing, had connections with Robert Dempster and the Perthshire Alyth Ploughman's Club and Socialist Union producing their socialist *Labour Leaflet* in Aberdeen in 1888. Leatham made Aberdeen a centre for the production of socialist literature between 1888 and 1893 and also produced Bruce Glasier's compilation of *Socialist Songs*.[46]

H. H. Champion visited Aberdeen under the auspices of the Scottish League and the SSF in 1887 and 1888. Indeed, Lowe made mention that Champion was in Scotland 'principally in Aberdeen', but also in Arbroath, Brechin and Dundee.[47] Champion returned in 1890 to address the May Day Rally, where he focused on the eight-hour day and independent labour representation. Later a Labour Committee was formed around John Gerrie. At the beginning of 1891 the Trades Council appointed a committee to co-operate with the Labour committee 'to draw up a programme of labour questions of pressing importance'. This committee recommended the calling of a national conference that would include anyone 'who was favourable to the labour interest, but was precluded from becoming a trade unionist'.[48] This was held in Edinburgh on 8 August 1891 and the agenda included discussions on labour members of parliament, legislation for the eight-hour day, payments for MPs and payment of election expenses. The meeting was also noted for its many attacks on the Liberal Party.[49]

While it is true that most of the 'major impediments to the legal status of trade unions' were swept away by the early 1880s, the demand for the eight-hour day continued to help build trade unionism. The eight-hour question became a national issue in Scotland and in the 1880s and 1890s Scottish workers, trade unionists and political activists became more closely associated with each other and the International Socialist movement over this matter. According to A. E. P. Duffy, the issue united 'many trade unions and socialist groups on one common platform'.[50] Scottish workers may have been wary of socialism but in campaigning for an eight-hour day they were at least beginning 'to understand each other'. The issue surfaced within the mining county unions during the early 1870s, but gathered pace with the formation of the Scottish Miners' National Federation in 1886. The result was the Miners' Eight Hour Bill which, when first presented to Parliament by Cunninghame Graham in 1887, obtained merely fifty-four votes. Six years later in 1893 it was carried by a majority of seventy-nine votes. According to Lowe, 'the change had been brought about because the miners made the question an article of faith at election times and refused to support any candidate not in favour of the measure'.[51] The trades councils also played their part in the 1880s, generating widespread support for the 'Eight Hour Bill' in Scotland, and by the 1890s they were discussing civil, social and political matters and extensively involved in political pressure group activities.[52]

Securing the Miners' Eight-Hour Bill was a great victory but the uniform eight-hour day was some way off, and while the issue solidified the miners it was 1909 before this turned into political support for the Labour Party. The 'eight-hour' question was associated with May Day celebrations across the world, and quoting from the Rev. William Mackay's History of the May Day, Lowe wrote:

> Karl Marx, it should be remembered, was a May child . . . and in his masterly 'Das Kapital', published in 1867, he made the proposition for an Eight Hours Law . . . It dates properly from the International of 1864 and . . . became consciously an International question and demand at the International Trade Union Congress of 1883 [sic, but likely meant 1889].

From 1890 all over the world International May Day demonstrations 'gave a mighty impetus to Socialism and the Eight Hours question' and in 1892, Lowe noted,

> In London, Glasgow and elsewhere the May Day demonstration was a conspicuous if not magnificent success. On Glasgow Green some eight or ten thousand persons took part more or less in that demonstration. What ever the

hackmen of the Capitalist press said to the contrary, it was a veritable triumph for the social idea, and an Eight Hour Day.

Lowe stressed the connecting link between trade unionists and socialists because 'once a year, for many years, workers of all phases of opinion had demonstrated side by side on this question with the result that the taboo on Socialism became milder'.[53]

The socialist and the SLP fought tirelessly on the eight-hour question, and it is evident that they attracted a significant degree of support from the Scottish trade union and labour movement. When surveying the 'List of Representatives' to the party's fifth annual conference in January 1894, there were forty-two trade union societies listed with a joint delegation of ninety-seven, and the Dundee, Edinburgh, Glasgow, Govan and Paisley Trades Councils were represented by twelve delegates. Five Co-operative branches sent thirteen delegates; the Women's Protective and Provident League and the Women's Labour Party had three each, as did the Edinburgh Fabian Society, the Edinburgh SSF and Glasgow SDF. There were five 'Georgite' groups including the Campsie Single Tax Association, the Henry George Institute (Glasgow), two Glasgow branches of the Scottish Land Restoration Union, the Land Nationalisation Society (Mid-Calder), and the Nationalisation of Labour Society (Glasgow). The Ruskin Society of Glasgow also attended, accounting for a total combined delegation of forty-six.

There were twenty-five branches of the SLP with a total delegation of seventy-five listed: eighteen branches were located in the west, of which nine were Glasgow branches; and seven in the east including Arbroath, Dundee and five Edinburgh branches. In total 217 delegates were listed for the SLP conference in January 1894 and, according to Lowe, 'the Labour movement in Scotland was in good heart, enthusiastic, and nimble on its feet, as becometh youth in the spring-time of a great cause'. The flush of youth was however fleeting, and before the year was out fifty-three delegates representing thirty-two branches from all over Scotland gathered together to officially 'wind up the Party'. Thus, the SLP passed away quietly and quickly faded from memory as all eyes turned in hope towards the ILP.[54] In terms of electoral politics, the ILP was to prove no less successful than the SLP. It ran candidates in elections in 1894 and ran five candidates in 1895, but thereafter, it barely existed as a credible political force. Indeed, it did not repeat that challenge on the same scale until 1918. Clearly, many Scottish working men stood aloof from independent labour politics during this period.[55]

GUN-RUNNING AND WORKERS' EDUCATION: WILLIAM MCKIE AND THE SDF

The SDF maintained a presence in Scotland in the 1890s and 1900s, and one of the leading lights in this organisation was John Leslie – Lowe's 'perfervid Irishman and a true poet'. Little has been written on a man who, with Willie Nairn, Robert Hutchison, John Armour, Bruce Glasier, Jim Connolly and John L. Mahon, was 'to the forefront' of SDF activities in Scotland. The work of David Saunders on the impact of the 1905 Russian revolution on Tyneside and the SDF's involvement in 'gun-running' draws Leslie into the picture[56] – the events surrounding which we will return to shortly. But a more detailed description of Leslie's life and work in Edinburgh is provided by William McKie, an active SDF member in Edinburgh from the early 1890s to the 1920s, before he left for America in 1927.[57] William McKie was nineteen years of age when he came to Edinburgh from Carlisle in 1893. He was involved in the Amalgamated Metalworkers' Society and was reading books on political economy, but not actively involved in politics at that point. In Carlisle he attended Methodist meetings with his father and remembered discussions on 'religion and workers' with well-known atheists:

> The tendency was regarding how religion actually related to man's existence. I don't think they had any thought about a change in society. As a matter of fact the Socialist Party even in my day had no conception of what socialism was like, how it was going to be carried through, except they wanted to pass laws and so forth. Somebody must have discussed socialism as developed by Marx, but in my young days I never came across anything until I was in Edinburgh, about 20 years old, that I actually heard about socialism.[58]

Once in Edinburgh McKie went to hear Keir Hardie speak and at one meeting asked Hardie a question about the role of religion and Labour Party recruitment. To which Hardie replied, 'Probably you are interested in doing something for the working man [but] it isn't the way out. It might help things but it isn't the way out'. McKie asked the question to Hardie because he was 'developing away from religion' and wanted to be sure 'he was going in the right direction'. A short time later he met John Leslie at a political meeting and thereafter helped to distribute literature. He became a member of the SDF towards the end of 1895. He was to describe John Leslie thus:

> An old Irish Fenian . . . an expert on Marx. He knew Marx. He [said] the first book you have to read is the *Communist Manifesto* and *Wage, Labour and*

Capital, . . . I read *Wage, Labour and Capital* . . . couldn't understand it from Latin. The Communist Manifesto, yes! That made an impression . . . [59]

He began to organise meetings for visiting speakers and came into immediate contact with a host of well-known names such as William Morris and Cunninghame Graham. In what must have been one of Morris's last appearances before his death in October 1896, McKie arranged a meeting at a theatre in Leith where only 'about 20 people turned up', whereupon Morris made the remark 'if the people won't come to Mohammed – Mohammed will go to the people'. He enquired where the working men of Leith congregated and was told 'down at the crossing'. Morris stood on a lemonade box 'donated by a local store' and gave his talk and before long attracted hundreds of listeners.[60]

McKie became the SDF propaganda secretary in 1898 and at the same time Leslie became organising secretary of the Scottish District Council of the SDF. It was McKie's responsibility to organise meetings not only in Edinburgh but elsewhere. There was a hard-core Edinburgh membership of about thirty and it usually met in Leslie's house. Notices of the meetings were posted around Edinburgh on the Saturday evening with an invitation to attend next day. One Sunday morning they were discussing Marx 'when a stranger came in' and got involved in a debate with Leslie. He was familiar with Marx but he was not as able to deal with Marxian theory as Leslie. He later introduced himself as H. G. Wells.

McKie also touched on the impact of the Russian Revolution in 1905 and the repercussions this had for Britain. He intimated that this event was important to the SDF, but beyond a comment about disagreements between 'Leibknecht' and 'Kautsky' he gave few details.[61] The SDF support for the Russian revolutionaries in fact saw them become involved in gun-running activities during 1906–7. This was also important in the Scottish context for it would seem that the SDF was beginning to recover from the loss of Scottish members following the Socialist Labour Party (SLP) split from the SDF in 1903. At the SDF conference in April 1905 it was stated that Scottish branches had become 'the weakest link in their chain' and that the Glasgow branches were 'demoralised' (this was due in part to trade depression at Glasgow) and that the Scottish District Council needed to be strengthened. To that end they selected Thomas Kennedy of Aberdeen, a regular contributor to the SDF's propaganda organ *Justice*, to work across a wide area in Scotland to retrieve the situation.[62] They had recovered sufficiently by 1906 to run Kennedy as an SDF/Labour candidate at Aberdeen during the general election in 1906 and he polled a respectable 2,000 votes. But the contest at Aberdeen was of particular importance for John Maclean who had joined the party after the SLP breakaway in 1903. He assisted Kennedy and in doing so got his first taste of parliamentary electioneering.[63]

As for the gun-running, David Saunders' research suggests that even before 1905 John Leslie had become involved in assisting British-based Russian emigrés to supply revolvers to Russia via Finland through the ports of Hull, Newcastle and Leith.[64] To continue the supply of arms to Russia, they needed to have bases in the coal ports exporting to the Russian Empire and for two years, with the help of the SDF, the operation went well:

> We take space in the business part of town. Steamers come from Antwerp or Hamburg, bring boxes of Mausers, Brownings and rifles, with ammunition, boxes of literature. The boxes are unpacked, the contents re-packed into little packages which it is possible to carry in one's hands, . . . The affair went pretty well. No suspicions. But then there was a little slip and the whole business went to pot.[65]

In the early months of 1907 the operation was exposed. According to *The Scotsman* the trade between the Leith side and Hamburg 'had been going on all winter' and on the occasion of the 'little slip' Edinburgh police intercepted a consignment containing 'three or four thousands rounds . . . pistols and two cases of ammunition clips for loading magazines of Mauser rifles'. It was reported that two men were arrested in connection with the arms seizure and that they had an association with SDF activity in Edinburgh, Leith, Glasgow, Sunderland and Newcastle.[66] Robert Hutchinson, who was active in the SDF on Tyneside, was linked, as was John Fyfe Reid who was arrested at Glasgow and charged with 'storing ammunition and explosives without a license'. According to information from a 'Glasgow man', Reid had taken possession of 'ten cases containing 25,000 cartridges' but the police only ever recovered six.[67]

The whole affair was shrouded in mystery and the Scottish police and the press could not get to the bottom of who was ultimately responsible for the operation, which perhaps explains why the authorities in England decided not to prosecute, while in Scotland fines were imposed rather than custodial sentences.[68] The Scottish gun-runners 'acted on instructions received from a mysterious person in Edinburgh, known as Denvers', but police operations Scotland failed to unmask him.[69] Saunders notes that Thomas Denvers was the name appended to the article 'The Cartridge Mystery' which appeared in a 'Tyneside' socialist organ in May 1907, and that *Justice* reported in June 1907 that Denvers delivered an address to a 'fairly good audience' at Methil in Fife. That the police authorities could not track this man down suggests that Denvers was a pseudonym and that others had adopted the pseudonym too to escape detection.

Saunders' desire to identity the leaders would help answer the question whether the epicentre of these gun-running activities was in fact Scotland rather than north-east England. He noted that one of the earliest printed accounts of the gun-running in 1906–7 'is almost entirely Scottish in its coverage'. He also noted that 'Scottish socialist' John Leslie openly stated in 1918 that he was actively involved in gun-running 'immediately prior to the outbreak of 1905–7 [and] during the height of the reactionary terror' (is there a suggestion that John Leslie was Denvers?).[70] Ian MacDougall's *Militant Miners: Recollections of John McArthur*, which focuses on Buckhaven in Fife, also makes note of SDF activities before the war and the active role played by the SDF in helping revolutionaries in Russia after 1905. He recalled some 'old hands' (old SDF members) explaining 'how they had tried to ship arms from Methil docks' but that because of an impending police search the shipment was dumped over the side into the docks.[71] Leslie's account, argued Saunders, 'strengthens the notion that Scots were sending arms to Russia before people started doing so in the north-east England', but more importantly, that evidence of gun-running supports Graham Johnson's recent assertion that the SDF in Britain 'was a genuinely revolutionary organisation'.[72]

William McKie says nothing about gun-running, but neither does he mention the SDF's disaffiliation from the Labour Party in August 1901 nor the SLP breakaway at Easter 1903. The two episodes have a connection in so far as the disaffiliation occurred at the same time as H. M. Hyndman resigned from the SDF Executive Committee citing a failure 'to detect among English workers' heightened class awareness, and that even SDF members 'left much to be desired in that respect':

> He was quite astonished at the ignorance and apathy of his countrymen, and deeply discouraged at the result of their long continued propaganda. Their only hope at present lay in political action, yet the majority of their organisation seemed wholly destitute of political aptitude.[73]

As reported in the establishment and socialist press, workers had rejected the 'revolutionary type of socialism in England'.[74] Members in Scotland would later reject entirely Hyndman's plea relating to political action to embrace industrial action in the form of American-style industrial unionism and the syndicalist ideas of American Marxist Daniel De Leon and the American Socialist Party.

McKie might not have mentioned gun-running but he did make many references to the arrival of John Maclean and, as befits a 'propaganda secretary', made special note of Maclean's determination to establish a Marxist economic class for workers. Unsurprisingly, McKie described Maclean 'as the most outstanding Marxist that we had in Britain':

> He had personality, was from the working class. He used to come from Glasgow . . . he'd stay with me over the weekend, and I'd have him speaking in Edinburgh about every other week . . . he'd be giving a lecture about polit-ical economy, tracing production, export and imports. And then he'd have a lecture on India and a lecture on the U.S.[75]

It was noted that he usually talked for 'half an hour' then opened up the topic for general discussion among the workmen when 'they would get up and express their opinion . . . it developed them getting to their feet and talking'.[76]

McKie's general discussion on workers' education noted the estab-lishment of the Workers' Education as Association (WEA) and the setting up of the Scottish Labour College. He dated the arrival of the WEA in Scotland 'as developing in 1904', set-up by the government the year before, to give 'workers education from an employers point of view'. Maclean and the SDF rejected this in favour of 'independent working class' education 'built on the class struggle [and] Marxism'.[77] The Labour College dates from 1916, and it is not always clear when McKie is discussing workers' education from before that date. But, according to Nan Milton and James Young, Maclean began lecturing on industrial and economic history classes from 1906. Indeed, in 1908 the Scottish ILP socialist weekly *Forward* suggested that Maclean was among 'the ablest expounders of the mysteries of Marx in Scotland'.[78]

Socialists had for many years been critical of the indoctrination asso-ciated with state education, and were fighting against this by setting up their own classes. The education establishment in Scotland 'felt threat-ened by the Scottish Labour College and John Maclean' for, as Young argues, 'they did not want working people getting their education from agitators'.[79] One reason why socialist and educator Alexander Dickinson sought election to the school board in Edinburgh in the 1890s was to challenge that establishment view head-on. It is also clear that the estab-lishment had felt threatened by economic Marxism for a generation or more before Maclean's arrival on the scene. Gilray noted that in the 1880s 'Socialism was a word of terror' and had been since the days of the Paris Commune. Professor W. B. Hodgson lectured on the 'Fear of Socialism' to the Literary Institute of Edinburgh in 1876, and two years

later he lectured again on the dangers of socialism to students studying 'Commercial and Political Economy' at Edinburgh University. He
stressed that he introduced the subject because the youth of the country
needed to be instructed in the 'true principles of economic science as a
counteractive to the seductive themes of Socialism'. The lecture was open
to the public and in the audience were the Rev. John Glasse of Edinburgh
and the Rev. Alexander Webster of Aberdeen who became leading figures
in the emergence of Socialism in their respective cities.[80]

THE INDEPENDENT LABOUR PARTY

Despite its lack of electoral success from the mid-1890s, the ILP was
nonetheless the leading political organisation associated with the trade
union and labour movement in Scotland, with a combined membership
greater than the SDF, the Fabians and the other socialist societies –
including the Clarion Fellowship – put together. In 1893 it decided
against calling itself 'a socialist party' in order to keep the trade unions
on side. But this set it on a collision course with its own rank and file and
the SDF, who disaffiliated in 1901, although it made it perfectly
amenable to the Fabian Society who drew ever closer in its efforts to halt
any further development of revolutionary Marxism within the movement. The ILP and its confused relationship with socialism and the trade
union movement remained a sticking point, however, although many
rank-and-file members proclaimed themselves socialist. By the twentieth
century Lenin's view of the ILP was that it 'was frequently independent
of socialism but depended upon the Liberals'. Indeed, according to Jim
Mortimer, 'this trend was reflected even more strongly in the Labour
Party after 1906'.[81] This is clearly seen in the many discussions that took
place within the ILP and the Labour Party (previously the LRC between
1900 and 1906), when in 1908, in debate on 'Socialism and the Trade
Unions', John Bruce Glasier stated:

> On behalf of the party (ILP) he could say that they did not wish to impose
> Socialism on those who were not prepared to declare for it. He was proud
> of Socialism. There was no hope for the world but through Socialism. But
> Socialism as a concrete power must not be forced upon Trade Unionists.[82]

Talk of splits from the Labour Party and divisions within the ILP by those
demanding 'a more clearly defined Socialist programme' were repeated the
following year at Edinburgh, when John Gilray delivered his 'short sketch
of the Socialist movement' in the city' to the seventeenth Annual
Conference of the ILP. The rank-and-file delegates argued for 'labour and

socialism', and one speaker proposed that the ILP secede from the national Labour Party because it was a 'non-Socialist Party . . . moving in the direction of the Liberal Party'. Another argued that the Labour Party 'was professedly afraid of the word Socialism', and one delegate suggested that the Labour Party in 1909 'was even further away from the Socialist movement than in 1906'. Robert Smillie of the Scottish Miners' Federation felt it should not dampen their enthusiasm for socialism to be associated with a 'non-Socialist body', and that they should work inside the Labour Party 'to convert it to Socialism'.[83] In this highly charged atmosphere the old socialist John Gilray spoke passionately about the problem of building socialism in the city of Edinburgh, noting that as socialists they had yet to convince the great majority of the electorate in Scotland to vote for them:

> Our own city is not taking the place in the march of towards Socialism as we would like it too, [but] it has yet done something. It has, for one thing, educated numbers in the principles of Socialism, and sent forth many to sow the seeds in more congenial soil, and in any case we grudge not the greater success of other towns – it will come our way yet . . . That which we call Socialism will inevitably come about.[84]

It would not come about as a result of that conference, however, for on the last day Keir Hardie, Philip Snowden, Ramsay MacDonald and Bruce Glasier all resigned from the National Administrative Council of the ILP over the disagreement about the ILP's links with the 'non-Socialist' Labour Party, and differences of opinion as to the methods and tactics adopted to achieve the goal of socialism within the ILP. The rank and file sought keener, more 'revolutionary methods' while the leadership gazed along the evolutionary path to socialism.[85] Keir Hardie was determined to fight any talk of a split in 1909, and despite the problems and division that existed within and between the SDF and the ILP members on both sides – including a reluctant John Maclean – most socialists sought the holy grail of 'Socialist unity'. Two years later, in October 1911, a Socialist Unity Conference was organised and members of the ILP, the Fabians and the Clarion Scouts met with the SDP (formerly the SDF). The outcome was not unity but the formation of the British Socialist Party (BSP) and it was mainly supported by old SDP members and a breakaway of some radical ILPers.

POSTSCRIPT: A HESITANT ADVANCE, 1910–14

To many rank-and-file members of socialist and labour movement in Scotland, the ILP was simply another version of the Liberal Party, but for the press and public the ILP was viewed as thoroughly socialist. According to a report in *The Times* in January 1909, which developed as a four-part serialisation of the 'Socialism Movement of Great Britain', the ILP's influence was being felt in both national and local government. Much of that advance was clearly taking place in the large industrial centres and colliery districts of England, although it was noted that in Scotland the ILP had twenty-three members elected to the school boards. *The Times* was impressed by the 'extensive and highly organised' ILP propaganda machine which produced a quite remarkable output of socialist literature, organised indoor educational classes and open-air propaganda meetings, and political conferences for trade unions. Indeed, in order to support this level of propaganda, the ILP maintained a directory containing the names of 848 propaganda speakers.[86]

This perceived level of success was evident, for example, in the relationship between the industrial and political wings of the trade union and labour movement in Edinburgh. This had been growing stronger since the 1880s and 1890s, and resulted in greater co-operation between the trades council and the socialist movement on the issue of 'independent labour'. The ILP in particular was useful to the trade unions, for while it was 'explicitly a socialist organisation', argued John Holford, it did not have 'a coherent political philosophy', and it was therefore more accessible, fluid and open, and in terms of propaganda (the housing issue, rents and prices) it stayed doggedly to the task at hand. When this overlapped with political issues dear to the heart of the trade union movement (the eight-hour day, health and safety legislation, trade union law), both organisations could and did work well together. Moreover, the industrial and the political bodies were not necessarily mutually exclusive for there was considerable overlap in the membership of working-class institutions. Both clearly gained through this relationship, and the ILP made some substantial electoral advances in Edinburgh before 1914: a labour councillor returned in 1909, two more in 1911, and a further three in 1913. A Labour parish councillor was elected in 1908, another was elected to the school board in 1911, and there were two Labour members on the Leith school board by the time of the Leith dock strike in 1913.

The SDP/BSP (not all SDF members went over to the BSP, and the SDP remained a political party until 1941) were clearly very active in Edinburgh and its industrial hinterland before 1914. They were also involved in providing Marxist education classes, which, according to William McKie, before 1914 included many dockers and miners from the Lothian pits. The ILP was likewise involved in providing workers' education mainly through propaganda meetings, but Holford argues that 'the most vital socialist party in Edinburgh' during the early party of the century 'was the Socialist Labour Party' (SLP). When it broke from the SDF in 1903, led by the Scottish branches, 'Edinburgh and Leith were at the head of this movement, and indeed the party's national headquarters, and its publishing house, were in Edinburgh until the war'. The SLP was the main representative of Marxist socialism in Edinburgh and it decried the SDF and the ILP commitment to change through constitutional means. The SLP was avowedly anti-parliamentary and believed that the innate conservatism of the trade union movement actually blocked the path to socialism.

This was all set to change after 1910 when De Leon gave his support to the Industrial Workers of the World, and this allowed the less doctrinaire SLP members to work with the unions, to personally become trade union members, and to involve themselves in campaigns which addressed industrial and political issues affecting the working class, in order to further progress and develop socialism. Others vehemently disagreed and felt they should adhere rigidly to the original and pure Marxist principles which the SLP had left the SDF to pursue in 1903: they should not become involved in what they termed then as 'shop stewardism'. Indeed, this was the line taken by an Edinburgh branch of the SLP and as a result it was were expelled from the main party in 1911: the members of the branch formed themselves into the British Section of the International Socialist Labour Party in June 1912. But the great majority of SLP members became more intimately involved with the trade union movement in Edinburgh and elsewhere, in particular with the NUR 'at the height of the unions' flirtation with syndicalism and industrial unionism'.[87]

Marxist economic classes were already well developed before the war and were made increasingly popular by popular lecturers such as John Maclean (SDF and BSP) and by the SLP's 'most accomplished propagandist', John S. Clarke. Indeed, when Clarke spoke at public meetings in working-class districts before the war, 'as many as 2,000 people at a time' turned out. Clarke also delivered a series of lectures on syndicalism to the No. 1 branch of the NUR between 1912 and 1913, which led Holford to suggest that syndicalism thereafter 'became the focal point of the railwaymen's revolutionary industrial unionism' in the city before the Great War.[88]

It was during the labour unrest that the trade union and labour movement in Dundee became much more organised and radicalised. The syndicalist-style carters' strike in 1911, the general strike and lockout of

30,000 textile workers, and the rent strike action in 1912 helped develop a strong bond of solidarity among a broad spectrum of the Dundee working class. Mary Brooksbank became a well-known left-political radical and communist in Dundee during and after the war, but she was just a 'barefooted wee lassie' when she witnessed demonstration by striking carters and dockers in December 1911. She remembered how they faced the police who stood at attention with batons drawn, and that it was the first time she had heard 'The Red Flag' sung. Indeed, some days later her mother heard her singing the song and remarked to her father 'Dae ye hear that ane singin' a Protestant hymn!' Her father explained the song's significance to his wife.[89]

Brooksbank's 'first lesson in class warfare' occurred in April the following year when she became involved in the wide spread Dundee textile workers' strike at the age of fourteen:

> At this time there was quite a spate of strikes. The miners' fight for a minimum wage, the seamen's fight for better conditions, and the railwaymen's fight for shorter hours coincided with the first decade of the Labour Party. There was a definite upsurge of political awareness amongst the mass of the people, and the need for independent political working class representation had grown.[90]

She had not fully realised the forces that would be arrayed against her and her fellow strikers, and she later wrote: 'Private property takes paramount place over ordinary people. Blacklegs were often escorted to work by the police, but strikers were not considered to require protection from the bosses.'[91] It was a lesson she never forgot.

Alex Wilkie had been a Labour Party MP (one of Dundee's two parliamentary representatives) since the general election of 1906, and along with John Barnes at Glasgow, was one of only two Labour candidates elected in Scotland in that year. Bob Stewart, a Marxist and a Scottish Prohibitionist Party (SPP) activist before the war and a leading Dundee communist after, described Wilkie as 'very much a Lib-Lab politician' who was essentially a by-product of Dundee's strong radical Liberal tradition. But he stood firmly 'on the Labour ticket' and his victory did mark the end of the Liberal-Labour unity in Dundee and 'the birth of organised independent working class political action'. Stewart was an active trade unionist and a shipyard shop steward, and in 1908 he was elected to the town council. He was involved in the labour unrest in Dundee as well as helping to organise the Rent Strike with the help of the BSP, the ILP and the Dundee Trades Council in 1912.[92] In 1908, Winston Churchill, then a Liberal, was elected as the city's second MP. The Labour Party had run a candidate against Churchill in that election, and while he came third behind the Conservative candidate he polled just under 25 per cent of the total votes cast (16,118) and was only 366 votes behind the Conservative candidate.[93] Clearly, as Brooksbank suggested, with one Labour candidate already elected in 1906, and with a sizeable vote for a second in 1908, Labour's vote was already growing in strength in Dundee before the war.

CONCLUSION

Progress was being made before 1914, and Scottish trade unionists and political radicals were able to unite when it mattered and overcome political and organisational differences. The Scottish Trades Councils in particular, dominated as they were by a Presbyterian, politically liberal, artisan elite, were helping to break down sectional, religious and ethnic divisions. Indeed, as the example of the NUDL shows, being Catholic and Irish was no barrier to trade-union organisation in Scotland, and in 1906 John Wheatley, an ILP member and socialist, formed the Catholic Socialist Society. These organisations and institutions co-existed side by side with mainstream industrial and political organisations and became part of a growing network of working-class organisations across Scotland. Other immigrant communities were likewise accommodated. Jewish immigrants to Glasgow in the 1880s and 1890s, who were overwhelmingly refugees fleeing the pogroms in Tsarist Russia, quickly formed themselves into trade unions once in Scotland. Branches of the International Cigarette Workers' Union and the International Tailors, Machinists and Pressers Union were formed in 1894 and affiliated to the Trades Council in Glasgow. Indeed, under the leadership of Maurice Hyman, many became 'revolutionary socialists' and through contact with their parent organisations in America maintained a clear internationalist perspective.[94] The Jewish Workers' Circle was established in Glasgow and its members joined the ILP, the BSP and the SLP, and a Lithuanian Socialist and Catholic press emerged from the mining communities in Lanarkshire and the Lothians, where leading Lithuanian socialist Vincas Mickevicius-Kapsukas maintained close links with Scottish and internationalist socialist movements.[95] In 1903 the Jewish Workers Co-operative Wholesale Society was formed, demonstrating that Jewish workers were embracing Scottish working-class values and culture.

Scots had an involvement with Russian revolutionaries between 1905 and 1907, and after their defeat came stories of 'Scots joining together with Baltic, Russian and Jewish comrades' under the banner of the 'United Committee to Aid Political Prisoners in Russia'. Such bodies ostensibly represented the interests of foreign workers but they co-existed with and fed into working-class industrial and political organisations taking shape across Scotland. This rendered the Scottish industrial landscape and the Scottish working class, from whatever ethnic, racial or religious background they came from, different and distinctive, and by definition so too were the institutions and the process of trade unionism that developed out of this structure.[96] Clearly, and as Christopher Harvie argued, because of Scotland's 'social, and even geographical position, the Scottish left was open to a wide variety of cosmopolitan influences', and this was reflected in the emergence of a Scottish socialism which, although 'difficult to organise', was nonetheless 'both more original and articulate' particularly when compared to its English counterpart.[97]

NOTES

1. Gall, *The Political Economy of Scotland*, p. 1.
2. Knox, *Industrial Nation*, p. 124.
3. Young, *The Rousing*, pp. 134, 148, 154.
4. Knox, *Industrial Nation*, pp. 18, 163–9.
5. Young, *Rousing*, pp. 165–6.
6. Harvie, 'Before the breakthrough', p. 18.
7. E. Belfort Bax, *Justice*, 8 February 1923.
8. K. Manton, 'The fellowship of the New Life: English Ethical Socialism Reconsidered', p. 285.
9. Knox, *Industrial Nation*, p. 166. John Gilray noted that on discovering the stigma associated with 'Socialism', Edinburgh University Socialist Society changed their name to Edinburgh University Reform Society in 1885: *Early Days of the Socialist Movement in Edinburgh*, p. 7.
10. Gilray, *Early Days*, pp. 1–2.
11. Ibid. pp. 2–3.
12. Young, *Rousing*, p. 145.
13. Lowe, *Souvenirs of Scottish Labour*, p. 1.
14. Gilray, *Early Days*, p. 11.
15. Lowe, *Souvenirs*, pp. 128–9.
16. Gilray, *Early Days*, p. 15: reference to the 'wind up' of SLP in Lowe, *Souvenirs*, p. 170.
17. Gilray, Early Days, pp. 8, 14.
18. Lowe, *Souvenirs*, p. 172.
19. Brown, 'Religion and the Development of an Urban Society, Glasgow 1780 to 1914, p. 516.
20. *The Scotsman*, 3 September 1888.
21. Gilray, *Early Days*, p. 10.

22. *The Glasgow Herald*, 1 September 1888.

23. *The Scotsman*, 3 September 1888.

24. Ibid.

25. Gilray, *Early Days*, p. 12.

26. Lowe, *Souvenirs*, p. 122.

27. Gilray, *Early Days*, pp. 8–10.

28. *The Scotsman*, 23 August 1887.

29. *The Scotsman*, 1 September 1887.

30. *The Scotsman*, 5 September 1887.

31. *The Scotsman*, 8 October 1887.

32. *The Scotsman*, 13 October 1887.

33. Report in *The Scotsman* variously over January 1888, see also Duncan, *The Mine Workers*; McKay, 'A Social History of the Scottish Shale Mining Community', McKay chapter in Cavanach, *Pumpherston. The Story of a Shale Oil Village*.

34. Gilray, *Early Days*, p. 16.

35. Lowe, *Souvenirs*, p. 132: *The Scotsman* also reported on Hamilton's campaign against Councillor Baillie Steel and his role in the Broxburn evictions.

36. *The Scotsman*, 1 and 2 November 1893.

37. Gilray, *Early Days*, p. 17.

38. Lowe, *Souvenirs*, pp. 125–32.

39. Gilray, *Early Days*, p. 22.

40. Knox, *Industrial Nation*, p. 168.

41. Christine Thomas, 'How the Labour Party was formed', p. 2.

42. Lowe, *Souvenirs*, p. v.

43. Ibid. p. 128.

44. Ibid. p. 168.

45. Ibid. p. 126.

46. The Voice of Radicalism: Socialism 1850–1900; Historic Collections – DISS – University of Aberdeen; Buckley, *Trade Unionism in Aberdeen,* and Duncan, *James Leatham*: Lowe, *Souvenirs*, pp. 122, 124. See also the Oxford DNB online: James Leatham by Rob Duncan.

47. Lowe, *Souvenirs,* p. 149.

48. Aberdeen Trades Council Minutes, 28 January 1891.

49. *The Scotsman*, 19 August 1891.

50. Duffy, 'The Eight-Hour Day Movement in Britain, 1886–1893'; quoted in Laybourn, *A History of British Trade Unionism*, p. 80 and p. 92, n. 11.

51. Lowe, *Souvenirs*, p. 17.

52. Fraser, 'Trade Councils', pp. 12–17.

53. Lowe, *Souvenirs*, pp. 147–8.

54. Ibid. pp. 160–70.

55. Smyth, *Labour in Glasgow*, pp. 134–6, 145.

56. D. Saunders, 'The 1905 Revolution on Tyneside', and 'A Russian Babel Revisited', p. 647. Saunders cites the recent work of Johnson, *Social*

Democratic Politics in Britain, where he confirms John Leslie's status as 'Organising Secretary of the Scottish District Council of the SDF' from 1908, p. 148. See also Lee and Archbold, *Social-Democracy in Britain: Fifty Years of the Socialist Movement,* pp. 148–54.

57. The McKie Papers, Nat Ganley Collection, Archives of Labour and Urban Affairs, Wayne State University: Box 33. Reference to Leslie as Connolly's uncle: Folder 17, p. 13; [among a collection of occasional loose pages in no particular sequence]. Note: I have worked on copies produced by Mike Smith, Reference Archivist at Wayne State University (January 1997) which were passed on by Professor Alan McKinlay, St Andrews University.
58. McKie Papers, Folder 26, pp. 3–4.
59. Ibid. Folder 17, p. 18. Note: page referring to Keir Hardie is unnumbered and part of a collection of occasional loose pages.
60. Ibid. pp. 5, 8.
61. Ibid. pp. 9–10.
62. *The Scotsman,* 22 April, and *Justice,* 27 April 1905.
63. Milton, *John Maclean,* pp. 33–4.
64. Saunders, '1905 Revolution', p. 21; note on Leslie's involvement, p. 29.
65. Saunders, '1905 Revolution', p. 24.
66. *The Glasgow Herald,* 16 April 1907.
67. *The Glasgow Herald,* 15, 16 April 1907.
68. Saunders, '1905 Revolution', pp. 26–7. Saunders points out that this was widely reported in the establishment socialist press, including *Justice* and *Forward,* variously between the arrests, trials and aftermath between April and July 1907.
69. *The Scotsman,* 17 April 1907.
70. Saunders refers here to an article by Leslie appearing in *Justice,* 5 September 1918.
71. MacDougall, *Militant Miners,* p. 10.
72. Saunders, '1905 Revolution', pp. 27, 29–30; also Johnson, *Social Democratic Politics.*
73. *The Scotsman,* 6 August 1901.
74. *Justice,* 8 August 1907 and *Forward,* 10 August 1907.
75. McKie Papers, Folder 17, occasional papers, not numbered.
76. Ibid. Folder 17, pp. 1–2, occasional papers.
77. Ibid. Folder 17, pp. 13–14, not in any particular sequence.
78. Young, *John Maclean,* pp. 23–4; Milton, *John Maclean,* p. 41.
79. Young, *John Maclean,* p. 31.
80. *The Scotsman,* 5 November 1878.
81. Jim Mortimer, 'The Formation of the Labour Party – Lessons for Today', p. 15.
82. *The Scotsman, The Glasgow Herald,* 22 January 1908: see also extensive reports in *Forward* and the *Labour Leader,* 25 January 1908.
83. *The Scotsman,* 12 April 1909.

84. Gilray, *Early Days*, pp. 21–2, 23.
85. Trouble had been brewing for some time considerable among the ranks of the ILP as to whether ILP members standing for election should be permitted to call themselves Independent Socialist Labour Party candidates. In the course of the discussion Keir Hardie stated that the day might well come but that at that juncture, the 'Socialist wing' they should not impose this on the trade union movement. The matter came to a head at the ILP conference at Edinburgh between Saturday, April 10 and Tuesday, 13 April 1909 and continued through to Keir Hardie's address on the so-called 'Labour Party Split' to the West London district branch of the ILP on 26 April. The matter was not to rest for some considerable time and was extensively reported, discussed and debated in *Forward* and the *Labour Leader* as well as in the *Clarion* which was the organ of the Social Democratic Party (previously the SDF), throughout April and May.
86. 'The Socialist Movement of Great Britain', article III, *The Times*, 12 January 1909.
87. Holford, *Reshaping Labour*, pp. 149–51.
88. Ibid. pp. 150, 181.
89. Brooksbank, *No Sae Lang Syne*, pp. 3–4, 10.
90. Ibid. pp. 3–4.
91. Ibid. pp. 20–1.
92. Stewart, *Breaking The Fetters*, see chapters 7 to 12.
93. Ibid. pp. 42–9.
94. Young, *The Rousing*, p. 155.
95. Thatcher, 'Representations of Scotland in Nache Slova during the First World War', pp. 144–5.
96. MacDougall, *Mid and East Lothian Miners*', p. 386; Rodgers, 'The Glasgow Jewry' and 'The Lanarkshire Lithuanians', in Kay (ed.), *The Complete Odyssey*, pp. 22–9; Kenefick, *Rebellious and Contrary*, chapter 5; Kenefick, 'Jewish and Catholic Irish Relations: The Glasgow Waterfront c. 1880 to 1914', pp. 215–34.
97. C. Harvie, 'Before the Breakthrough', p. 18.

4

Red Scotland, c. 1910 to 1932:
Themes and Issues

THE LABOUR UNREST, 1910–14

In describing the upsurge in trade unionism and political action in relation to the new unionism, the preceding chapters have already discussed
some of the main contributing causes associated with industrial and
social unrest. These include a growing sense of worker alienation, the
impact of technological and scientific management, employment insecu-
rity, employers' anti-unionism, falling real wages, poor housing and
overcrowding, and increased levels of poverty.[1] These factors are of
course equally applicable to the discussion of the causes of the labour
unrest of 1910–14 and need not be repeated here. There is some considerable debate regarding the extent to which the new unionism was influenced by socialist and labour politics, and some of the evidence presented
suggested that by sponsoring political action, socialists did come into
closer contact with ordinary workers and trade-unionists. For example,
the politics of Irish Home Rule and land reform was integral to the formation of the National Union of Dock Labourers (NUDL) in Glasgow
in 1889, and the demand for the shorter working week and state intervention on the railways helped to radicalise the railwaymen in the 1890s
and thereafter encourage the growth of industrial unionism. But while
contemporary opinion were certainly of the view that the new unionism
was 'politically inspired', historical opinion would argue that improvements in the economy were largely responsible for the upsurge in both
trade unionism and strike activity.

The political dimension to labour unrest is less contentious in so far
as socialism and syndicalism were considered to be important contributing factors between 1910 and 1914. The syndicalist movement in Britain,
for example, had an organisational structure and a distinctive political
ideology and strategy 'as important as that of France', and the Socialist
Labour Party (SLP) and the British Socialist Party (BSP) were thought to

be important conduits in promoting socialist and syndicalist ideas.[2] The strike at the previously peaceful Singer factory in Clydebank in 1911 was influenced by socialist and syndicalist ideas and came to epitomise the escalating breakdown in capital-labour relations experienced at this time. The press clearly held this view, and while some reports verged on the 'wildly sensationalist', socialism, syndicalism and industrial unionism were consistently blamed for fuelling the discontent among the labouring masses. At the time of the national strike of seamen and dockers in August 1911, *The Glasgow Herald* reported,

> That Glasgow had felt the surge of a movement that has swept the great centres of population throughout the country, . . . The restraints imposed by the older and more respectable type of trade unionism are flouted by workers who have come under the spell of incendiary advisers like those who made the Confederation of Labour a menace to the structure of French society, . . . The present situation is the gravest that has been known for a century.[3]

In January 1912, the same broadsheet blamed a worsening situation 'on the fermentation of a socialist leaven on untutored minds', and reporting on an escalation in the frequency of labour disputes proclaimed 'that practically every outstanding upheaval of recent days has been an insurrection'.[4] The ILP organ *Forward* reported that the widespread use of sympathetic action had ensured a great victory for the seamen and dockers of Clydeside during 1911. Indeed, Emanuel Shinwell asserted that this type of direct action 'helped sow the seeds of revolution on the Clyde'. 'Socialism had rarely been mentioned', he argued, 'but its principles and ideas have been expressed at every turn'.[5] George Carson, secretary to the Glasgow Trades Council, felt that that it was 'no exaggeration to say that in number and magnitude . . . never in the history of the labour movement had such an upheaval taken place'.[6] *The Scotsman* observed that even schoolchildren had been caught up in this mood of revolt by 'imitating their elders' and striking across the country during September 1911 against corporal punishment and homework.[7] The sudden and swift upsurge in trade unionism among a growing body of workers from 1911 – including many unorganised female and unskilled workers – further fuelled the fires of discontent, and was of such a scale that John Maclean felt sure that Scotland was 'in the rapids of revolution'. Two years on H. G. Wells wrote of the labour unrest in a similar manner:

> The discontent of the labouring mass of the community is deep and increasing. It may be that we are in the opening phase of a real and irreparable class war . . . New and strange urgencies are at work in our midst, forces for which the word revolutionary is only too faithfully appropriate.[8]

G. D. H. Cole stressed that 'the unrest was real, possessing both direction and determinism, and without doubt was syndicalist in form', and David Shackleton of the Home Office, the Association of the Chambers of Commerce, and the Employers' Parliamentary Council openly expressed their fears over the rising tide of militancy and the increased use of the sympathy strike and direct action.[9]

Among labour and social historians, however, there is still considerable disagreement regarding the ideological impact of socialism and syndicalism during the labour unrest. Bob Holton, for example, argued that there was a palpable 'proto-syndicalist mood of revolt' evident in Britain before 1914 as more workers became embroiled in spontaneous and unofficial industrial action.[10] Richard Price suggested that syndicalist ideas permeated almost all trade unions to some extent during the labour unrest,[11] and Raymond Challinor and Michael Haynes developed similar lines of argument.[12] According to Henry Pelling and Hugh Clegg, however, syndicalism played little part in influencing the trade union movement or in encouraging industrial action over the period 1910–14.[13] Politically, there may have been a distinct shift to the left but no large union held revolutionary aims and of the fourteen main strikes in Britain between 1910 and 1019 only two had any significant syndicalist influence. James Hinton, Keith Burgess and Bill Knox all agree that there was a definite surge in class consciousness, and a fracturing of relatively peaceful industrial relations at the time of the labour unrest, but that capitalism was never seriously threatened by this challenge.[14] Indeed, Keith Laybourn asserted:

> [That it] is difficult, if not impossible, to believe that syndicalism was in any sense pervasive among the British working class . . . the impact of syndicalism has been exaggerated [for] [t]here was little threat to the industrial status quo before 1914.[15]

In line with E. H. Hunt's analysis of the unrest, Laybourn concluded that there was little or no support for syndicalism beyond South Wales, the Midlands or Ireland.[16] Moreover, as noted by Phillip Leng, even in locations where there was an active syndicalist leadership, the rank and file were still more concerned with 'gaining higher wages than overthrowing capital'.[17]

Opinions vary too regarding the nature of the labour unrest and the manner in which levels of collective organisation, wage rates, strike propensity and employers' responses showed marked geographical variations before 1914.[18] John Benson suggests that a great many workers were simply unaffected by trade unionism, labour disputes and politics

Table 4.1   Unemployment and Sequestrations for Non-Payment of Rent on Clydeside, 1910–14.

	I (% unemployed in Britain)	II (% unemployed in Clyde Engineering)	III (% unemployed in the Clyde Shipyards)	IV (Sequestration for rent arrears, Glasgow)
1900	2.5			10,818
1901	3.3			10,878
1902	4.0			11,409
1903	4.7	6.5	11.4	13,092
1904	6.0	9.3	16.0	14,517
1905	5.0	7.2	11.4	15,020
1906	3.6	4.0	7.5	14,528
1907	3.7	5.0	9.0	15,602
1908	7.8	19.8	24.2	20,858
1909	7.7	17.9	22.1	21,517
1910	4.7	6.3	14.7	19,556
1911	3.0	3.4	1.8	16,450
1912	3.2	4.2	2.1	11,239
1913	2.1	2.2	1.0	4,522
1914	3.3			3,660

Source: Column I J. E. Cronin, *Industrial Conflict in Modern Britain* (1979); Columns II–IV J. H. Treble, 'Unemployment in Glasgow 1903–1910: Anatomy of a Crisis', *Scottish Labour History Society Journal*, 29, 1990, p. 39 and also W. Kenefick and A. McIvor, *Roots of Red Clydeside?: Labour Unrest and Industrial Relations in West Scotland* (1996), p. 27.

before World War One.[19] James Young would readily identify with this perspective in so far as he viewed the labour unrest in 'ca' canny Scotland' as far less intense than in England. Indeed, Hamish Fraser suggested that most of the salient features of the labour unrest in Britain were already apparent by around 1907. He noted that the economy was beginning to move out of recession by 1907, that the three main railway unions re-launched their demand for the eight- and ten-hour day and improved pay and conditions, and there were clear signs of rising discontent among the engineers and textiles workers and in the mining industry from 1907. Thus, he concluded, 'any attempt to identify the unrest of 1910–13 as a unique phenomenon needs to be treated with considerable caution'.[20]

The validity of Fraser's argument is less viable, however, when the unrest is considered from a west of Scotland perspective. Table 4.1 is extracted from the Glasgow Labour History Workshop (GLHW) study and demonstrates that the economic malaise on Clydeside was much deeper than in other areas of Britain, and that between 1907 and 1910 unemployment on Clydeside was felt in almost every trade. *The Glasgow Herald* reported in 1908, for example, that almost 2,000 dockers were idle, and for those still in work wages were half their former level. If there was a general improvement in trade in Britain from 1907, shipyard and engineering workers did not feel the affects of it until after 1909, and the revival in the fortunes of the carters, dockers and seamen can be more or less precisely dated to 1911. The national rate of unemployment in Britain stood at 7 per cent in 1907 rising to 9 per cent in 1909, before falling to 5.5 per cent in 1910 (2 per cent higher than in 1903). But on Clydeside, as Jim Treble noted, unemployment remained well above the British national average. General and casual labour suffered considerably and, as a result, the total number of applications for relief works in Glasgow, Govan and Partick increased from 7,906 to over 14,000 between 1907 and 1908 alone. It was the same at Dundee where 'unemployment was rampant' and workers were in such 'a desperate position' that relief work had to be arranged 'and soup kitchens erected'.[21]

The years 1911–14 were especially important for the carters, dockers and seamen. The Shipping Federation was, as ever, in a position of great strength and it dominated industrial relations. Indeed, it epitomised the anti-union mind-set that typified much of Clydeside capital. The Federation demonstrated its determination to defeat the dockers at Dundee by converting the port to free labour status in 1904. It also played a leading role in the dockers' and transport workers' strike at Belfast in 1907, where it threatened to 'raise its own police force' if the local authorities did not make provision for sufficient police to guard its 'free labourers'. This led to 2,600 British troops being brought into Belfast and, over several days during August 1907, the police baton-charged strikers, troops charged with fixed bayonets and two people were shot dead.[22] The Federation made an equally determined stand against the fledgling SUDL and the recently reformed Seamen's Union at Glasgow in 1911, it mounted a counter-attack on the SUDL at Ardrossan in 1912, and challenged the NUDL at Leith in 1913. It failed on each occasion.[23]

However, Ronald Johnson, in his seminal work *Clydeside Capital 1870–1920* (East Linton, 2000), asserted that any distinctive 'oppositional attitude' to trade unionism in the west of Scotland had largely evaporated by the early years of the twentieth century. Thus, it would be wrong to argue that employer authoritarianism was a prime causal factor in the upsurge of workers' radicalism on Clydeside. Johnson does not deny that there were strong employer associations operating on Clydeside, but he does suggests that many functioned merely as short-term

Table 4.2   Strike Activity in the West of Scotland, 1910–14.

	1910	1911	1912	1913	1914	Total	%
Mining	3	16	8	15	11	53	20.3
Shipbuilding & engineering	3	10	13	11	16	53	20.3
Transport	6	20	9	6	7	48	18.4
Textiles	1	6	12	2	7	28	10.7
Metals	1	2	12	3	8	26	10.0
Construction	–	–	5	6	1	12	4.6
Printing	1	1	–	2	3	7	2.7
Chemicals	–	1	2	3	–	6	2.3
Timber & furniture	–	2	2	2	–	6	2.3
Glass & pottery	1	1	3	–	–	5	1.9
Municipal	–	1	1	2	1	5	1.9
Food	1	1	2	–	–	4	1.5
Retail	–	–	–	3	–	3	1.2
Miscellaneous	–	–	1	3	1	5	1.9
Number of strikes recorded	17	61	70	58	55	261	

Source: *The Glasgow Herald* and *Forward*, 1910–14. Strikes enumerated within the geographical region comprising Renfrewshire, Dunbartonshire, Lanarkshire and Ayrshire. Industrial classification is that adopted by C. H. Lee, *British Regional Employment Statistics*, (1979); figures for 1914 cover January to July only. W. Kenefick and A. McIvor, *Roots of Red Clydeside?: Labour Unrest and Industrial Relations in West Scotland* (1996); GLHW study, chapter 1, p. 22.

coalitions at times of industrial strife, and generally broke up when the immediate danger has faded. The engineering employers' federation was an exception, he noted, as it went from strength to strength throughout the period 1870–20. The authoritarian Clydeside employer was 'a nineteenth century phenomenon, but a twentieth century myth'.[24] Johnson makes only a few references to the Shipping Federation, and it is in relation to the port transport industry that his main argument, while generally convincing, begins to break down. Like the engineering employers, the Shipping Federation went from strength to strength between 1890 and 1914 and went largely unchallenged until the labour unrest.[25]

It is clear that Fraser, like many other historians, generally supports the notion that the labour unrest was over by 1913 and that levels of industrial unrest had slowed down and tailed off by then. Official statistics do suggest such a decline, but the findings of the GHLW study seriously challenge this perspective.

Table 4.3 Comparison between Board of Trade and GLHW Figures for
Strike Incidence, 1910–14.

	Board of Trade	Glasgow Labour History Workshop
1910	11	17
1911	24	43
1912	41	70
1913	49	58
1914	6	55

Source: W. Kenefick and A. McIvor, *Roots of Red Clydeside?: Labour Unrest and
Industrial Relations in West Scotland* (1996); GLHW study, chapter 1, p. 24.

Table 4.3 compares the Board of Trade figures, which represent the
whole of Scotland, and the strikes identified by GLHW based on their
examination of sources local to the west of Scotland: comprising
Ayrshire, Dunbartonshire, Lanarkshire and Renfrewshire. Not only does
the GLHW study reveal a much higher level of strike activity than the
officials records suggest, they also demonstrate clearly that the labour
unrest continued well into 1914.

GEORGE DANGERFIELD AND THE EVEN STRANGER DEATH OF LIBERAL SCOTLAND

A sense of the escalating crisis taken place during the labour unrest is
considered in George Dangerfield's classic treatise, *The Strange Death of
Liberal England* (1935), which is widely disregarded by most historians.
Dangerfield confirms the general view that the government and press
believed the labour unrest had abated somewhat by the autumn of 1913.
But in November 1913, Sir George Askwith, of the Board of Trade,
warned that 'Within a comparatively short time there may be movements
in this country coming to a head of which recent events have been a small
foreshadowing'. By the early months of 1914, the Statistical Department
of the Board of Trade noted 'a positive fever of small strikes – so small
as to be imperceptible', but it was 'spreading through the country'
nonetheless. By July no less than 937 'little strikes' had taken place and
Sir George Askwith 'began to wonder just how the storm would burst
and from what quarter it would come'.

Dangerfield made some interesting observations about Askwith and
the material contained in his book, *Industrial Problems and Dispute*,
published in 1920. Askwith referred to the link between the labour
unrest and low wages, but also commented that the 'desire for solidarity

among the rank and file' was clearly obvious. His brief account of 1914, suggested Dangerfield, conveyed 'a pregnant atmosphere of bewilderment and mystery. Something was stirring which . . . his reason could not elucidate nor his imagination apprehend'. 'It was not simply a desire for shorter hours, better wages, and improved conditions of labour which threaten once again to convulse the country's industry; it was a fever, effervescence; and the causes of it were hidden from him.' Askwith also remarked on the network of employers' associations spreading across the country, and federated trade unions, but felt strongly that the employers 'from indifference, or fearfulness, or greed' simply refused to meet their workers halfway. Dangerfield also made an interesting comment on Ramsey Macdonald's *Social Unrest* (1913), where in one essay MacDonald 'expressed both veneration for the aristocracy and hatred for the *parvenu*'. This left Dangerfield uncertain 'whether its author was a Tory with Socialist leanings or a Socialist with a Tory imagination'.[26]

Dangerfield suggested Askwith 'must have been struck' by the resemblance between the 'swiftness of these small strikes' and 'the tactics of Syndicalism'. Dangerfield also considered that the Triple Industrial Alliance was one of the most potent weapons developed by the labour movement before 1914. This had come about as a result of rank-and-file agitation among the miners, railwaymen and transport workers, for left to its own devices the Trades Union Congress (TUC) 'would never have forged so potent a weapon'. The miners were one third of the Alliance and had need of such a weapon, for their anger was not simply focused on shorter hours, or increased wages, but on the social conditions experienced in the mining communities and the dangers they faced daily below ground. It was breaches in safety regulations that were to blame for 440 lives lost at Senghedydd in Wales in October 1913. At the subsequent accident inquest, the Senghedydd mine manager, appearing on seventeen different counts of negligence, was fined 'exactly £22!' Miners' lives at one shilling and one quarter of a penny each, reported the labour press. 'If legislation could not do better than this', Dangerfield argued, 'it was clear that the Government needed another lesson, for many other mines were hardly any better protected.[27] It was at the same mine where seventy-eight men died in May 1901, prompting the King to send his condolences in which he stated that he 'deeply grieved to hear of the terrible disaster'.[28] Over 500 miners lost their lives, over twelve years, in just one pit, and elsewhere other disasters and industrial accidents resulted in thousands of disablements and deaths.

Dangerfield's treatment of the labour unrest is sympathetic to the needs and desires of workers, and refreshing also in so far as he takes

Table 4.4 Disablement and Fatalities in Maritime, Mining and Rail
Transport, 1909–14.

Industrial Sector	Number of Disablements	Number of Fatalities
Railways	135,394	2,425
Maritime shipping and docks)	124,598	3,934
Mining	997,642	8,877

Source: Home Office Workmen's Compensation Statistics, 1909–14 [Cd 5386; 5896;
6493; 7088; 7669 and 8079]: and W. Kenefick, *Rebellious and Contrary: The
Glasgow Dockers, 1853–1932* (East Linton, 2000); Appendix Table VI (i) to (vi),
pp. 259–260.

account of how 'non-economic issues' such as occupational heath and
safety could occupy the minds of rank-and-file workers and not just the
trade union leadership. As Table 4.4 shows, there is no denying that the
industries represented by the Triple Industrial Alliance had an abominable health and safety record.

Dangerfield was particularly critical of British employers, noting how
the railway employers behaved 'in a vindictive manner' after the railway
strike of 1911, applying dismissal and punishments for all manner of
minor infractions in direct violation of the terms that ended the dispute.
Like the miners, the railwaymen demanded a shorter working week, and
this claim had, since the 1870s, been made as much on safety grounds as
on any other. Dangerfield also noted the role of the Shipping Federation
and how the National Transport Workers' Federation had emerged in an
attempt to combat its influence on the maritime trades. Under the Triple
Alliance banner, the miners, transport workers and railwaymen had the
potential to call all their workers out on a general strike. By July 1914
there were ominous signs that a wider unrest was brewing, and from the
engineers to the general labourers, wrote Askwith, 'there rose and
increased the alarming cry of "Wait till Autumn"'.[29]

The big push towards a general strike came ironically from the
Scottish coal-owners, when they declared in July that they would no
longer pay a previously agreed district minimum day wage. It was
evident, argued Dangerfield, that to the miners' rank and file this was the
final challenge and that the Miners' Federation would have to take issue
with the Scottish coal-owners. Had this happened, and the transport
workers and the railwaymen joined in, it was forecast that by October
at the very latest 'there would be an appalling national struggle over the
question of the living wage'. Britain went to war on 4 August 1914, and

so 'the great General Strike of 1914, forestalled by some bullets at Sarajevo . . . slipped away into the limbo of unfinished argument'. But as far as Dangerfield was concerned: 'The spirit of the workers in 1914 had never since been equalled'.[30]

Dangerfield's thoughts on the labour unrest barely figures in any discussion within labour historiography, and when they are noted, they are usually disparaged and maligned. Revolution forestalled only by the firing of some bullets at Sarajevo! It is hardly creditable. But the evidence from the GLHW demonstrated that strikes were on the increase in the west of Scotland between 1910 and 1914, and in the months before the First World War this 'class conflict' reached unprecedented heights. Echoing the thoughts of George Dangerfield, J. R. Richmond, an engineering employer, noted in his presidential address to Glasgow University Engineering Society after war had been declared noted:

> The position just before the outbreak of war was [that] inroads on the powers of management in the shops had become so serious that, had war not intervened, the autumn of 1914 would probably have seen an industrial disturbance of the first magnitude.[31]

The labour unrest still clearly generates considerable historical debate, and opinions differ regarding the main causes of unrest, the impact or otherwise of socialism and syndicalism and, as with the discussion on the new unionism, when the labour unrest actually began and when it ended. More importantly, was the labour unrest simply part of a longer-term development of the trade union and labour movement in Scotland, or was it, as Dangerfield argues, more indicative of a wider crisis affecting Edwardian society in the years before the Great War?

RED CLYDE AND THE WIDER IMPACT OF THE GREAT WAR

In the introduction to the recent seminal work *Scotland and the Great War* (1999) – the only one-volume study of the impact of the Great War on Scotland to date – Elaine McFarland wrote that 'in historiographical terms, the Great War was remarkable for the speed at which it was written into formal "history"'. Much of this historiography was, and still is, as McFarland suggested, caught up in the heroics of war – the brave and the good, those who fell at the front lines and those who courageously fought the war on the home front. Over the last decade or so, however, this view has undergone some revisionism to the point where both the 'heroic and the anti-heroic' are being discussed more rigorously in order to generate a more balanced perspective of the impact of war and changing social attitudes. All of which, suggested McFarland, leads to a clearer 'separation between the military and the social historical perspective'. And yet the Scottish experience is still nevertheless 'seldom disaggregated' from the British, or even the international historiographical overviews of the Great War, and Scottish historians have generally been slow to take up this challenge 'beyond the implications for labour relations on "Red Clydeside"' – a point we shall return to shortly.[32]

But much was to change after August 1914. Before the war the average law-abiding British citizen thought little about the liberty and freedom implicit in living out their day-to-day life. They had no need to carry an identity card, did not need a passport to travel abroad, and did not require permission to leave the country. A British citizen enjoyed one other important freedom:

> Unlike the countries of the European continent, the state did not require its citizens to perform military service . . . [he] could enlist, if he chose, in the regular army, the navy, or the territorials. He could also ignore, if he chose, the demands of national defence.

During the Great War the people of Britain were expected to become 'active citizens' and to place their personal wants and desires below the needs of the state. Indeed, the state was to establish a hold over its citizens during the war, which although relaxed in peacetime, was 'never to be removed'.[33]

The First World War brought the labour unrest to a fairly abrupt halt as the nation as a whole patriotically mobilised behind the war effort. The British public seldom wavered in its support of British war aims in the military arena, and it was prepared to accept limitations on their liberties at home in order to ensure victory for Britain and the Empire. Between 1915 and 1916, however, the attitude of workers began to change. They had shown their loyalty and proved their patriotism time and again, and they had accepted the demands and constraints that the war effort placed on them. Wages were rising rapidly during the war, but so too were prices, and greater competition in the housing market meant significant increases in rents. Some individuals had prospered because of the war, and the employers and landlords were accused of 'profiteering' at the workers' expense. This sense of outrage was keenly felt on Clydeside where the war 'played a critical role in incubating Clydeside workers' grievances, raising class awareness and drawing workers away from Liberalism towards the left'.[34]

The first major wartime strike took place over the issue of dilution (deskilling) on the Clyde in 1915, and a 'rent strike' involving up to 20,000 people threatened to further destabilise an already tense situation.

Indeed, it was the issue of dilution and de-skilling in the munitions factories that led to the emergence of the radical shop stewards' movement. The rent issue was resolved in 1915 with the introduction of the Rent Restriction Act, which froze rents for the duration of hostilities. It did not alter the fact that there was an acute shortage of housing, and neither the issue of dilution nor the accusations of wartime profiteering went away. Indeed, these issues were seized on by the political left and the ILP in particular in order to raise public awareness of the real cost of war. Meanwhile the shop stewards, 'many of whom were Marxist, syndicalists and Independent Labour Party socialists', went on to form the Clyde Workers' Committee (CWC), which the authorities viewed with grave suspicion. In the escalating disputes that followed, the CWC directly challenged the authority of the state, and its syndicalist and revolutionary leaders were accused of turning loyal and patriotic workers against the war effort. Between March and April 1916, ten CWC shop stewards were arrested, convicted of sedition and deported to Edinburgh.[35]

It seemed that a degree of peace and stability returned to the Clyde after the deportations, but what occurred on the Clyde had not gone unnoticed outside Scotland. For the editors of the Paris-based Russian Social Democratic newspaper *Nashe Slovo,* it was 'evidence of potential for revolution'. *Nashe Slovo* (Our Word) was the 'most frequently published, widely circulated, and influential Russian international broadsheet of the First World War' and its 'illustrious editors' included Julius Martov and Leon Trotsky. According to Ian Thatcher, between April 1915 and July 1916, twenty-three articles on Scotland appeared in *Nashe Slovo,* with and the 'heaviest concentration of these between January and July 1916'. It was the strikes in April of 1915 that first attracted attention, and the arrest of the workers' leaders and the suppression and closure of the *Worker* – the CWC propaganda organ – was followed with great interest. It was clear that the editors of *Nashe Slovo* saw the CWC as the basis of a strong workers' movement in Scotland, that the Scots had strong links with international socialism, and that 'the cause of the Russian Revolution (the 1905 Revolution) was close to the hearts of the Scottish workers'. This was clear in their support of the 'United Committee to Aid Political Prisoners in Russia', under whose auspices the Scots joined together with Baltic, Russian and Jewish comrades. It was reported that at the May Day Rally at Glasgow in 1915, the 'international sympathies' of the Scottish people were 'not only revealed in speeches being made in Russian, Yiddish, Lithuanian and Polish alongside English', but that through a sale of 'red bow ties' £5 and 7 shillings were raised to help the fund for political prisoners in Russia.

The arrest and internment of Peter Petroff in Glasgow in January 1916, 'until his repatriation to Bolshevik Russian in 1918', was reported as an illustration of 'the most sustained treatment of Scottish help to Russian Revolutionaries'. Petroff was a close friend and comrade of John Maclean and he was by then a leading and prominent figure in the BSP in London. But it was in Glasgow that he was arrested. A report appeared in February 'recounting specific acts by Scottish workers in Petroff's defence':

> A meeting of several hundred delegates issued a unanimous protest against the arrest; a circular explaining the affair and containing the workers' appeals was published and circulated; speeches were made at meetings attended by thousands of workers.

According to *Nashe Slovo*, the 'Petroff Affair' had intensified worker-government antagonisms to the point at which 'the growing revolutionary-proletarian movement in Scotland [would] have to face the test of history'.[36]

Nashe Slovo made special mention of Scotland's revolutionaries, most notably John Maclean and his role in the provision of Marxist education classes across Scotland. The example of the Scottish workers' willingness to become involved in direct action (rent strikes and unofficial industrial disputes, for example), the presence of syndicalist shop stewards and the formation of the CWC, the role of a Marxist and socialist leadership, Marxist education and the socialist press were seen as a model that could be replicated across Britain, and thereafter assist in radicalising a much broader swathe of the British working class. There was debate and discussion as to the exact nature of Scotland's revolutionary potential, particularly as the leading Marxist party, the BSP, was divided between pro-war 'social patriots' and anti-war 'internationalists'. But based on the views of Peter Petroff, it was made clear that the Scottish District Council of the BSP in Scotland was staunchly anti-war and it concluded that the BSP in Scotland 'was clearly Marxist in character'.[37]

The issue of Red Clyde is a broad, wide-ranging and much contested topic of interest, and the literature on the subject is now fairly extensive. It is therefore not the intention here to delve much further into this matter. For anyone wishing to learn more about the historiography of 'Red Clydeside', there is arguably no better starting point than the full, comprehensive and detailed overview of this topic provided by Terry Brotherstone and John Foster.[38] It is more important to outline how events taking place in Scotland were viewed in an international context and as part of an international movement because, as Brotherstone suggests any discussion on Red Clydeside 'must be grounded in an analysis of international and not merely national or local developments'. This is an important point, for it not only focuses on the role of John Maclean, as did many of the reports in *Nashe Slovo*, but also on the relationship with Russia after October 1917:

> Maclean's central importance lies precisely in his struggle in practice to establish the interconnectedness of Red Clydeside with the world-wide historical process of which the Russian Revolution proved, at that period, to be the climax.[39]

But something needs to be said briefly about the perceived 'mythical' or 'legendary' Red Clyde as promulgated in the theories of a growing number of historians by the 1980s. The most notable is Iain Mclean, but as he stated in the introduction to the 1999 edition of *The Legend of Red Clydeside*, 'what happened, and didn't happen, and nearly happened, and might have happened, in the street the streets and munitions factories of Glasgow between 1914 and 1922, was already a legend long before I chose my title'. McLean was in truth building on a body of work that had been 'reassessing the validity of revolutionary Red Clydeside' since the 1960s. John Maclean, 'briefly Soviet consul in Glasgow in 1918', 'may have come to be venerated' by a host of Scottish and international radicals and socialists thereafter, but the end result was still the same: 'The heroics of the Red Clyde, faithfully retained by further generations of activist, masked a fundamental defeat'. A legend was thus born to explain the revolution that never was.[40] McLean's first edition was described by one reviewer as 'an important piece of historical research', 'difficult to refute', and one that would 'put paid to the myth of 'Red Clydeside', which, even by 1918 had in any case become 'a sour journalistic cliché'.[41]

McLean identified with two distinctive and separate 'Red Clydesides', and stressed that each 'had little in common' with the other. They therefore did not form one cohesive and distinctive movement. The second Red Clyde 'entailed a broadening of Labour's social base', and was 'more open and inclusive' as a result, but when compared to the first it had little impact beyond the General Election of 1922. The newly elected 'Red Clydesiders' may have made the House of Commons 'a more colourful and livelier place' by their presence, but over the longer term this was thought 'counter-productive'. Lenin's communist administration, and some British government officials, may have felt that Scotland was on the threshold of revolution after the war, but the Red Clydeside 'constructed by the excitable minds of John Maclean and Sir Basil Thompson', argued

McLean, quite simply 'never existed'. Thus, discounting Glasgow's wartime militancy as something of a chimera, McLean concluded that the main achievement of Red Clyde was the 1924 Housing Act and it was this that would stand as Red Clydesiders' monument.[42]

It is clear, however, that McLean's view – which was originally based on a PhD thesis produced in the early 1970s – has proven 'remarkably influential and resilient', and has clearly prejudiced many other historians. Chris Harvie's *No Gods and Precious Few Heroes*, with its 'curt dismissal of Clydeside's radical reputation', is one example, and McLean's influence is evident too in the work of Michael Lynch and T. C. Smout. Lynch dismissed Red Clydeside, in a manner reminiscent of McLean, as a 'lost revolution', 'the revolution that never was', and wrote that the failure in 1919 had since 'become the talisman of a Left trying to retrace its own footsteps'.[43] In an article on 'Perspectives on Scottish Identity' (1994), Smout argued that Scottish history could be 'boiled down to half a dozen "mythic" episodes' – one of these was 'the tragic defeat by an Anglicised set of employers on Red Clydeside'.[44] But as Smyth points out,

> McLean's revisionism has come in for some sustained criticism by other historians who insist that the war-time unrest was both more prolonged and more significant than McLean allows and was also responsible for the post-war shift in political loyalties towards labour.[45]

Brotherstone describes the revisionists, or 'de-mythologisers', as the 'New Orthodoxy', and a prime example of their work was *The ILP on Clydeside, 1893–1932: From Foundation to Disintegration* (Manchester, 1991), edited by Alan McKinlay and Bob Morris. The book and its contributors clearly validate the phenomenon that was Red Clydeside, but conclude that it was the ILP who were 'mainly responsible for the *real* Red Clyde'. As there was ultimately no revolution on Clydeside, this version of Red Clyde was 'definitely to be disassociated from aspirations of Bolshevik internationalism'. The '*real* Red Clyde' referred, therefore, to the activities and propaganda of the ILP, the substantial contribution it made 'to the development of Labour politics' in Scotland, and 'the emergence of the Labour Party as a second major force in Parliament'.[46]

This 'revisionist' view of Red Clyde largely ignores the contribution of the smaller parties of the socialist and revolutionary left in Scotland, such as the British Socialist Party (BSP) and the Socialist Labour Party (SLP) and, by focusing on the developments that led to Labour's electoral success in 1922, it downplays the role of the socialist and the revolutionary leftists who joined with the Communist Party in 1920–1, and their role in the Red Clyde movement. More to the point, the revisionist view, like that of McLean and the other Red Clyde debunkers, also tends to ignore the impact of the No-Conscription Fellowship (NCF) and Scotland's conscientious objectors, their relationship with the ILP and involvement in its political advancement during the First World War, and indeed, the example they provided for a generation of left-activists who followed. Lastly, Mclean and Harvie's somewhat narrow view reinforces the conviction that little of significance occurred within the trade union and labour movement before 1914. Viewed from a broader geographical perspective, and adopting an approach that examines the actions and activities of workers beyond the west of Scotland, there is sufficient 'prima facie evidence', as Gregor Gall recently suggested, to proclaim that Scotland was both 'Radical' and 'Red' between the 1870s and the 1920s.[47] The matter should not simply be measured in relation to events taking place on Clydeside before 1914, or on the streets and munitions factories of Glasgow during and after the Great War.

There was a small, but significant, anti-war movement in Scotland during the war which operated across the whole country. But, as yet there has been no comprehensive account published on the Scottish war resisters between 1914 and 1918, and it is only relatively recently, in *Scotland and the Great War*, that this topic has received any attention.[48] This important aspect of Scotland's social history of the Great War examines the attitude of the church, the press and public to the war, and the ferocity of opinion publicly vented at Scottish war resisters. In telling the story of the war resisters, it can be demonstrated that the Scottish left did not simply 'jettison internationalist and anti-militarist perspectives at the outbreak of the war'. On the contrary 'these years saw the consolidation of an ethical and political outlook on which future generations of Scottish socialists could draw'.[49] International Socialism may have failed with the outbreak of war in 1914, but British war resisters 'provided a stirring tradition for the second and third generations of Socialists to follow'.[50]

NOTES

1. GLHW, *The Singer Strike*; on housing, Melling, *Rent Strikes: People's Struggle For Housing in West Scotland 1890–1916*.
2. Kenefick and McIvor, *Roots of Red Clydeside*, pp. 5–6, 32–7.
3. *The Glasgow Herald*, 15 August 1911.
4. *The Glasgow Herald*, 31 January 1912.
5. *Forward*, 12 August 1911.
6. Reported in Glasgow Trades Council, *Annual Reports*, 1911–12; quoted in Smyth, *Labour in Glasgow*, pp. 73–4.

7. *The Scotsman*, 16 September 1911.

8. Quoted in Kenefick, 'A Struggle for Control: the importance of the Great Unrest at Glasgow harbour, 1911 to 1912', p. 148.

9. *Roots of Red Clydeside*, p. 35; Askwith, *Industrial Problems and Disputes* (1920).

10. Holton, *British Syndicalism*, p. 269; see also Holton's reappraisal in Mommsen and Husung, *The Development of Trade Unionism in GB and Germany, 1880–1914*. To a large extent, Holton's views echo those of G. D. H. Cole, writing in the 1930s: see for example, G. D. H. Cole, *The World of Labour* (1913).

11. Price, *Labour in British Society* (1986); Price, *Masters, Unions and Men* (1980), pp. 236–67.

12. Challinor, *The Origins of British Bolshevism* (1977); Haynes, 'The British Working Class in Revolt, 1910–14', *International Socialism*.

13. Pelling, *A History of British Trade Unionism*; Clegg, *A History of British Trade Unionism*.

14. Hinton, *Labour and Socialism*; Burgess, *The Challenge of Labour*; Gore, 'Rank-and-File Dissent'; Knox, *Industrial Nation*; and White, '1910–1914 Reconsidered'.

15. Laybourn, *A History of British Trade Unionism*, pp. 104, 119.

16. Hunt, *British Labour History*, p. 329.

17. Leng, *The Welsh Dockers*, p. 51.

18. Morris, *Atlas of Industrialising Britain*, p. 193; Hunt, *Regional Wage Variations in Britain*; Church, 'Edwardian Labour Unrest and Coalfield Militancy, 1890–1914'; Laybourn, *A History*, pp. 107–8: see also Devlin and Renfrew, in Kenefick and McIvor, *Roots of Red Clydeside*, chapters 3 and 7.

19. Benson, *The Working Class in Britain*, pp. 174–206.

20. Fraser, *British Trade Unionism*, pp. 111–14.

21. Treble, 'Unemployment in Glasgow', p. 12; Kenefick, *Rebellious and Contrary*, pp. 204–9; and for Dundee, Stewart, *Breaking the Fetters*, pp. 44–5.

22. Gray, *City in Revolt*, pp. 59–60, 143, 154–68.

23. Kenefick, 'Ardrossan, the Key to the Clyde', pp. 1–20 and 'A Struggle for Control', pp. 129–52 in *Rebellious and Contrary*, pp. 212–27.

24. Johnson, *Clydeside Capital 1870–1920*.

25. Kenefick, *Rebellious and Contrary*, pp. 177–8, 216–17.

26. Dangerfield, *The Strange Death of Liberal England*, pp. 312–13.

27. Ibid. p. 318.

28. *The Scotsman*, *The Glasgow Herald* and *The Times* invariably all ran with this story as did the socialist weeklies during late May 1901, and later during October 1913.

29. Dangerfield, *The Strange Death*, p. 319.

30. Ibid. p. 320.

31. McKinlay, 'Philosphers in Overalls? Craft and Class on Clydeside, c. 1900–1914', p. 102.
32. Macdonald and McFarland (eds), *Scotland and the Great War*, pp. 3–4: Foster, 'Red Clyde, Red Scotland', pp. 106–24
33. Taylor, *English History, 1914 to 1945*, pp. 1–2.
34. McIvor, 'Red Dawn Fades', p. 9.
35. Ibid.
36. Thatcher, 'Representations of Scotland in *Nashe Slovo*', pp. 142–5.
37. Ibid. pp. 145–57.
38. Brotherstone, 'Does Red Clydeside Really Matter Anymore?'; Foster, 'Red Clyde, Red Scotland'.
39. Brotherstone, 'Does Red Clydeside Really Matter Anymore?', pp. 60, 67.
40. Harvie, *Few Gods and Precious Few Heroes*, pp. 16–23.
41. Brotherstone, 'Does Red Clydeside Really Matter Anymore?', pp. 57–8.
42. McLean, *The Legend of Red Clydeside*, pp. 239–41.
43. Lynch, *Scotland: A New History*, pp. 424–47; Brotherstone, 'Does Red Clydeside Really Matter Anymore?', pp. 53–6.
44. Smout, 'Perspectives on Scottish Identity', p. 108.
45. Smyth, *Labour in Glasgow*, introduction, pp. 3–4; see also p. 4, n. 14 for a list of McLean's critics.
46. Brotherstone, 'Does Red Clydeside Really Matter Anymore?', pp. 64–5.
47. Gall, *Political Economy of Scotland*, p. 6.
48. Kenefick, 'War Resisters and Anti-Conscription in Scotland: an ILP Perspective', pp. 59–80.
49. McFarland, Introduction, *Scotland and the Great War*, p. 6.
50. Hayes, *Conscription Conflict*, pp. 248, 257, 266.

5

Labour Unrest, 1910 to 1914

INTRODUCTION

In the *Roots of Red Clydeside 1910–1914?: Labour Unrest in Industrial Relations in West Scotland*, William Kenefick and Arthur McIvor argued that while Scottish labour history had developed significantly over the previous thirty years, weaknesses still persisted and coverage in certain areas was patchy. It was noted, for example, that in Scottish labour history there had been too much focus 'upon the lives of male, skilled, protestant workers' and, more specifically, that too little attention had been paid to the role of Scots workers during the 'labour unrest' of 1910 and 1914. The book was intended to address both these weaknesses. The publication was the end-product of a project that began ten years earlier when the Glasgow Labour History Workshop (GLHW) was established at Strathclyde University in 1986. Three years later they produced their first publication, *The Singers Strike, Clydebank, 1911*. This book told the story of the confrontation between a group of Red Clydesiders and their struggle against rapacious and 'fiercely anti-trade unionist American employers'. Importantly, the GLHW established that women played a key role in this dispute and that the workforce was closely associated with the Industrial Workers of Great Britain (IWGB), and the revolutionary Socialist Labour Party (SLP). The details of this strike had been largely lost to posterity, although at the time it provoked widespread interest across Britain, America and the Continent. Indeed, the SLP organ *The Socialist* reported that 'in the History of Labour' the Singers strike ranked 'alongside the Dockers Strike of 1889, and the Engineers' Lockout of 1897'.[1] In researching the *Singers Strike*, however, it became clear that little was known about the activities of Scottish workers during 'labour unrest' for they were mentioned rarely in British labour historiography, and were simply ignored in general Scottish social histories.[2] This neglect could be justified if the labour unrest of 1910–14 had been unimportant in Scotland, but their research clearly demonstrated that this was not the case. In uncovering the role of revolutionary socialists, the influence of American-style syndicalism and industrial unionism, and the participation of a large body of female workers, the GLHW identified new dimensions in the nature of the labour struggle in Scotland before the First World War.[3]

Since 1996 there has been a reasonable body of research produced on the experience of the unskilled, non-Protestant and women workers, including the work of James Smyth on women and the Irish in Glasgow, William Kenefick's work on Irish Catholic involvement in the emergent dock unionism on the Clyde, Ann Marie Hughes' examination of Clydeside women and the ILP, and Neil Raffeek's path-breaking oral history-based research on women, socialism and the Communist Party in Scotland since 1919.[4] Other than *Roots of Red Clydeside*, however, there have been no further published studies specifically focused on labour unrest in Scotland, and more importantly little consideration of how the experience of unrest affected workers beyond the Clydeside region of Scotland. This chapter introduces new research on strike activity in the east of Scotland and in dovetailing this with the GLHW study presents a fuller picture of the extent and nature of the labour unrest across Scotland.

THE LABOUR UNREST BEYOND THE WEST OF SCOTLAND

A Year of Few Strikes – 1910

If the columns of *The Scotsman* are to be believed, there were few strikes to report during 1910 and those strikes identified were mainly local in character. Aberdeenshire settmakers were involved in the lockout of early January, and there was a dispute involving printworkers in Edinburgh in May. The only other strike of note also occurred in May and involved woodyard workers at Bo'ness, where it was reported that the employers brought in 100 blacklegs from Glasgow organised by the 'well-known west of Scotland strike-breaker' (probably Graham Hunter). The strike involved 'several hundred strikers, male and female', and there were several disturbances due to the presence of blacklegs, which on at least one occasion resulted in a police baton charge.[5] But there were only around seven or eight reports on trade disputes over the first half of 1910.

Most reports referred to larger strikes such as the Northumberland mining disputes and the Welsh mining disputes at the beginning and the end of the year; and between times there was trouble at the Ayrshire mines, and in and around Edinburgh and Leith increased activity on the part of the railwaymen and the Seamen's Union. The main industrial dispute took place in shipbuilding and engineering, and was precipitated by an employers' lockout in September 1910. It included yards in Glasgow, Govan and Greenock and in the east, Aberdeen, Dundee and Edinburgh. The *Dundee Courier* reported on the impact of the lockout in Dundee at the Caledon and Panmuir shipyards, where it was noted that the Dundee boilermakers were initially against the dispute (because Dundee was just recovering from a downturn in trade). The determination of the employers' federation to draw the union into a fight had hardened their resolve.[6] They refused 'to place their union at the mercy of the federation' and in October the Dundee boilermakers – in line with the national vote – rejected a ballot which would have empowered their executive to negotiate with the employers.[7]

The press commented that there were a 'latter-day tendencies' among trade unionists to be 'directed, or misdirected, by Socialistic influences'.[8] The shipyard dispute was a good example, for when a second ballot was rejected in early November, by an even bigger majority than the first ballot, it seemed that the boilermakers' officials had little influence over the rank and file. A third ballot was finally agreed in mid-December and the boilermakers' national dispute in Scotland was over. Ironically, the Dundee boilermakers, who had initially been against strike action, voted against the third ballot and against the instructions of their union's executive.[9] Because of the actions of the Engineering Employers' Federation during the shipyard lockout, the boilermakers of Dundee had moved to a more militant position. The local press had initially been sympathetic but when Dundee voted against the final ballot this mood changed. The Dundee *Advertiser* could only conclude that this 'worrying and puzzling' development formed part of the 'crest of a deep wave of social and industrial unrest' affecting labour across the country.[10] There was another dispute of note at Dundee during September of 1910. It was reported as a 'wildcat' strike and involved seventy apprentice engineers employed at Caledon shipyard. It was unofficial, had no union support, and a settlement was brokered locally. The apprentices were back at work within the week, but it was viewed as another worrying development in labour relations in Dundee.[11]

The fight for a 'living wage' – 1911

When the year 1911 opened, the outlook for labour relations on the east of Scotland looked peaceful enough. The Singer strike at Clydebank during March and April was a worrying development, but as far as the press was concerned all seemed well with the world. But this masked two important disputes which went largely undetected. The first involved a strike at Cox's mill in Lochee in Dundee where the whole mill complex was shut down because of a reduction of two workers in one spinning squad. Over 80 per cent of the mill workers were members of the Jute and Flax Workers' Union and the Dundee press were critical of Mr Cox, the mill owner, for his heavy-handed attitude in refusing to meet with the union organiser and end the dispute. The strikers returned to work three weeks later on the condition that the two workers considered excess to requirements were found alternative employment.[12]

The second important dispute was the strike of Kirkcaldy male 'powerloom tenters' which began almost unnoticed in early January 1911. This dispute received little press attention, and it was only when reporting on a series of strikes among female textile workers at Kirkcaldy later in June that it became clear that the powerloom tenters' dispute was still unresolved. Also in Fife, another dispute involved 'a strike of women and girls' at Dunfermline, which became protracted because the women refused to discuss any matter relating to the strike without their trade union representative being present.[13] The powerloom tenters' dispute was unresolved when the press reported on the growing discontent among female textile workers at Kirkcaldy during October. Indeed, there was a 'great demonstration' held in the town and the Rev. William Milne, of the United Free Church, spoke in support of the workers, stating that 'The Church must come out and show her sympathy with the working people of our land in their great effort to reach something like a living wage', and that in Kirkcaldy 'workers were far below the living wage in very many circumstances'.[14] The strike started in early October and was not settled until mid-December, and it was only at this juncture that the eleven-month powerloom tenters' dispute was finally resolved.[15]

During 1911 there were several national disputes among railwaymen, dockers and seamen. Around 16,000 railwaymen came out across Scotland in August 1911, and although 54,000 working-days were lost to the strike action, the dispute was over more or less before it began. The strike resulted in a great victory for the railwaymen, but the brevity of the dispute moved *The Scotsman* to report that 'in industrial disputes Scottish workmen do not as a rule become unduly excited'. A series of short, sharp strikes, of the type Dangerfield would later associate with the syndicalist-style direct action, was initiated by the recently formed Scottish Union of Dock Labourers across Clydeside in the summer of

1911, and this culminated in a national dispute involving 13,000 dockers and seamen in August that year.[16]

The dockers' and seamen's dispute was the result of the widespread penetration of trade unionism among maritime and port transport workers across Scotland in 1911, and it was to prove particularly important to trade union development at Dundee. Workers at Dundee had become much more radicalised since the boilermakers' strike the year before. The year opened with the dispute that shut down the Cox's Mill complex when two workers were made unemployed, and by September 1911 even the schoolchildren of Dundee were on strike. School strikes were taking place all over the country from London to Dublin, and from Paisley to Aberdeen, but at Dundee the local press reported 'that the strike took on a more serious face'. For example, on 14 September the press reported that a gang of over 1,500 schoolchildren 'attacked schools with sticks and stones' at the Hilltown, Dens Road and Blackness Road, and the previous evening eight schools had been targeted. It was stressed that this 'new outburst [was] not a natural act of revolt, it [was] simply a matter of imitation'. Indeed, the Educational Institute of Scotland (EIS) thought that the press had 'unwittingly' helped spread the epidemic by printing details of the strikes, so much so that 'a game of follow the leader' had ensued.[17] The strike was widespread but short-lived, and after a week children across the country were back behind their desks.

From an east coast perspective the big story of 1911 was the events surrounding the carters' and dockers' strike at Dundee during December. The strike was important for two reasons. First, the unrest was generally referred to in the Dundee press as the 'Carters' Strike', and was the cause of a famous Dundee split from the Scottish Horse and Motormen's Association (SHMA) by Peter Gillespie, something of a syndicalist sympathiser who opposed the 'non-political' industrial strategies of the SHMA and its leader Hugh Lyons. The split in itself is something of a side-issue, however, for it was the impact of the strike on Dundee workers which makes it important. Alan Bell demonstrated that the strike was 'of some considerable scope' and consequence and during one week in late December 600 carters and 700 dockers brought Dundee to a standstill. Due to a lack of raw materials, 30,000 people were unable to work as the strike forced the closure of virtually all of Dundee's vast textile industry, yet these workers took to the streets in support of the strikers. The authorities responded to the strike with a dual approach, involving an arbitration process and the drafting-in of extra police 'and three hundred troops of the Black Watch'. The strike was important for various reasons. It was conducted and organised locally by Peter Gillespie and, while the SHMA took no part in it, it was supported by Dundee's biggest union, the District Union of Jute and Flax Workers, and the Dundee Trades Council which held street collections 'to give all classes an opportunity of assisting the men on strike'.[18] Cargoes of materials bound for Dundee were also blocked at Leith, and Shinwell ensured that no blacklegs would leave Glasgow bound for Dundee (although the NUDL could not halt the flow of blacklegs from Aberdeen). The camaraderie among a broad swathe of Dundee workers was at that time exceptional, so much so that *Forward* proclaimed the strike 'a glorious lesson in solidarity'.[19]

The other dimension to the strike was the role of the dockers. The national press clearly saw them as a key element of the strike principally because of the role of the SUDL, its connection with the Seamen's Union and the National Transport Workers' Federation (NTWF). The SUDL reorganised Dundee and, in doing so, re-established a link between Dundee and Glasgow that went back to the new unionist days (a link probably explained by the presence of the Irish). In 1904, however, Dundee became a free labour port and supported the Shipping Federation and its offshoot, the Free Labour Bureau. Indeed, in June 1911, six month before the carter's and dockers' strike broke out, the Free Labour Bureau published its *Annual Reports* wherein it was stated with some confidence that 1,235 dockers at Dundee (this would have included port carters) had 'signed the free labour pledge'. 'A number of trivial claims had been dealt with', but there had been no labour disputes at the port. Six months on and Dundee was no longer a Federation free port, and in the meantime, reported *The Scotsman*, Dundee dockers had earned a 'regrettable' reputation for 'disorderliness'.[20] This was somewhat ironic, for it was only in August that the same broadsheet asserted that Scottish workers as a rule did not get 'unduly excited' when it came to industrial matters. Indeed, looking back over the year, *The Scotsman* had shifted its opinion to entirely the other extreme regarding the nature of industrial disputes, arguing that 'The Labour Unrest has been recruited from a vague Syndicalism of the French Socialists, who suggest that the universal strike is the best means of bringing "capitalism" to its knees'. It would seem that they thought the recent dock strike at Dundee was such an example of syndicalism at work.[21]

A RISING STRIKE FEVER – 1912

The New Year brought no respite. Dock carters and 'young mill "hecklers"' came out at Montrose and linoleum hand printers went on strike at Kirkcaldy.[22] But attention quickly turned to Dundee where on 11 January, between thirty and forty female weavers at the Grimond Bowbridge plant went on strike over pay and conditions. Within a few days some 1,200 workers, mostly women and members of the Jute and Flax Workers' Union, were affected by the dispute. The women were offered the opportunity to return to work, but on a vote elected to stay out on strike, and they were joined by twenty male polishers from the Bowbridge plant. The Dundee Trades Council became involved, as did the ILP, and Dundee carters' leader Peter Gillespie spoke in support of the women and their struggle for 'better wages'. It was also stated that the 'Clyde was to render assisstance' after Mr Sime, the Jute and Flax workers' leader, read a reply to a telegram sent by him to Shinwell, Tom Mann, A.W. French (Scottish Seaman's Union) and Joe Houghton asking that they block any raw materials or goods going to or dispatched from Grimonds' works via Glasgow and the west coast ports. Shinwell replied: 'Best wishes for success. Clyde transport workers will render every possible assistance.' The employers came back with an offer of an increase in wages. All but eight of the 560 women workers present at a specially convened strike meeting rejected the employers' offer. [23]

As the strike entered its second week, it was noted that Grimond's had managed to transport goods bound for America to Glasgow docks, but that Joe Houghton of the SUDL 'would ensure they would go no further'.[24] He also noted that he was 'keeping an eye' on goods intended for London, and if necessary would request the assistance of Ben Tillett of the London dockers. There were 2,000 workers out as the dispute entered the third week and on 24 January the *Courier* reported on another development taking place at Dundee, when it was noted that at a meeting in the Gillfillan UP Hall, tenants had decided to go on a rent strike. The report stated that the hall held 2,000 people and was so full the doors had to be close leaving a further 1,000 people assembled outside.[25]

Within days of the rent strike decision, the Jute and Flax Workers' Union had brought out a further 500 workers at Grimond's Maxwelltown carpet works. The dispute was escalating and, as the strike moved into its fourth week, it was reported that the Scottish ironmoulders had voted overwhelmingly for a national strike action, and that 'war had begun on the Clyde' as a new shipping dispute got underway.[26] On 1 February, the Bowbridge women workers voted overwhelmingly to remain on strike, and it was announced that the employers and the union had brokered a deal to bring the dispute to an end. The workers returned, having gained more or less what they set out to achieve.[27] Workers at other mills now demanded wages increases and, during the last week in February, 900 people were on strike. At one meeting of the Jute and Flax Workers' Union held on 28 February it was reported that other Dundee textile workers' wanted to come out and support those on strike because Jute union members still at work felt like they were acting and behaving as 'blacklegs'. It was pointed out that they were not blacklegging because the union had asked them to remain at work.[28]

The Dundee newspapers reported that the outbreak of 'strike fever' affecting Dundee was perhaps due to the fact that workers were in receipt of strike pay, and thus saw the dispute 'as an excuse for a holiday'. Viewed from this perspective, there were 15,000 mill operatives on 'holiday' in Dundee by 1 March. A photograph of a group of strikers was pictured in the *Courier* the following day below the banner headline 'Dundee Under Strike Spell'.[29] Within a few days twenty-four separate mills and factories were affected and 18,000 workers were in dispute.[30] The number on strike increased to 25,000 after the massive Camperdown works shut down and when Baxter's millworkers became involved, a total of 30,000 workers were in dispute in Dundee.[31] By the time the dispute entered its third week, however, there were reports of Dundee workers going back to work on the old terms. Beyond Dundee, the labour troubles in the mines had improved after the employers accepted the imposition of the miners' minimum day wage. Tom Mann's arrest for inciting 'mutiny' was also making headlines as the press once again turned their attentions to the thorny issue of syndicalism. The Dundee *Advertiser* noted a correspondence from the Industrial Workers of the World (IWW) that the public could no longer doubt 'the power of syndicalism', and that they had convinced the railwaymen to come out if they were asked to 'transport troops' to any area affected by strike action.[32] Meanwhile in Dundee, some of the textile workers were still on strike, but as March came to a close, most seemed eager to return to work. By then workers at Cox's mill had been locked out, and employers at three other mills did likewise when 2,000 jute workers at Lochee refused to return to work under the old terms. On 26 March the talk in Dundee was about the impending threat of a city-wide lockout. It was clear by this juncture that the dispute was beginning to take a toll, for between 1,200 and 1,300 hungry children were being provided with breakfast by the Dundee ILP 'in order to keep up their spirits'. At the same time it was reported that Mr Williamson of the Dundee School Board proposed to instruct children 'under their control' that 'strikes were mischievous' and produced nothing of real benefit to strikers.[33] The jute workers of Lochee clearly disregarded Williamson's views and remained on strike. The employers demanded they resume work immediately. The Lochee strikers refused, and on 4 April 30,000 workers were locked out by the employers.[34]

The press were also reporting on miners rioting across the Fife coal fields. It was noted that a miners' ballot had produced a two to one majority against calling off the national strike action, and that in Fife the majority was higher still. The worst of the rioting took place at Lochgelly, where strikers managed to 'wreck' the pithead, and 350 policemen were drafted in to restore order. Indeed, even when the issue was ostensibly resolved and the Fife and Kinross Miners' Association agreed to restart work on 9 April, the Lochgelly miners refused to go back, and the following day 2,000 miners at Cowdenbeath decided to join them.[35] As the miners' troubles continued, industrial peace returned to Dundee after the lock out was called off on 15 April. The employers and the Jute and Flax Workers' Union brokered a peace deal and the Lochee workers received a slight advance on wages.[36]

The experience on the picket lines had clearly radicalised Dundee workers, and this was further demonstrated in the threat to initiate a rent strike during January and March 1912. According to Ann Petrie, when Dundee landlords moved to raise rents by as much as 10 per cent in early January 1912 – the only area in Scotland to attempt such a high increase – tenants became incensed, and with the help of Dundee Trades Council, the BSP and the Scottish Prohibitionist Party (SPP) they organised rent strike meetings. The authorities and the landlords capitulated fairly quickly on the matter and Dundee tenants did not have to make good their threat. The SPP propaganda organ *The Prohibitionist* bemoaned this fact, stating that by calling off the threatened rent strike, 'Dundee workers had again shown themselves to be extremely poor combatants of oppression'.[37] But as Petrie argued, after it was agreed to increase rents by 2.75 per cent rather than 10 per cent as originally proposed, the potential strikers had in effect achieved their goal.[38]

The question that might be asked is whether such rent strike action would have ever been contemplated had Dundee workers not experienced the labour unrest at such close quarters between September 1910 and the early months of 1912. It is also clear that with literally tens of thousands of workers on strike or locked out between February and April of 1912, they evidently had other things on their mind. The Jute and Flax Workers' minutes show that a hard core of mill workers, particularly those at Lochee – who were responsible for the earlier strike in January – did not want to end the dispute, and only returned to work reluctantly. It is perhaps typical of *The Prohibitionist* to decry Dundee workers as 'poor combatants of oppression' when anything between 15,000 and 30,000 had for many weeks been directly involved in an industrial dispute of the first magnitude. Only the Scottish coalminers could call out more workers during 1912 and over a much shorter time period. The next nearest action in terms of numbers was the seamen and dockers' strike and the Scottish railwaymen's dispute in August 1911, which involved 13,000 and 16,000 workers respectively. The railwaymen were not out for long and the seamen and dockers were out for little more than a fortnight, and in total 168,000 working days were lost to strike action. This pales into insignificance when compared to the 1,064,000 days lost to the strike at Dundee during February and April 1912, and this does not include the protracted strike action taken during January of that year.[39]

Until the end of April 1912 there were thirty separate strikes recorded across east Scotland, and apart from the Dundee mill strikes and the Scottish miners' strike, most were fairly short in duration, involving not more than sixty workers. There were strikes of joiners at Perth and Dunfermline, lithographers and upholsters in Edinburgh, disputes involving dockers at Kirkcaldy, Methil and Leith docks, quarry settmakers at Dalbeattie and Aberdeen, and linoleum printers at Kirkcaldy. There were twelve disputes between May and July, but these strikes were generally lengthier and involved more workers. For example, 200 dye workers at Perth went on strike between June and July; Densfield works at Dundee was closed in June in a dispute affecting 300 workers; 150 engineers went on strike at Edinburgh's Rosebank ironworks; and in June there was a dispute involving typefounders in Edinburgh which was not finally settled until September. In July there were 150 ship painters and carpenters on strike at the Caledon shipyard in Dundee, and towards the end of July even Dundee doctors were on strike.[40]

On 7 August, Dundee was hit by another strike wave when 250 apprentices at Caledon shipyard come out on strike over a deduction in their wages due to the working of the new National Insurance Act. Within a week apprentices at Kirkcaldy, Aberdeen and Glasgow were on strike. On 13 August the employers issued an ultimatum to the strikers to return to work, but this was uniformly ignored. Indeed, the following day apprentices at Monifieth and Arbroath joined the strike. By 16 August well over 5,000 apprentices were out across Scotland: 2,500 at Glasgow; 1,000 at Dundee; 500 at Edinburgh and Leith; 500 at Aberdeen; 300 at Coatbridge; 150 at Airdrie and Johnston; 150 at Kilmarnock; 100 at

Motherwell and 100 from the Clyde ports. When the strike entered its third week, the Dundee press reported, with subdued sense of pride, that the strike was 'waning in the west', but 'holding strong in Dundee and Monifieth'. They returned to work the following week after almost four weeks in dispute.

The apprentice boys' strike was number forty-six in the list of sixty-five disputes that took place across the east of Scotland during 1912, and one of twenty-five to take place in Dundee (or its immediate environs). More generally, there were strikes of carters at Kirkcaldy, Dundee, Leith and Montrose, dockers at Granton, Leith and Methil, and a strike among the Forth coaltrimmers. During September there was a large strike involving some 3,000 workers at Rosyth dockyard, another involving 200 leather workers at Arbroath, and in October 300 riveters were on strike at Dundee. Before the year was out carters and busmen were out at Edinburgh and Leith, and in Kirkcaldy 300 carters of all classes were in dispute. All in all, 1912 had been an eventful year for workers across Scotland, but the strike and lockout of 30,000 millworkers at Dundee stands out as the single biggest strike to affect one area during 1912. Indeed, it was the single most significant strike of its type to affect Scotland between 1910 and 1914.

A RECORD YEAR FOR STRIKES – 1913

The year 1913 opened up quietly enough, and with January and February relatively calm in terms of the industrial unrest it offered some hope that the worst of the labour troubles were over. There was a strike of 3,500 carters at Glasgow between January and February, and on the other side of the country Perth painters were on strike, there were textile disputes at Hawick and Blairgowrie, strikes among irondressers at Arbroath and Dundee, and one strike of 120 chippers and painters at Leith docks. But when compared to the opening months of 1912, workers seemed somewhat subdued, and from that standpoint the carters' dispute could well have been viewed as an aberration.[41] That was to change in April, however, when there was a virtual flood of strike activity across Scotland, precipitated by a dispute by granite and quarryworkers in Aberdeenshire – the first and only large-scale strike of significance to take place in the north east during the labour unrest.[42]

The next big dispute was the ironworkers' strike at the Falkirk during May and July of 1913, and this was precipitated by a strike of 170 pattern makers. The men ignored the demand of the employers that they return to work, and as a result, on Friday, 30 May the Central Ironmoulders'

Employers Association declared a district-wide lockout. But by then 3,000 men were already on a general strike in the Falkirk district well before the ink was dry on the lockout notices. The disputes then spread to foundries at Bonnybridge and Bo'ness and came to involve 4,000 workers.[43] The general ironworkers' strike was not resolved until the end of July when the patternmakers finally returned to work and the lockout was called off.

Of the twenty-nine strikes that took place between the beginning of April and the end of July, twenty-two were relatively small strikes and were settled fairly quickly. They were also generally settled in favour of the workers. Other disputes took longer to resolve, however. For example, a strike of Dundee hosepipe weavers was in its ninth week before it was settled in June, and around the same time 300 pit-prop workers at Bo'ness returned to work after four weeks on strike. There was also a strike of similar size and duration among pit-prop workers at Grangemouth. Among specific groups of workers, disputes arose among female fish curers in Buckie; in the north-east among fishermen of the Highlands Fishermen's Union; in Bo'ness and Kirkcaldy pottery workers; in Bo'ness and Grangemouth sawmillers; in Arbroath and Forfar carters and motormen; building workers in Dundee, Dunfermline, Kirkcaldy, Pitlochriy and Peterhead; dockers and harbour labourers in Grangemouth, Granton, Kirkcaldy, Leith and Thurso; boat carpenters at Banff; and in Dunfermline and Kirkcaldy there were strikes among female winders and linoleum printers.[44]

The above chronicle gives a flavour of the geographical spread of strike activity and the many types of different workers now involved in industrial dispute. It should be noted too that while many of these strike started as economic disputes, they often ended in demands for trade union recognition, the exclusion of non-union labour, or as part of a broader campaign of sympathetic action. Indeed, the series of strikes among a broad swathe of workers at Kirkcaldy from 1911 onwards demonstrated that this type of workers' response was a direct result of a greater and more intense involvement in industrial action. This was not dissimilar to the radicalising affect of industrial unrest at the time of the Dundee carters' and dockers' strike in December 1911, or the Dundee mill strikes during the early months of 1912, when workers became involved in picket line action.

The Leith dockers' strike between 26 June and 14 August 1913 was to have a similar impact and was another good example of workers' solidarity in action. The seven-week dispute involved 4,000 workers and was widely reported in the Scottish press, and within a few days the *Leith*

Observer was reporting that business at the port was at a standstill. The dockers were represented by the NUDL which submitted a request for a rise of 'a penny per hour' on the day rate, an increase in the piecework rates for handling 'dirty cargo' and a one o'clock stop on Saturday. Crucially, they demanded an end to the employment of non-union labour. The powerful Leith Dock Employers Association was not prepared to concede to these 'unreasonable' demands, and with the assistance of the Shipping Federation brought in 450 'free labourers' to the port in the first week of the strike. The free labourers were housed on Federation free-labour ships, the *Lady Jocelyn* and the *Paris*, and were drawn initially from Berwick, Cardiff, Liverpool, Middlesbrough and Newcastle. Their numbers were later increased to 600 when a further 150 men were brought in from Manchester. They were protected day and night by the Edinburgh and Leith constabulary, augmented by a force of 150 policemen form Glasgow, Lanarkshire, the Lothians and latterly Aberdeen.

The dockers could not gain entry into the docklands which were surrounded by a perimeter wall. They placed pickets on the dock gates on a eight-hour three-shift system, and there were also squads of flying pickets. Only six pickets at any given time were allowed within the dock perimeter wall, and always under tight police escort, as they vainly attempted to persuade the free labourers to stop work. The docklands were publicly owned and this raised the question of the legality of closing off the dockers' access to the port. The Dock Commission argued, however, that it was duty-bound to protect that property and those working on it, and thus access continued to be restricted to all but the police, free labourers, federation and harbour officials, and those issued with a valid permit. As a result of their actions the railwaymen and the seamen became involved, and for the duration of the strike 200 carters and 600 seamen refused to handle any cargo or work any boat operated by free labour. The Lothian Miners also backed the dockers, despite the fact that the coal embargo imposed by the NUDL directly affected them and was the cause of considerable unemployment. Dockers at Grangemouth, Granton and Kirkcaldy all refused to handle cargo diverted from Leith.[45]

In early July it was reported that a 'strike epidemic' was affecting Leith when female ropeworkers went on strike and, more disturbingly for the Shipping Federation, when the shipmasters' and mates' went on strike over pay and conditions. The latter action prompted the *Leith Observer* to report: 'All this has brought about a state of matters unprecedented not only in the history of Leith, but in any part of the country.' The *Leith*

Observer reported that the free labourers 'were hardly an energetic lot' and that it took them all day to do what an ordinary docker did in a few hours.[46] The cost of maintaining and protecting such a strike-breaking force was enormous, and the press reported that it was clearly costing the employers much more than the increase in wages requested by the dockers. This only heightened an already tense situation, and over three nights between 16 and 18 July there was serious rioting around the docks. Indeed, there was so much damage caused that the *Leith Observer* commented tersely that the only trade 'doing brisk business' in Leith were the glaziers. The disturbances got progressively more violent and there were numerous cases reported of molestation of free labourers, while in another incident an unsuccessful attempt was made to blow up the perimeter wall with gelignite. At the request of the Midlothian authorities, on the night of 17 July six naval gunboats found their way into Leith harbour, and this prompted many angry responses that sailors and marines should not be used in such fashion, for to do so 'was a disgrace to the King's uniform'. Questions were put to the Secretary of the Admiralty in Parliament asking why gunboats were sent to Leith. He replied that 'they had been called upon for aid, but fortunately it did not take an active form', and the gunboats had been withdrawn on 19 July in any case. One MP expressed surprise 'that the Navy could interfere in a labour dispute, at the behest of a local authority, but only report on the incident after the action had been taken'.[47]

It was widely reported that the union officials did their 'level best' to avoid the use of violence during the dispute, but given the forces arrayed against the dockers at the port, it was perhaps inevitable that disturbances would take place. It was also reported widely in the press that the police had provoked the strikers on many occasions and were the cause of many disturbances around the port. On 4 August, George Barnes MP raised the issue of 'police brutality' at Leith in a debate in the House of Commons, and noted that the authorities had failed 'to take any notice of their conduct'. The police imported into Leith were 'most untrustworthy', and as many were raw recruits 'they were altogether unsuitable for the purpose'. He also pointed to evidence 'that the police provoked a disturbance' during August because they had 'come to an agreement with the dock-owners and commissioners to stamp out the strike'.[48]

Just after the mid-July riots the Edinburgh tramwaymen and the Leith boilermakers came out on strike, and although not directly connected to the dock dispute they joined forces with the dockers, seamen and firemen, and various other 'trades societies', on a demonstration through Leith on 20 July 1913. It was a lengthy procession reported *The Scotsman*:

> Fully fifteen minutes was occupied in passing a given point, and those who took part were marching about six abreast. There were about 3,000 dockers on strike, and they mustered strongly for the demonstration. Sailors and firemen, of whom there are said to be about 600 at present in Leith . . . were also largely represented. It was estimated that about 500 tramwaymen attended, and about 150 boilermakers took part . . . A feature of special interest . . . was a company of about 350 children of Leith strikers who marched at the front under the charge of Miss C. M. M'Nab and Mrs J. Cruikshanks (Labour members of the Leith School Board), and Madame Sorgue, who has been taking a special interest in the dockers.

A number of mill girls were among the demonstration, and there were several bands including the Wallyford Miners' Band and the Celtic Pipe Band. A number of banner and trade emblems were carried: one read, 'Leith Dockers' Strike – We protest against the use of armed forces of the Crown to assist the employers', and another simply stated, 'Leith Dockers – We are out for a living wage'. On the end of a staff was carried 'a loaf of bread, painted to represent it as green with mould and a placard underneath bore the words – "Our share of the profits."' The tramwaymen then peeled off to march onto Edinburgh, while the dockers and the other marchers headed to the 'Links' at Leith Walk. They broke into two platforms, and gathered around each were crowds of 6,000 and 7,000 respectively. The police reported afterwards, 'That there had never been a meeting held at the port of such dimensions and of so orderly a nature'. There were speeches made at both platforms, and the French anarcho-syndicalist Madame Sorgue, and the leader of the French dockers, advised the men to stand firm. Another speaker added that the workers of Edinburgh should not simply confine their fight to the industrial arena, but also go into the political arena and vote for labour candidates in elections. James Airlie of the boilermakers' union noted that the army had been used by the employers twenty times in industrial disputes over recent years, but only used once in a war.[49]

The tramwaymen's strike was settled on 2 August, but they promised financial support and the Amalgamated Society of Engineers (ASE) agreed to levy each member in order to provide 'practical support' for the 'splendid fight' the dockers were mounting. The Leith and Edinburgh Trades Councils also assisted the strikers, and they were supported by labour members on Leith and Edinburgh councils and their respective school boards. As the strike entered the sixth week, the first of the

dockers charged for their part in the 'July Riots' appeared before the
Sheriff court. They were found guilty and fined for interfering with the free
labourers' 'right to work'. Under the pseudonym 'Leith Laddie', the *Leith
Observer* printed a fairly lengthy letter condemning the opinions of
Sheriff Guy and his 'right to work' decree. He asked whether it was legitimate that 'Scabs had the right to interfere in an industrial dispute, and
the use of His Majesty's forces in protecting them'. They were simply
traitors to their fellow working men. It was the introduction of Scab
labour that was the 'cause of rioting and bloodshed throughout the
country', he argued, they were 'worms' protected by the armed forces.
This was not a 'fair fight' for Scabs 'had no right to work in an industrial
dispute': 'The day was when Britishers boasted of "never hitting below
the belt." The greed for gold has blinded all sense of fair play, but the end
of it all will be – take my word for it – Revolution!' He concluded that
the shipowners had it in their power to end the dispute, but instead chose
to 'fan the flames'. As an 'on-looker', as an 'observer', his sympathies
were with the dockers'.[50]

The dockers had little hope of winning against the might of the
Shipping Federation, and on 14 August James O'Connor Kessack
informed a mass meeting of dockers, held at the Gaiety Theatre, that
another Federation 'depot ship', carrying 300 fresh men, was on its way
from Newcastle. On the advice of the NUDL leadership, the meeting
decided by a large majority to end the strike, but for those waiting
outside the decision came as a surprise, 'for they had not anticipated that
the strike would end so suddenly'. The dockers returned to work on the
same conditions as before, but the 'free labourers' would be dispatched
from Leith immediately in preparation for a return to normal working.
The great Leith dock strike was over, but there was still considerable
fallout from the dispute, not least among those men who were still
appearing before the courts charged with rioting, and there were still
many questions being raised in Parliament about the conduct of the
police and the use of gunboats and troops during industrial disputes.[51]

The Struggle Intensifies – September to December 1913

By the closing months of 1913 the press were reporting a strike epidemic
breaking out all over the country. *The Scotsman* reported that 'September
was making a bold bid for a record in the number of trade disputes', and
noted that for the whole of Britain there were already 102 disputes
involving 80,626 persons, accounting for 801,600 days lost, and it was
only mid-September. The use of sympathy action had increased and the

newspaper gave an example of how this worked in practice by profiling the impact of the Dublin transport strike, which had escalated into a lockout of 20,000 men and women. Liverpool railwaymen refused to handle goods diverted from Dublin, and so 3,000 left work. In Birmingham 7,000 were on strike for similar reasons after a 'dozen men' were dismissed for refusing to handle goods from Dublin. Almost immediately 300 men went on strike, and a procession was formed which visited each goods yard in the city in turn, until its ranks were swelled with up to 7,000 strikers. Dublin, Liverpool and Birmingham were threatened with paralysis 'because of a dispute between Dublin employers and Mr Larkin of the Irish Transport and General Workers' Union', and in total 30,000 workers were now idle. What made matters worse was that the sympathy action was rank-and-file inspired, although *The Scotsman* took some solace form the fact that the unrest was not simply confined to Britain – it was 'a world-wide spirit'.

The press noted the words of Keir Hardie who argued that it had become fashionable 'even among socialists' to decry strikes, 'but the day of the strike is far from over' and it would remain so until socialism provided the right conditions for industrial and social peace.[52] Many labour and trade union leaders disliked the use of sympathy action and what they termed as 'Larkinism' in describing how Larkin pandered to the dictatorship of the rank and file. The rank and file, however, clearly agreed with the sentiments expressed by Keir Hardie, and other labour MPs such as George Barnes, as demonstrated in the resolution passed by the Kirkcaldy District Trades and Labour Council condemning Philip Snowden and Ramsey Macdonald, among others, for their hostile attitude to the use of the sympathetic strike in connection with the labour troubles at Dublin. Indeed, during October *The Scotsman* reported on 'Edinburgh Labourists' support for Larkin and the Dublin workers, and noted that the Edinburgh Trades Council, local branches of the ILP, the BSP, Edinburgh University Fabian Society, the Women Workers' Union and the Women's Labour League formed a central committee 'for the purposes of collecting money in support of the Dublin strikers'. It was also noted that plans had been made to bring a large number of children from Dublin to Edinburgh during the remainder of the strike, and that a meeting of socialists in Kirkcaldy, chaired by Mr James Buchanan (Edinburgh ILP), had voted likewise. They all proclaimed their support for Jim Larkin and his industrial tactics in Ireland.[53]

When Larkin was arrested and found guilty for sedition there was uproar across Scotland at what was perceived as an 'unjust sentence'. As a result of considerable pressure from the trade union and labour movement in Britain, Larkin was released from prison in December. Shortly after his release he spoke to a meeting attended by 3,000 people at Glasgow, at which Tom Johnston presided. Cunninghame Graham moved a motion in support of Larkin, his work with Irish workers, and his role in the Dublin dispute, and John Wheatley seconded the resolution. Larkin spoke that his fight against the English trade union leaders was a fight against 'dictators' who would disregard the rank and file: 'They must be shifted, and shifted by the rank and file', he argued.[54]

The following evening he addressed an audience of between 6,000 and 7,000 men and women at Edinburgh's Waverley Market. It was chaired by James Campbell who stated that 'every Trade Union, Labour and Socialist organisation in the city had co-operated in making arrangements for the meeting', and added:

> That Mr Jim Larkin had done something for the city that had never been done before. He had brought them altogether. The working classes in this country would not exchange Jim Larkin for all the politicians whoever filled the cabinet. They welcomed Mr Larkin with open arms regardless of any official reproach.

Cunninghame Graham addressed this meeting too and spoke 'on the meaning of Larkinism':

> It stood for revolt. It stood for their Indian fellow-subject in the Transvaal. It stood against the intolerable tyranny dictated by the oil capitalists in America in regard to Mexico. It stood for freedom of the weak and oppressed. It was because Larkin was a man of frontal attack that he was the leader of the labour movement today.

When Larkin rose to address the gathering he was cheered loudly. He began by stating that he had no pretension to be a leader or a spokesman of the working class, 'but he had a message to deliver':

> There was a platform upon which both Scottish and Irish workers could stand and agree to work together and that platform was not only broad enough for the Celt, but for the Saxon or any other race. It was the platform of human liberty.[55]

By mid-December 1913, the news columns were filled with renewed fears of syndicalism and of the possibility that it had influenced the municipal strike among corporation workers at Leeds. In Scotland the bookbinders were on strike at Aberdeen, Glasgow and Edinburgh, and the carters were out again at Dundee. The year 1913 was memorable because there were more strikes recorded, and more working days lost in disputes affecting more workers than in any year since official records began in 1888.

The Dublin transport strike started in September and continued well into December, and even after it was ostensibly settled there were many scuffles and skirmishes associated with the dispute taking place during January 1914. A railway strike spread rapidly across South Wales in connection with the Dublin dispute in December, when local shop stewards called the railwaymen out in direct opposition to the instructions of the NUS leadership. Some 5,000 Leeds corporation workmen went on strike on 12 December for a rise in wages, and 300 members of the Gasworkers' Union joined in unofficial sympathy action in what was a rank-and-file-led dispute.

'Larkinism' meant 'direct action', and according to the press 'direct action' was the cause of the disputes at Dublin, South Wales and Leeds. These and many other disputes were clearly 'outbreaks of syndicalism'.[56] Far from marking the end of the labour unrest, the year 1913 was to signal an increase in strike activity which would continue through to the outbreak of war in August 1914.

The Short, Sharp Strike – 1914

When the light dawned on New Year's Day 1914 the press were consumed by reports of unrest both at home and abroad. There were labour troubles across Natal, widespread unrest in the Transvaal led by syndicalist-inspired Scots, and in New Zealand 'Red Federationist' waterfront workers were also on strike. In February *Forward* carried a report on the 'brutal treatment' of 'Lanarkshire miners' (and ex-members of the Lanarkshire Miners' Union) involved in a strike, which by then was almost eighteen months in duration, on Vancouver Island in British Columbia, Canada. The municipal strike at Leeds was unresolved, many Dublin waterfront workers still refused to go back to work, Blackburn corporation workers were also on strike, and Liverpool docks were once again at a standstill. In Scotland, the Dundee trawl fishermen's strike had just ended, but at Anstruther, Leslie, Methil and Thornton in Fife, 200 firemen of the North British Railway Company were on strike. London coalworkers were in dispute, and military personnel and student volunteers were loading and discharging coal during January, and by the end of January 100,000 building workers were involved in a dispute affecting the whole of London, in a strike supported by the Labour Party and endorsed by Keir Hardie.[57]

In east Scotland Perth dyers were in dispute throughout January and February; this was followed by a three-week strike of joiners in the town which ended in March, and a painters' strike involving over 1,000 members of the Edinburgh and Leith Painters' Association took place in April. During May there was a series of strikes including Dalkeith joiners, the Scottish basketmakers, linoleum workers at Kirkcaldy, and Aberdeen ship painters; Fife and Kinross miners were on strike over the use of non-union labour and the demand for a four-day working week, and there was a threat of a general strike of bricklayers and labourers which would affect Edinburgh and Leith and much of the Lothians. Edinburgh and Leith coopers were on strike during May and in a lockout by mid-June, just as the riveters and platers came out on strike at the Leith shipyards.

By mid-June the main story was the London building trade lockout which was in its twenty-first week at that juncture, and reported as ranking among 'one of the most protracted and costliest disputes of the last twenty years'. It involved directly 45,000 workers and accounted for working days lost of 4,720,000, and 30,000 workers had been made unemployed for anything between four and twenty weeks as a result of the employers' lockout. A protracted plumbers' strike at Galashiels was finally settled in July, just as Kirkcaldy pottery workers came out on strike in a dispute that was not settled until the end of August after Britain declared war.

There was a steady increase in strike activity across Britain, and on 6 July, just under a month before the outbreak of war, between 7,000 and 8,000 ASE members at the Woolwich Arsenal came out on strike over the sacking of one man. In tones reminiscent of statements made at the time of the Singer strike at Clydebank three years before, the strikers proclaimed 'that an injury to one was an injury to all'. The London Labour Protection League promised support and quickly came out in sympathy action and on 7 July 12,000 workers were on strike. The matter was widely reported, but The Scotsman's angle on the issue was interesting:

> Woolwich Arsenal is the scene of the latest of those 'one man' strikes which are becoming a feature of modern industrial life. On account of the dismissal of a single fitter, practically the whole of his fellow-workers have laid down their tools . . . and there are threats of extending the strike to other Government factories.[58]

Workers at Plymouth, Devonport, Portsmouth and Enfield all voted to strike in sympathy, but the issue was resolved within a few days and resulted in 'a complete victory for the men'. By mid-July, when the Falkirk joiners returned to work after several weeks on strike, there was

Table 5.1   Comparison of Board of Trade, GLHW and Strike Incidence
across East Scotland, 1910–14.

	B of T	(a) GLHW	(b) § East Scotland	Total (a) and (b)
1910	11	17	8	25
1911	24	43	21	64
1912	41	70	65	135
1913	49	58	51	109
1914	6	55	24	79

Note: § Denotes trawl of columns of *The Scotsman* for evidence of strike activity for the
entire period January 1910 to August 1914. The *Dundee Courier* and *Dundee
Advertiser* were consulted widely for the period 1910 to 1912 and January/February
1914, and the *Leith Observer* was used to cover the period of the Leith dockers' strike
in 1913.

talk of a Scottish mining lockout. On 23 July the Miners' Federation of
Great Britain gave full backing to the Scottish Miners' Federation to take
immediate action to resist any further reduction in wages in Scotland. A
marine engineering strike was still ongoing in August and was only
settled days before war was declared. The National Federation of
Building Trade Employers voted by an 'over-whelming majority' to call
a national lockout across Britain for 16 August 1914. Because of the war
this threat was never made good and from late August through until the
early months of 1915 the industrial unrest finally subsided.

POSTSCRIPT: THE POLITICS OF UNREST

In November 1914 the Board of Trade made a special report into the
widespread labour unrest that had taken place over the period 1908–13.
The report tended to be somewhat upbeat when compared to the
alarmist prognosis of an impending industrial revolt and social discontent of the first order that had been predicted before the war. Indeed,
between 12 January and 24 February 1914, the Dundee *Courier* printed
no less than thirteen separate articles on the threat of syndicalism to
Scotland as a result of labour unrest.[59] By November, however, safe in
the knowledge that a labour peace had been guaranteed at a time of war,
the press were happy to accept 'that this period of unrest synchronised
with a period of expanding employment and upward movement in
wages'. Thus, the political dimension to the labour unrest had been
dismissed.

Table 5.1 above gives a good indication of the level of strike activity
across Scotland and includes figures for the Glasgow Labour History

Workshop for the period as a whole. It is clear that there was a significantly higher level of unrest recorded for this period than noted by the
Board of Trade (B of T). It should be noted that the B of T did not include
short strikes of less than a day in duration, and this would account for
some of the shortfall. But a good many of the strikes included in these
figures were significantly longer and did not become part of the official
record. Part of the explanation lies in the manner in which the data were
collected, for the B of T relied on both the employers and trade unions
returning information of a strike or dispute and very often this did not
happen. They only included verifiable or agreed statistical information
so as to correctly compute the numbers on workers on strike, disputes
taking place, the firms or trade unions involved, the cause and outcome
of a particular dispute, and days lost to strike action. The statistics above
indicate that the east of Scotland was less strike-prone than the west of
the country, but taken together the figures demonstrate a consistently
high incidence of strike activity across Scotland over the period as a
whole. More importantly, there was no sign that the labour unrest had
diminished in the months before the war. If anything, the statistical
analysis would suggest that labour unrest was intensifying.

But was there ever a political dimension to the strike activity experienced during the labour unrest? The SLP and the BSP were both influenced in some form or another by syndicalist ideas, and they were closely
involved in the Singer strike at Clydebank in 1911, and in the provision
of Marxist education classes in the area. William McKie spoke of the
success of SDP Marxist classes at Edinburgh, and more widely among
miners in the Lothians, and Fife and Kinross, and he stated that dockers
from Leith regularly attended classes.[60] Marxist classes were made
popular by lecturers such as John Maclean (SDF and BSP) and the SLP's
'most accomplished propagandist' John S. Clarke, who delivered a series
of lectures on syndicalism to Edinburgh workmen and in particular the
railwaymen during the years before the war.[61]

Syndicalism was generally regarded as having played little part in
influencing the trade unions or industrial action between 1910 and 1914,
although there was a decisive shift to the left. Indeed, where Dangerfield
saw danger in the form of the Triple Industrial Alliance, historians would
generally view the organisation as a failure. Indeed, this was demonstrated to some extent at the time of the Leith dock strike in 1913, where
there was clear and widespread support among the rank and file of the
miners, seamen and railwaymen for some form of united action. But the
Triple Alliance was not invoked, nor even considered, on that occasion,
despite the presence of the Shipping Federation. Indeed, the NTWF was

largely uninvolved in the dispute. Examples such as this suggest there was little support for syndicalist-style direct action beyond South Wales, the Midlands and with Larkin in Ireland.

The situation with the South Wales miners was clearly different. They formed the South Wales Reform Committee, and published the *Miners' Next Step* to promote their syndicalist programme. This organ asserted among other things that miners' leaders should be more militant, that the rank and file should be encouraged to take more independent industrial and political action, and that they should work towards building a trade union structure 'far more centralised' than anything that had existed hitherto in mining.[62] This ambitious programme had wider support beyond South Wales. John McArthur, a Buckhaven miner and left-radical socialist, noted that a Reform Committee was established in Fife. It was a fairly loose organisation of BSP members, but it did meet regularly. McArthur noted that the SDF had branches at Buckhaven and Methil for many years before the war, but that the SLP played an important role in providing Marxian education, that the ILP was active around East Wemyss, Cowdenbeath, Kelty and Dunfermline, and that the BSP was particularly well organised in Kirkcaldy.[63]

The SDF also published its own monthly 'Socialist' bulletin, it had representatives on Buckhaven school board and on the town council, and it advertised its activities in Fife by placing notices of meetings and in the local newspapers. The *Leven Advertiser and Wemyss Gazette* noted one such meeting in May 1910 and, in reporting the proceedings, declared it 'a vigorous campaign for socialism'. The main speaker on that occasion was Jack William, the old socialist agitator of the Trafalgar Square riots of 1887, and the following month Willie Crawford (later the ILP and editor of *Forward*) was the main speaker.[64] Indeed, the available evidence points to Fife as being something of a radical left hotspot, and Kirkcaldy one of the most radical towns in Fife. Of the twenty-eight strikes recorded for Fife over the period 1910–14, sixteen took place in Kirkcaldy, and these included the eleven-month powerloom tenters' strike (the dispute of the longest duration to take place in Scotland during the labour unrest), and a two-month strike among female millworkers during 1911.

In 1912, eleven disputes took place in Fife, including the strike at Rosyth dockyard which involved 3,000 workers. But with six strikes among carters, dockers, building workers, and female pottery and textile workers, Kirkcaldy again topped the league for industrial strife in Fife in 1912. The workers of Kirkcaldy certainly approved of direct action, and this was made clear when the Kirkcaldy District Trades and Labour

Council condemned Philip Snowden and Ramsey Macdonald for berating the use of the sympathetic strikes during the 1913 Dublin transport strike.[65] All the major left-political parties were active in Fife, and given the existence of a Miners' Reform Committee, however unorganised, and a clear link with South Wales, it may well prove to be the case that syndicalism did play a role in influencing the labour unrest in Fife. However, as Ian Hutchison suggests, it was not perhaps the most productive ground for the ILP in its attempts to muster electoral support much before 1914.[66]

Were workers more concerned with gaining higher wages than overthrowing capital? Given the weight of the quantitative evidence produced in the *Roots of Red Clydeside*, it is clear that workers were attempting to overturn the reduction in real wages that had been occurring during the first decade of the twentieth century, and that this can explain much of the upsurge in trade unionism and strike activity that took place later during 1910 and 1914. It is also the case that many workers were still wedded to the politics of Liberalism, and many were suspicious of left-wing politics. Workers were not perhaps advocating the overthrow of capital, but they were laying down a serious challenge by joining trade unions in greater numbers than at any time in British history (including the expansion experienced during the war years), and they were willing to become involved in political action. Indeed, from 1911 onward an essential component part of literally every transport workers' strike in Scotland was the role played by well-known syndicalist and socialists propagandists such as Madame Sorgue, Tom Mann, Joseph Houghton, Manny Shinwell and John Maclean (to name only a few), in providing workers with the moral, ethical and political support for industrial action. When such luminaries visited town, they invariably addressed large audiences augmented by workers who were not directly involved in a particular dispute, and in many instances they encouraged unorganised workers to take sympathetic action in support.

In another example, a dispute at the port of Ardrossan on the Clyde coast began in October 1912 when twenty coaltrimmers went on strike over a wages issue. They were joined by 180 other workers who had already successfully secured their own wage demands some time earlier, but joined the dispute over the employment of non-union labour. Very soon the entire port was at a standstill, and the strike escalated to involve the Shipping Federation, the Free Labour Association, the SUDL and the Seamen's Union. Indeed, when addressing the Glasgow Trades Council in December 1912, Joe Houghton referred to Ardrossan as 'the Key to the Clyde', for he believed that if the Shipping Federation converted

Ardrossan to a 'free port' the rest of the Clyde would quickly follow.[67] Madame Sorgue, Ben Tillett and Joe Houghton addressed the strikers and the townspeople of Ardrossan, and when Tom Mann visited he spoke of syndicalism and said that 'real solidarity was only achievable within one organisation. Workers would thus control industry once released from the control of the capitalist'.[68] The local community rallied to the dockers' cause and actively took part in demonstration and meetings throughout the ten-week strike, raising funds to assist the strikers and their families and attending meetings to raise public awareness of their cause. The strike ended in something of a compromise in January 1913, but the port's trade union status had been assured, and thereafter Ardrossan was recognised as a bastion of dock trade unionism.[69]

We find a similar type of community consciousness developing through the use of sympathetic action at the time of the Dundee carters' and dockers' strike in 1911, when even some unorganised sections of the female labour force came out in support. There is clear evidence of the widespread use of sympathy action among a broad range of workers at Kirkcaldy during 1912, and during the Kilbirnie networkers' dispute between April and September 1913, when striking women workers joined with iron and foundry workers, and local miners, in solidarity demonstrations in the area. These are only a few examples of successful sympathetic action, and much more research is needed into this type of dispute. But in the final analysis, the sympathy strike showed no signs of abating before 1914, despite of protestations of the press, public and leading members of the trade union movement.

Indeed, it was because of the cautious and conservative leadership roles played by men such as Hugh Lyons (carters), James Sexton (dockers) and Havelock Wilson (seamen), that Peter Gillespie's North of Scotland Horse and Motormen, Joe Houghton's Scottish Union of Dock Labourers, and Manny Shinwell's British Seafarers' Union came into existence in Scotland. Lyons, Sexton and Wilson, in particular, were ever critical of Jim Larkin's more aggressive industrial relations style, but were aware that it was popular among the rank and file. Sexton fought a running battle with Larkin, when he was national organiser of the NUDL, over the extent to which union funds could be used to encourage such action. Indeed, it led to Larkin being arrested, charged and tried for fraud in 1909, and Sexton appeared at the trial as a leading prosecution witness. It was further evidence of the rightward drift of a cadre of trade union leaders, many of whom came to prominence during the new unionism, who were unwilling to sanction aggressive trade unionism and the use of direct action during the labour unrest. A similar tendency was evident with the Seamen's Union, which Havelock Wilson single-hand-edly converted into a virtual company by 1914, much to the disgust of socialists such as Shinwell on the Clyde. Indeed, given the perceived syndicalist tendencies of the NTWF, Scottish carters' leader Hugh Lyons severed his connection with the organisation in 1912, and went onto transform the Scottish Horse and Motormen into a non-partisan industrial union.[70]

CONCLUSIONS

Given such examples of disunity, it is understandable that historians argue that there is little solid evidence of a viable syndicalist influence within trade unions, and that, contrary to Dangerfield's judgment, there was no 'crisis' in Edwardian society before 1914.[71] Moreover, as argued by Kenefick and McIvor, in order to put the labour unrest in a clearer perspective, historians need to consider moving away from 'labour' towards social and 'working class' history. John Benson persuasively demonstrated just how little most workers were affected by trade unions, labour politics or strike action before World War One.[72] And from a Scottish perspective, James Young would readily identify with this view in so far as he saw the unrest in Scotland as far less intense than in England. But in Scotland the labour unrest clearly affected a wide variety of different types of workers and to an extent addresses some of the points raised by Benson, and Young clearly underestimated the depth and breadth of strike activity in Scotland at this time. The Glasgow Labour History Workshop study demonstrated that workers in the industrial region of west Scotland were particularly strike-prone and liable to take direct and unofficial action, and the evidence presented here for east Scotland generally supports this conclusion.

According to Bob Holton, there is evidence that syndicalism did strike a chord in areas such as South Wales and Liverpool, and Keith Laybourn extends this to the Midlands and Ireland, while both identify a strong 'proto-syndicalist' undercurrent among transport workers and miners.[73] Some of the evidence presented here notes a similar tendency among workers in east Scotland, and in particular the textile and mining areas of Fife, and among railwaymen in Edinburgh. For those who would argue that the year 1913 marked the end of the labour unrest, however, the evidence presented here would suggest otherwise. Indeed, in November 1914 the Board of Trade concluded that 'During the first seven months of 1914 the time lost owing to labour disputes was even greater than in 1913, but since the beginning of the war the majority of the outstanding differences have been settled'.[74] The war had brought the labour unrest more or less to an immediate halt, and talk of syndicalism and socialist-inspired revolt faded somewhat from memory as workers began to concentrate ever more on the war effort. But it was an uneasy peace, for the experience of war aggravated workers' grievances and reawakened in many a rebelliousness that had been growing and developing during the years before the First World War.

NOTES

1. *The Socialist*, no. 107, vol. IX, July 1911.
2. For example, Smout, *A Century of the Scottish People, 1830–1950* (1986); Cage, *The Working Class in Glasgow*: see also Marwick, *A Short History of Labour in Scotland*.
3. 'Roots of Red Clydeside', in Duncan and McIvor (eds), *Militant Workers*; Kenefick and McIvor, *Roots of Red Clydeside*, chapter 1.
4. Smyth, *Labour in Glasgow*; Kenefick, *Rebellious and Contrary*; Hughes, 'The Politics of the Kitchen and dissenting domestics'; Rafeek, 'Radicalism Continued 1919–1945'.
5. *The Scotsman*, 31 May 1910.
6. Dundee Labour History Group was established in 1998 along the same lines as the Glasgow Labour History Workshop collective. It was more or less wound up in 2001.
7. *Courier*, 10–14 October 1910.
8. *The Scotsman*, 12 October 1910.
9. Widely reported through the press from 14 December 1910.
10. *Advertiser*, 15 December 1910.
11. *Courier*, 26 December 1910.
12. *Courier* and *Advertiser*, between 23 February and 20 March 1910.
13. *The Scotsman*, 20 June 1911.
14. *The Scotsman*, 14 October 1911.
15. *The Scotsman*, 19 December 1911.
16. Kenefick, *Rebellious and Contrary*, pp. 212–16.
17. Reported widely by the press and almost every provincial newspaper, 11–15 September 1911.
18. *Courier*, 20, 21 December 1911.
19. Bell, 'A Glorious Lesson in Solidarity'.
20. Free Labour Bureau *Annual Reports, The Scotsman*, 15 June and 26 December 1911.
21. *The Scotsman*, 26 December 1911.
22. *Advertiser*, 3–4, 6, 9–10 January 1912.
23. *Advertiser*, 18 January 1912.
24. *Courier*, 20 January 1912.

25. *Courier*, 24 January 1912.
26. *Advertiser*, 29 January 1912.
27. *Courier*, 1–3 February, 1912. For details of settlement, see Jute and Flax Workers' Committee Minutes, 1911–1912, 6 February 1912: Dundee City Archives; GD/JF/1/7.
28. Jute and Flax Workers' Committee Minutes, 26 February 1912.
29. *Courier* and the *Advertiser*, 2 March 1912.
30. *Advertiser*, 4 March 1912.
31. *Courier*, 9 March; *Advertiser*, 13 March 1912.
32. *Courier*, 23 March 1912.
33. *Courier*, *Advertiser*, 26 March 1912.
34. *Courier*, 4 April 1912.
35. *Courier*, 9 April 1912.
36. Ibid. and *Advertiser*, 16 April 1912.
37. *The Prohibitionist*, 9 March 1912.
38. Petrie, 'The 1915 Dundee Rent Strike'.
39. Kenefick and McIvor, *Roots of Red Clydeside*, Table 1.2, p. 23.
40. Reported mostly by the Dundee *Courier* and the *Advertiser*, between January and July 1912: see also *The Scotsman*.
41. *The Scotsman*, 7, 11 January and 3–4, 14, 19 March 1913.
42. Kenefick, 'Aberdeen Was More Red Than Glasgow', pp. 176–7.
43. *The Scotsman*, 19, 27, 30 May 1913.
44. *The Scotsman*, between 1 April and 31 July 1913.
45. *Leith Observer*, 28 June, 5 July 1913.
46. *Leith Observer*, 5, 12 July 1913.
47. *Leith Observer*, 19, 26 July and 2, 9 August 1913.
48. *Leith Observer*, 9 August 1913.
49. *The Scotsman*, 31 July 1913.
50. *Leith Observer*, 9 August 1913.
51. *Leith Observer*, 16 August 1913.
52. *The Scotsman* and *The Times*, 31 September 1913, and *The Scotsman*, 3 October 1913.
53. *The Scotsman*, 17 October 1913.
54. *The Glasgow Herald*, 12 December 1913.
55. *The Scotsman*, 13 December 1913.
56. All the national daily newspapers and the socialist weeklies were reporting these events. On the question of the general strike action generally, the socialist press seemed divided. Keir Hardie and George Barnes MB were uncomfortable with unofficial action, but were supportive of workers' right to strike. Others were less convinced and this was the topic of much debate in the columns of *Forward* and the *Labour Leader*. James O'Connar Kessack of the NUDL supported a worker's right to take strike action, but not at the behest of syndicalists, and his superior James Sexton had no time for the industrial relations strategy promoted by Larkin. This placed him in

direct opposition to Joe Houghton of the SUDL, and many other rank-and-file transport workers in Scotland and Ireland.

57. *Forward*, 21, 28 February 1914.
58. *The Scotsman*, 7 July 1914.
59. *Courier*, 12, 14, 16–17, 22, 28 January, and 2, 7, 9–10, 16, 21, 24 February 1914.
60. Nat Ganley Collection; Box 33, Folder 17, miscellaneous papers, pp. 1–5 (page 4 missing).
61. Holford, *Reshaping Labour*, see pp. 150, 181.
62. Laybourn, *British Trade Unionism*, p. 104.
63. MacDougall, *Militant Miners*, pp. 3, 10–11, 18, 20, 23–4.
64. *Leven Advertiser and Wemyss Gazette*, 11 May, and 29 June, 1910. I would like to thank Heather Simpson for drawing my attention to this material.
65. *The Scotsman*, 3 October 1913.
66. Hutchison, 'Scottish Politics', in MacDonald and McFarland, *Scotland and the Great War*, pp. 39–41.
67. Kenefick, *The Key to the Clyde*, p. 1.
68. *Ardrossan and Saltcoats Herald*, 16 November and 20 December 1912.
69. Kenefick, *The Key to the Clyde*, pp. 19–20.
70. Coates and Topham, *The Making of the Transport and General Workers' Union*; Lyon, *The History of the Scottish Horse and Motormen's Association*; Tuckett, *The Scottish Carter*.
71. See O'Day, *The Edwardian Age: Conflict and Stability*.
72. Benson, *Working Class in Britain*, pp. 174–206.
73. Holton, *British Syndicalism*, pp. 19–21, 77–88, 97–103, 127–9, 167–9.
74. Reported in *The Times*, *The Glasgow Herald* and *The Scotsman*, 9, 10, December, 1914.

6

War Resisters and Anti-conscription

INTRODUCTION

From the commencement of hostilities on 4 August 1914, the Independent Labour Party (ILP) dismissed the claim that Britain's war was a 'just cause', and it held consistently to that line from then through to armistice on 11 November 1918. In the propaganda paper *Forward*, the ILP asserted form the start that the war was being fought to satisfy the lust for industrial profit on the one hand, and the desire to promote the rise of the British military state on the other. 'The Alliance between "Holy Russia", Cut Throat Servia [*sic*], Protestant Britain, "Heathen Japan", and "Catholic" France' was evidence enough to demonstrate the duplicitous and self-serving actions of British diplomacy in the run-up to the crisis.[1]

As war hysteria quickly reached fever pitch, the government was urged to take every necessary action to ensure a British victory. The state rapidly took control of the railways, impounded enemy ships, interned aliens and mobilised the territorials. Against this background, many in the ILP feared the inevitable growth in state power the longer the war continued. Already, political propaganda and social and economic coercion followed in the wake of the government's war recruitment campaign, typified in the immediate calls to introduce conscription. On this last issue the ILP was resolute, for if compulsory military service were introduced it would lead inexorably to the militarisation of civil and industrial society. Should the state procure such powers, the result would be 'the negation of all law', the denial of the right of conscience and the curtailment of the individual freedoms.[2]

The No-Conscription Fellowship (NCF), formed in November 1914, was also prominent in the anti-war campaign and 'bore the brunt of the struggle against conscription'. After conscription was introduced, the NCF and its members became conscientious objectors (COs), three-quarters of whom were political objectors, and most 'owed their primary allegiance to the ILP'. In the long-term the NCF was to win the argument against British militarism. International socialism clearly failed on the outbreak of war, and it was 'British war resisters' who were to provide 'a stirring tradition for the second and third generations of Socialists to follow'.[3] The Military Service Acts of January and May 1916 provided for the full exemption of COs on moral, religious and political grounds, but many still found themselves in prison over the exercise of conscience. Indeed, five months after the war had ended, *Forward* was campaigning for the release of the COs who were still in prison, prompting W. J. Chamberlain to declare, in March 1919, that these men were 'victims of the most scandalous persecution since the sixteenth century'.[4] It seemed certain that the ILP would suffer in taking an anti-war position. By the armistice of 1918, however, the number of Scottish ILP branches had more than doubled and membership was three times its pre-war level. In contrast, elsewhere in Britain the ILP never fully recovered from the loss of branches and members sustained during the war years.[5]

So why was the ILP in Scotland so successful, and what part did the NCF play in this political phenomenon? This chapter will attempt to shed some light on this subject by examining in detail the role of Scottish war resisters and the 'anti-war' movement in Scotland, and the attitude of the press and the public towards Scotland anti-militarists. Clearly, the ILP's triumph can be partly explained by its successful 'exploitation of welfare issues' and 'workers' grievances' during the war, but the active opposition to war played by the NCF also helped to raise the ILP's profile, and particularly so in Aberdeen and Dundee.[6] Despite the clamour for war in Scotland, and vitriolic attacks on the ILP and its membership, the party held the anti-militarist line, and through *Forward* gave the people of Scotland the opportunity to consider a critique of the war at a time when few dissenting voices were heard.

SCOTLAND AND WAR HYSTERIA

It had never been in doubt that the Scots responded in great numbers to the call to arms at the onset of war in 1914. The *Daily Record* reported that within two days of war being declared, and over the first weekend of war, 6,000 men 'from all classes' enlisted in Glasgow alone.[7] By December 1914, 25 per cent of the male labour force of western Scotland had signed up.[8] The Scottish press reported with great pride the country's high voluntary recruitment levels, and in November 1914 the *Dundee*

Advertiser proclaimed: 'All honour to the lads who have put Scotland in the front this time . . . We must not let the sons of the Rose or the Leek or the Shamrock get in front of the proud Thistle.'[9] Derek Young would argue that there has been a tendency to 'overstate' Scotland's contribution to voluntary levels of recruitment, and he would urge caution in relying on information gleaned from the pages of the establishment press. But over the first few months of the war and 'for much of the period prior to the introduction of conscription', military recruitment in Scotland was generally brisk.[10]

So how do we explain this early and relatively high level of recruitment? Chris Harvie suggested that 'it is difficult to assign precise motives, but the fear of unemployment was probably as great as patriotic enthusiasm and solidarity with "Brave Little Belgium"'. He noted, for example, that in the Lothian coalfields, where the overseas market for coal had already collapsed because of the war, 36 per cent of miners had volunteered. In contrast, in the Ayrshire coalfields, where trade had not been so adversely affected, only 20 per cent of miners signed up. In the agricultural districts of north-east Scotland, despite being 'strong territorial country', mobilisation was delayed somewhat because the 'war coincided with the harvest'. Economic factors clearly held back recruitment in some areas, but 'following one's pals' remained a powerful component in the decision to join-up – as was the general expectation of a short war.[11] Even when it became clear that the war would not be over by Christmas, and that the loss of life would be greater than first imagined, few argued for a peaceful end to the hostilities between Britain and Germany. That stall was clearly setout at the very start of the conflict, and Germany's guilt was early established, when *The Glasgow Herald* asserted in August 1914: 'Germany is the criminal. Let Germany pay the penalty.'[12]

Such anti-German sentiments were prevalent throughout British society, and were often seen at their most vociferous within the ranks of the labour and trade union movement. While not all of its members were 'Hun-hating jingoistic super-patriots' who, like Ben Tillett, wished to have the Germans 'eliminated from civilisation', many were, nevertheless, convinced that the war was justified and that it was necessary to defeat Germany at all costs.[13] Despite the resolution passed by the Second International at Basle in 1912, declaring its members' opposition to war, no action of that type was ever taken and few suggested that it should be. As Nan Milton has argued, the Second International had failed its first test, and 'failed dismally'. Writing of the life and times of her father, leading BSP member John Maclean, she stressed:

In Britain the socialist movement as a whole responded 'gallantly' to the Liberal government's appeal to protect 'poor little Belgium' and to 'fight for democracy' against the threatening Prussian despotism. The TUC, the co-operative movement and the Labour Party unreservedly gave their services in the cause of the allies, the TUC promising complete industrial peace for the duration of the war.[14]

Milton asserted that the ILP, despite taking a 'fairly strong pacifist line' on the war, still tended to sit on the fence on the major issues, and thereafter retreated from the public gaze into the intimacy of local halls 'where they could reach nobody but the converted'.

Milton's censures aside, the ILP's strong 'anti-war' line was clearly and consistently evident in the weekly columns of *Forward*. In contrast, the BSP organ *Justice* was being used by her father's former colleagues, Robert Blatchford and H. M. Hyndman, 'for both blatant and subtle war propaganda'. Moreover, as she herself notes, many members of the BSP in Scotland, and in Glasgow, rejected Maclean and remained loyal to Hyndman, resulting in a definite split in the ranks of the BSP. Some ILP members did support the war and others left the party because of its stand, but there was no definitive split within the ILP ranks such as occurred with the BSP. Fife miners' leader John McArthur recalled the BSP split and how the Buckhaven branch remained loyal to Hyndman, while the Kirkcaldy branch split 'in line with Maclean and Gallagher'. Because of its opposition to war McArthur and two friends joined the Kirkcaldy branch:

> We were not conscious socialists, but we believed the war was creating terrible misery and hardship . . . The purpose of the war, and what would arise from it, was occupying our thoughts more and more. In the main our opposition to the war took a semi-pacifist line: we would refuse to go into the army on the grounds that it was an imperialist war.[15]

Clearly, the cause of socialism suffered a setback because of the war. *The Glasgow Herald*, which before the war had published many articles and reports warning of the evils of socialism, by August 1914 could claim with some justification: 'Scratch a Socialist and find a patriot'.[16] *Forward*, unhappy with such sentiment, attempted to play down the working class zeal for war, by arguing that socialists too were patriots, not because they supported war, but rather because they opposed it. They did not want war, they wanted peace, and a land to defend 'not that of the capitalist, but one which all shared equally'.

There was also practical support for peace. The Glasgow ILP, John MacLean and the anti-war BSP faction, and the Peace Society helped organise a peace demonstration in Glasgow within a week of the war being declared.[17] *Forward* reported, 'the gathering was cosmopolitan in character and included doctors and dock labourers and rebels of every possible brand from the mild peace advocates to the wildest of revolutionaries'. The meeting heard various speakers pronounce that 'the war was simply the outcome of Capitalism, Militarism and Secret Diplomacy', and agreed a resolution calling on the government to sue for a peaceful settlement to the war, and in support of 'International Socialism'. Below the report it was noted that the meeting was 'boycotted by the Capitalist Press'.[18] There were similar meetings organised across Scotland. But generally, unless noted in the columns of *Forward,* the *Labour Leader,* and some other socialist weeklies, the anti-war movement received little or no press coverage. Although over 5,000 turned out for the Glasgow Peace Demonstration, they were nevertheless a dedicated minority. The ILP also suffered because it openly opposed the Labour Party's support for the war and its decision to become actively involved in the government's recruitment campaign.

By February 1915 the ILP was already detecting a change in the attitude of people. Willie Stewart, by then Scottish organiser of the ILP, was to write that the party had been caught in the full glare of public interest because it had come out so openly against the Labour Party. But this strategy had been necessary, he claimed, in order to preserve the ILP as 'a socialist organisation'. The initial impulse of that crisis had passed and so 'the work of Socialism could be revived', and their efforts in the fight against the war could now be renewed. He nevertheless urged caution, and wondered 'would the people listen?':

> With our hospitals filled with broken men, with bereaved families in every street . . . in every village and hamlet, how can we expect people to listen to the arguments about the rights and wrongs of war? We shall be misunderstood and will only increase the mental pain . . . We must be tender and considerate to the feelings of our fellow workers, however hot our wrath against the war-makers.

Things had already improved for the party since the early days of the war, and in time they would get their message across – not least when war-weariness set in. The ILP's experience over the next four years was to prove Stewart correct.[19]

THE ANTI-WAR MOVEMENT AND THE SHADOW OF CONSCRIPTION

By September 1914 the columns of *Forward* were regularly reporting on the rift between the ILP and the Labour Party over the decision to back

Lord Kitchener's recruitment campaign. The National Administration Council of the ILP quickly mobilised its own campaign. It advised its members not to take part in any recruiting campaign, to stand firm, and 'Remain true to the goals of International Socialism and in all conscience remain firm in its opposition to war'.[20] This was repeated by the Rev. James Barr, a leading Scottish war resister and ex-president of the Peace Society. In what would prove to be the first *Forward* article to tackle the question of conscience, set against the prevailing pro-war mood of the nation, he asked:

> What is a man if he cannot abandon himself to the natural rage, and identify himself to the full with the popular passion, if he does not 'cry havoc, and let slip the dogs of war,' if, above all, he hints that there may be just something to be said for the other side, and that the whole war might someway have been avoided, he is at once set down as unpatriotic, cranky, and absolute impossible man in a time of war.[21]

Barr went on to dismiss suggestions that the war was inevitable, for 'To say this . . . was to renounce faith in God and man, and the future of our race.' Who did the war benefit, and who gained from waging war?:

> No one but the British, American, French and German industrialists, financed by British, French and German banks . . . [and] if Britain and Germany can federate to sell implements of destruction, can they not unite together in a bond of eternal peace.

Barr clearly articulated the moral and political objections to war, illustrating how the two strands could be seen to be part of one over-arching philosophy. This was in essence the philosophical and ideological position adopted by the ILP before the war, and was to be developed and extended during the conflict. By the end of October 1914, it was being reported throughout the press, and announced from every recruitment platform, that enlistment levels had fallen slightly, which prompted a terse comment from the editors of *Forward*, that the cannon fodder 'was rather backward in coming forward'. This line of reasoning angered one reader, who, writing under the lofty pseudonym '*Deep thinker from Larkhall*', believed he knew exactly why recruitment levels were tailing off: 'Lanarkshire miners have got the fighting spirit implanted within their breasts. If that has been diminished to a great extent, it is vastly due to bastard Socialism and the deficiencies of Christian teaching'. So there we have it, replied the editors of *Forward*, 'Christian teaching results in fighting spirit'.[22] There was a serious side to this issue, for even a slight fall in recruitment raised anew the issue of conscription. In reality, recruitment levels were still relatively stable. But during the early months of 1915, the recruitment rate fell from 300,000 to around 120,000 per month.[23] The government needed to balance both military and civil needs and was not at that time unduly troubled by falling recruitment levels. But for the pro-conscriptionists, and supporters of compulsory military service, such news was a godsend.

If the matter had been left to the Scottish press corps, the decision to introduce compulsory military service would have been a foregone conclusion. *The Glasgow Herald* ran a leading article on December 1914, which put the question of conscription to its readership with the comment: 'Is it unfair?'[24] It would seem that they had already decided in favour of the matter some weeks earlier, when it was reported that they made no apologies for stating that 'if voluntarism did not work, then conscription, or something approaching conscription, was the only alternative'.[25] The *Daily Record* ran similar articles, including one under the headline: 'Should our boy go to war'. In this issue they invited two parents to put their views on the matter, and suggested that these issues were actually being debated seriously. But nothing could have been further from the truth, for the 'boy' in question was left in no doubt that it was his duty to enlist.[26]

In the meantime, the Labour Party had swung determinedly towards the pro-war position, although it asserted that conscription was not considered an option. Its support for the war effort was noted in a letter printed in *Forward*, sent by a regular contributor who wrote under the pseudonym 'Rob Roy':

> We are not discussing whether we should be at war or not. We are in it . . . [and] to get well through, to avoid Belgian risks [*sic*], we require sufficient soldiers. The Labour Party accepted responsibility for finding them, and its members have courageously played their part. If they hadn't, if they had adopted the attitude of some socialists, would conscription not already be upon us? Has not the slow, sure commonsense of the Labour Party washed-up better than the theories of its critics?

The ILP recognised that this was aimed principally at them, and the sentiments expressed in the letter were thought 'quite disingenuous' in tone. The editors of *Forward* argued that the main aim of the letter was to place the Labour Party in the right, and 'some socialists' in the wrong. The editorial went on at some length, raking over many old coals, but the main argument was clearly put: 'that there was no evidence to suggest that the recruiting energies of the Labour Party [had] saved the country from conscription'. Restating its anti-war position, it argued that, unlike the Labour Party, it would never deviate from that line: 'The Anti-War Socialists will fight against Conscription if ever it is proposed. The Labour Party has given away their right to do so, and, on their present line of action, should not desire to do so!'[27]

Acting almost as a postscript, one short letter appeared in that same November edition of *Forward*. Under the heading 'The Question of Conscription', it suggested that 'it might be as well for us who refuse to take the part of a combatant in the present war to form ourselves into a body to consider the matter'.[28] At this point the anti-conscription movement was more or less still at an embryonic stage of development in Scotland. But in November 1914 Fenner Brockway wrote to the *Labour Leader*, inviting young men to form an organisation 'suggesting joint action for mutual help and encouragement'. The No-Conscription Fellowship was formed as a result.[29] Believing it was only a matter of time before compulsory military service was introduced, the aim of the NCF was to create an organisation to offer support, guidance and direction for those men who would refuse military service if it were imposed by the state.[30]

According to John Rae, 'this fusion of idealism with the promise of active resistance attracted young men with a variety of religious and political views'. The British Socialist Party produced many COs, as too did the Socialist Labour Party, the Socialist Party of Great Britain and the Industrial Workers of the World.[31] Yet it was the young men of the ILP who were to provide the initiative and leadership of the organisation. According to Rae, 'the most fertile source of political objection in the First World War was the ILP', and while political objection to conscription was by no means restricted to the ILP, there was little doubt that it was 'the best organised and most active group'.[32] Indeed, after conscription was finally introduced in January 1916, it has been estimated that 'almost seventy percent of conscientious objection cases involved ILP members'.[33]

In January 1915, Bruce Glasier, a leading ILP member, travelled north to gauge how the ILP's pacifist position was being received by the wider Scottish public. He made the following observations:

My mission has been somewhat in the nature of that of an Apostle among the Primitive Churches in Pagan Rome. For the present the ILP Branches are almost as sharply isolated from the surrounding population as were the Christian communities of Ephesus, Galicia, and Corinth in Apostolic days. Though not under any formal interdict as a seditious organisation, the ILP is nonetheless regarded with grave suspicion as a pestilentially pacifist faction, as a damper of the war enthusiasm of the nation, and a noxious shrub in the glowing flowerbed of British patriotism.

Despite this situation, however, he noted that the branches were bearing up well, although membership had fallen off slightly. He praised the Dundee, Leith and Glasgow branches, in particular, for holding regular lectures and propaganda meetings in their areas. He did note that 'two comrades in Bo'ness tended towards the Labour Party line on recruitment', but that overall, the situation in Scotland was very encouraging:

> The unanimity and steadfastness of the Branches in their adhesion to International principles, and the opposition to Militarism in all its forms, amidst the thunderstorm of war passion that has swept the country and the civilised world, must be reckoned one of the most distinctive and memorable events in the life of the ILP and the history of the Socialist movement. I can remember no occasion during the 21 years existence of the ILP where such virtual complete unity has been displayed in its ranks on any question critically affecting the party or the nation.[34]

Glasier then went on to suggest that the 'Anti-War feeling in Scotland was more energetic and aggressive than in English Branches'. He attributed this attitude 'to the keener dialectical habit of the Scottish mind', and to the courageous and brilliant 'Red Flag propaganda of *Forward*'. He concluded:

> I have never felt more reassured of the spirit and power of the ILP than now in beholding the Scottish branches bearing the banners of their Socialist faith unfalteringly against the almost universal crash of religion and politics.[35]

For Glasier at least, the anti-war position of the ILP in Scotland was holding well against the 'super-patriotism' so evident throughout the rest of Scottish society.

Not only were there major ideological differences between the ILP and other political groups, not least the Labour Party, but on the issue of morality and the war there were often serious divergences of opinion between the ILP and various religious bodies in Scotland. The Glasgow Study group, a Christian pacifist organisation, was particularly influential in promoting the pacifist position, but in the case of the large denominations, ecclesiastical support for the war was evident and more typical.[36] This found voice, for example, in the Bishop of Edinburgh's *Quarterly Letter* in 1914, and the Very Rev. Sir George Adam Smith's Address to the Moderator of the Church of Scotland in 1916, which he used to denounce COs, while another Presbyterian minister described COs as 'the dregs of the community'.[37] Indeed, it should not be forgotten that it was the Anglican Bishop of London who first used the term 'conchies' to describe conscientious objectors. It was for that reason, perhaps, that *Forward* was particularly anxious to give full coverage to pacifist clergymen, and certainly one of the most politically articulate was James Barr. But there were others. The Rev. J. E. McIntyre, of the United Free Church, Motherwell, praised those who opposed war in an address entitled 'Blessed are the Peacemakers'. The complete text of his speech was reprinted in *Forward*, and in conclusion he asked: 'Would Christ have gone to War?' In reply, he answered, 'I cannot think so!'[38] Another sermon reported in full was that of the Rev. Malcolm MacCallum, 'the 'Old Crofters venerable champion', who warned his congregation: 'Beware of the Churches as presently organised for this war was neither God's War nor a Holy War! It was a war of sinful men . . . between misguided brothers'.[39] It was such sentiments as these that added a spiritual and moral resonance to the ILP's anti-war propaganda.

THE PRESS, THE WAR AND PUBLIC OPINION

Prior to the introduction of conscription in January 1916, many in Scotland held to the belief that compulsion was wrong and that voluntarism was the preferred method of military recruitment. Others were less convinced, and would have extended the principle into the industrial arena. As *The Glasgow Herald* reported in May 1915:

> With national service for the period of the war we should also secure military discipline, and the entire munitions industry would be dealt with precisely as if it were labour performed in the trenches or on the battleships.[40]

Predating the main period of the Red Clyde unrest, such talk did not augur well for the future of industrial relations. It was this very concern that led others to wholly reject military conscription. In the early months of 1916, a series of articles appeared in the Dundee *People's Journal*, which stated that 'military compulsion was wrong' because logic dictated that civil and industrial conscription would follow, for in it would lie 'Britain's most deadly peril'. The Munitions Act was seen already as a major source of trouble and had shown that workers did not readily accept forms of coercion: 'Let any who doubts this go down to the Clyde and find out the spirit of the workers there'.[41]

During the previous month a large 'Free Speech and No-Conscription Demonstration' was held at Glasgow, the ILP organised a similar event in Motherwell, and towards the end of the month 'excited scenes' were reported at a No-Conscription meeting at Rutherglen, when a 'strongly organised force of patriots' attempted to wreck the event. The patriots were ejected, but they gathered outside to assail the local councillors who were speaking at the meeting. 'A body guard of at least 1,000 men' was reported to have escorted the councillors safely home. 'It was a crowning triumph to a long series of local victories won by the Rutherglen Socialists', reported *Forward*.[42]

Typically, the press and public opinion sided with the 'patriots', and all over the country, in theatres and dancehalls, pubs, clubs and factory floors, at greyhound tracks and football grounds, the recruiters set about their task. The army was quick to mobilise female public opinion, and even the Mothers' Union produced a recruiting poster showing their members bravely pointing their sons in the direction of the recruiting offices. The *Active Service League* and the *Order of the White Feather* were organisations formed in the days after war was declared to persuade the manhood of Britain to enlist *en masse*. The *Bystander* commented tersely in September 1914: 'Men who put on uniforms as a result of exhortation by squires, parsons, retired-officers . . . politicians, cartoonists, poets, music-hall singers and women are not volunteers; they are conscripts!' Whether driven by genuine patriotism or the weight of militant pro-war opinion, by the end of December 1914, over 1.2 million British and Irish men had enlisted.

So were these men swept along by patriotic jingoism, an earnest desire to 'stand up for plucky little Belgium'? Was it an attempt to escape the dull monotony of the farm and field, or the poverty and low wages of the grimy urban landscape of workshops and factories? Was it the intense social pressure that was exerted: were the recruits shamed and cajoled into 'taking the King's shilling' by white-feather wielding females? In Ian MacDougall's *'Hard Work, Ye Ken'*, Midlothian female farmworker Agnes Tod recalled:

> I remember very well the 1914 war breaking out. And all the young chaps – although they could have stayed on because the army didn't take farm folk – oh, they were getting handed white feathers and a' this sort of thing . . . It was the young ladies, farmers' daughters, they were going round handing them white feathers . . . (There were eighteen young men in total) . . . none were really of age to go . . . None of them came back. None. They were all killed.[43]

In the battle to win the hearts and minds of the people of Scotland, and encourage them to expose the shirkers in their midst, few newspapers could beat the antics of the Dundee *People's Journal*. In an article 'Conscription for Women' in November 1915, the paper came to the following conclusion:

> The day is fast approaching when a girl who fiddles away at fancy work when she might be making shells . . . will as much be an object of public scorn and

as much deserving of compulsory treatment as the 'nut' who carries a golf club when he ought to be handling a rifle'.[44]

In January 1916, as the paper invited comments on the conscriptions debate, just days before conscription was introduced, the editors invited readers from all around Scotland to submit poems, in the style of the 'Bard, Rabbie Burns', against the men who refused to fight, more commonly referred to as 'shirkers'. Below are reproduced five of the ten winning entries:

People's Journal Poetry Competition – January 1916

First prize of 10 shillings went to a Mr W. L. Laurie, Aberdeenshire:

Ye guid for naithing, lazy lout,
Hoo can ye shirk whilst heroes shout,
And see them fall in some fell bout
Through shells and gases?
Had I my way, I'd tak' ye a'
And line ye up in ae big raw
Then wi' 'Mons Meg' the lot I'd blaw
To hell and blazes.

Mr T. D. Shaw, Scotstoun, Glasgow won 5 shillings for his effort:

Shame on ye, man: gae hide yer face,
Puir sample o' the British race,
The firin' lines yer proper place
At sic a time.
When oor brave lads frae toon and glen
'Midst bluid and fire oor hames defen'
Frae Huns, vile hate ayont oor ken,
Then toe the line.

There was also 'A New Double Stanza to Scots Wha Hae':

Men unworthy o' the name,
Trembling, hide their heads at hame,
Theirs be everlasting shame,
Regret and Misery.
Scotland's God look on them now;
Licht within their heart a low;
Send then forth resolved to bow,
Nevermore to kneel.

And the 'Shirkers Prayer'!

> O shirker, dae ye no think shame
> Tae bear that unco cooardly name?
> This nicht afore ye sleep at hame,
> Pit up this prayer –
> Lord, hear me when I cry tae Thee.
> Oh tak', the chicken-he'rt frae me.
> In khaki, Lord, I fain wad be,
> An' shirk nae mair.

And finally, Mr Thomas Anderson, Coatbridge:

> Lads, why should you, like whipped curs,
> Stand back still undecided,
> Till branded by the conscript mark,
> Your from the men divided?
> Be Britons still: Be Britons true.
> Wake up now, be Attested!
> And teach the Huns that not by them
> Can honour be molested.

Half the entries were by women. But the theme is a common one: those who did not sign up, for whatever reason, were shirkers and cowards, and if all else failed they would in the end be caught once conscription was introduced.[45]

After conscription was introduced, the readership of the *People's Journal* were asked to consider another series of questions: 'What is a conscientious objector?'. And more searchingly: 'Were such men sane?' They called on various authorities to help answer such questions, and under the banner heading put the question: 'THE CONSCIENTIOUS OBJECTOR: IS THERE A KINK IN HIS CONSTITUTION?':

> If you examine the list of conscientious objectors you will find that there are extremely few men from the working-classes among them. The conscientious objector usually belongs to the middle and upper strata of society. Why? Because the industrial and urban workers were used to the brutalities of life, having seen or experienced depravity in one or more forms. Such men can easily believe the stories of German brutalities and degradation on Belgium women and children.

Your average CO was, concluded this particular expert, 'a man who had been wrapped up all his life in cotton wool', and therefore most likely the son of the middling to upper classes. There then followed the 'remarkable statement' by a doctor from Morningside in Edinburgh, who presented his views under the heading: 'HUMAN WHITE RABBITS':

> There are some women and some men . . . who ought never to marry . . . because they are physical and mental nonentities. When a girl of a simpering doll type mates with an effeminate, anaemic man, the children that result are just too often the sort that will grow into conscientious objectors.
>
> . . . Personally, I must say that I pity rather than condemn many of these conscientious objectors. They are men without masculinity; they have women's hearts in men's bodies.
>
> . . . What we ought to do with these sensitive souled faddists is difficult to say, but we certainly ought not to let them remain in our midsts and proceed with their work to produce a race of human white rabbits.

He stated that the COs should be told to clear out and deported, but not be allowed to shelter in our colonies. The doctor then proceeded to divide COs into two basic types: liars and lunatics. A medical test had to found which would separate the two. Once this was confirmed, the lunatics would be institutionalised, and the liar then sent onto the front![46]

The readership of the *People's Journal* had all manner of ideas as to how best treat COs, including levying a special 'disloyalty tax' on war resistors.[47] It is also clear that they supported the work of the Dundee tribunals with some degree of relish. Indeed, by way of an example, there was a case raised in the House of Commons in May 1916, regarding the action of a Dundee employer. It was noted that his employees had gone on strike, and rather than resort to the usual means of dealing with disputes 'he informed the Military Authorities'. The men were called up under the terms of the Military Service Act. The trade union and labour movement protested, but public opinion was firmly on the side of the employers.[48] Dundee was a centre of war patriotism, but perhaps because of such 'vindictiveness', it was no accident that it was also destined to become a stronghold of both the NCF and the ILP. Whatever the local press might report, it did not seem to make much impact on the anti-war movement in the city.

EXPLOITING WARTIME DISCONTENT

Opposition to war and the pursuit of peace was still the main aim of the ILP, but as James Maxton argued, 'the war also brought with it new opportunities to proclaim the socialist message'. Concerns over the rising cost of food, fuel and housing, the militaristic invasions of civil rights and liberty, and threats of compulsion and conscription were the type of issues the ILP was to exploit to its benefit. In championing such causes, Willie Stewart felt sure that 1915 would become 'memorable for other things than the war'.[49]

One topic that was to take up the attentions of the ILP was the concern over the issue of wartime evictions – particularly those of the families of men in military service – and *Forward* reported on cases from Kilsyth to Sutherland. A Kilsyth woman had her husband and her two sons fighting at the front, but it did not stop her factor removing half of the thatched roof of her cottage in an attempt to put pressure on her to leave. And it was reported that the Sutherland estate was proposing to evict crofters in the parish of Clyne in order to extend the Brora golf course. While the crofters were serving at the front, the petition was already before the Scottish Land Court. So much for the flag-waving patriotism of the landlords, reported *Forward*.[50]

That the ILP was a cause of great concern to many in Scotland could be seen in the reaction of the country's press to the party's annual conference in April 1915. The *Edinburgh Evening Dispatch* castigated ILP delegates as 'enemies of their country', while the *Sutherland Echo* was particularly vitriolic and had but one regret:

> That there [were] no legal powers for seizing such men, putting them under the grimmest of drill sergeants for severe and rapid training, and hurrying them to the hottest place at the front. This would probably have been done in Germany, and very properly too.[51]

So much for the country's hatred of 'Prussianism', noted *Forward*, and the propaganda which pilloried Germany for its 'inherent inhumanity'. The Dundee *Courier* castigated the conference 'as a gathering of cranks', while the *Aberdeen Free Press* considered the whole conference as 'deplorable . . . one jarring hole in the unexampled display of national unity'.[52] The *Edinburgh Evening News* noted that there had been strenuous efforts made to deny the ILP a public meeting place, but it asserted that this was wrong: 'After all, Britain is not Germany'.[53] More perceptively, perhaps, the *Aberdeen Evening Express* reported that 'when the backwash of the war began to perturb the nation', more people would have sympathy with the ILP line.[54]

By May and June, such criticisms were put to one side as relations with the Labour Party sunk to an all-time low following Arthur Henderson's decision to join the new Coalition Ministry. Underlying this concern was the issue of conscription. Willie Stewart asked: 'Are they joining the Government, as they started their recruitment campaign, to save the country from conscription?' He noted that the Labour Party now sided with tariff reformers, anti-Home Rulers, imperialists and Conscriptionists, which was 'reason enough for not joining the government', concluded Stewart.[55] By early June 1915, it was clear that the issue of military and industrial conscription was to be used to front the ILP's anti-war propaganda campaign.[56] And it was gaining momentum!

CONSCRIPTION BECOMES A REALITY

Despite the National Registration Act of June 1915, which was intended to encourage voluntary enlistment, recruitment levels fell to around 80,000 per month before the end of January 1916.[57] The National Military Service Act was introduced in January 1916, and imposed conscription upon single men aged eighteen to forty-one, with exemption clauses covering those in ill-health, engaged in work of national importance, or acting as sole supporter with dependants. It also maintained the right to refuse military service on conscientious grounds, and started objectors were to be heard by local tribunals which could grant military exemption on a temporary, conditional or absolute basis. Problems operating the Act meant that by March 1916, out of the 193,891 single men called up for military service, 57,416 did not appear. As a result, the conscriptionists turned their attentions to married men and extended the Military Service Act in May, 1916.[58]

Over a year before, the MP W. C Anderson in an address to the National Council of the ILP, warned that conscription would lead to the 'militarisation of the whole working class', and maintained that the organised workers had been 'emphatic in their declarations against it'. The National Council added that the Labour Party, speaking from platforms all over the country, encouraged men to sign up in order to spare the country from conscription. They had done so believing they had preserved the manhood of the country from the oppression of military service. This was a betrayal of those men.[59] Political opposition to conscription had indeed been growing and, as Anderson suggested, the trade union movement came out against it. Not a single delegate spoke in favour of it at the Trade Union Congress (TUC) conference in 1915, and the conference unanimously rejected any policy of forced service.[60] In January 1916 the Scottish TUC passed an anti-conscription resolution by sixty-six votes to forty-six, and the Glasgow Labour Party and the Scottish Labour Conference also rejected conscription.[61] Once conscription became law, however, workers were left with two choices: to oppose it, or to accept the democratic decision and the will of Parliament. Many complied, but joined campaigns for the repeal of the Military Service Act and, in September 1917, the TUC passed a unanimous resolution against both military and industrial conscription. A later Labour conference in January 1918 demanded the absolute withdrawal of the Military Service Acts.[62]

In the meantime, the ILP and the No-Conscription Fellowship were growing in strength, and in the early months of 1915 the Glasgow branch of the No-Conscription Fellowship was formed. The meeting had been organised by the BSP, and was widely advertised in both the *Labour Leader* and *Forward*.[63] By the first anniversary of the start of the war, the NCF had expanded and had set up branches in many locations around the country, and this paralleled the network of ILP branches that were forming across Scotland. A branch of the NCF was set up in Dundee, for example, following a large ILP meeting there in November 1915, and from then on the city became a stronghold of the ILP, the NCF and a growing pacifist movement.

By the end of 1915 the ILP had begun a register of its own for COs and it claimed to speak for 10,000 men in Scotland. Some trade unions were also organising non-conscription registers, including the Gasworkers Union of Scotland, the Shop Assistants Union, the Glasgow branch of the Workers' Union, the Leith Dockers, the Central Iron Moulders, and the Clydebank Trades Council. Moreover, Aberdeen, Dundee, and Kirkintilloch Labour Representation Committees (LRCs) declared that they would help to organise resisters' registers if the support of the Scottish Labour Party was forthcoming. But the best organised was Glasgow, where the ILP set in motion a series of demonstrations and meetings on the topics of conscription and 'Freedom of Speech'. On 18 December 1915 7,000 people were reported to have turned out for a 'Free Speech and No Conscription Demonstration', addressed by a whole host of well-known speakers, including John Maclean, Manny Shinwell, Helen Crawfurd and Willie Gallacher.[64] In short, the ILP had fought hard, along with the NCF, the BSP and other groups such as the Union of Democratic Control, to ensure that conscription was not introduced, and once it had been imposed they worked tirelessly for its repeal.[65]

Once conscription was introduced, it created further problems between the Labour Party and the ILP. During March, 1916, as the readers of the *People's Journal* grappled with the notion that COs were either 'liars' or 'lunatics', local Labour MP Alexander Wilkie was having problems with Dundee LRC. Because Wilkie backed conscription, he was informed that the LRC would not be supporting his candidature in the future. Wilkie replied with some veiled threat of 'having martial law enforced', which the secretary of the Dundee LRC, James Fraser, noted was typical of the 'pseudo-patriotic verbiage they had come to expect from such Labour MPs who were in support of the government at any cost'.[66] In July 1916 there was a special report in *Forward* on the COs turned down at Dundee, and this made some interesting reading:

- Ewan G. Carr, President of Dundee LRC, and Secretary of the Scottish Section of the ILP Scouts.
- Andrew Henderson, Vice-President of the Dundee LRC, Cooperationist, Trade Unionist, Socialist, and 'promising propagandist'.
- Stewart Campbell and William Adamson, Dundee Socialist Sunday School.
- Sandy Ross, ex-Glasgow policeman and 'champion literature seller North of the Forth'.
- Alexander Dewar, Prohibitionist and Socialist.
- Bob Stewart, ex-town councillor, Prohibitionist, Socialist, and International Protagonist.

Stewart came in for some special praise as a 'clever writer and convincing speaker', who refused non-combatant service on the grounds that it simply meant 'holding the jackets of another to fight'.[67] The following September it was reported that Bob Stewart was at the CO labour camp at Dyce, Aberdeen where around 250–500, mainly English, COs were engaged in 'hard labour'.[68]

By this time *Forward* and the *Labour Leader* were running regular reports on the treatment of conscientious objectors, both at the tribunals and at the hands of the military. One typical report noted the case of a man claiming exemption because he had a crippled brother and mother to look after. He was given a temporary exemption of three months, despite also having four brothers at the front. In contrast, a riding instructor was given six months' exemption, because he trained horses used by officers on their return from France.[69] The master of the Berwickshire Fox Hounds claimed exemption for one of his huntsmen, and in the process he drew the attention of the tribunal to a War Office letter, stating the desirability of keeping a large number of light animals suitable for the army. His huntsman was given a complete exemption.[70]

In *Forward's* new feature 'Round the Tribunals', it reported on what appeared in other papers around the country. One report from *The Glasgow Herald* noted the case of a dowager marchioness, who claimed exemption for her chauffeur (aged twenty-eight) because he was 'indispensable in running her down to her "war work" at the hospital'. In that same edition of *Forward*, James Maxton gave an example of how he filled in his exemption application form in preparation for his appearance before the tribunals, in which he simply stated:

> I am a Socialist and a member of a Socialist organisation. As such I have worked to establish a better system of society, which would make for the peace and brotherhood of peoples of all lands. To take part in a war would be for me a desertion of these ideals, and I must therefore decline to take part.

Willie Stewart similarly pleaded to 'tribunal members' to 'do no outrage to the one supreme product of human growth and development – the human conscience'.[71] Such sentiments apparently fell on deaf ears within the tribunals in Scotland, which seemed to display 'a particular vindictiveness' as illustrated in the selection of cases noted by *Forward*.[72] One report, from the *Highland News*, noted the words of the local tribune upon hearing the case of a religious objector, who claimed absolute exemption because 'he could obey only the Lord'. The Chairman dismissed his claim and stated: 'You are the most awful pack that ever walked this earth. To think that you would not stand up and defend our women and children from the ravages of the Germans. Is this Christianity? It is acting with the devil in the place of Christ.'[73] In other instances, it seemed as if the 'good tribunes' simply toyed with those who came before them. Mr Spence, of the Dundee Tribunal, heard the case of a draper's assistant claiming exemption on religious grounds. When asked what his religion was, he replied 'spiritualist'. On hearing this, Mr Spence concluded, 'you are the very man for the front. You might come in contact with a few of them there'. His case was dismissed.[74] Another tribunal member, on hearing the statement that Christ told us to love our enemies, replied, 'we can love our enemies and kill them at the same time'.[75]

Despite outbursts of ridicule and verbal abuse, the Scottish tribunals were not always consistent in their deliberations, and on one occasion twenty-one ILP COs were given exemption on political grounds.[76] Decisions often depended on where the tribunal met, and how many cases they had to hear. One of the reasons that the Glasgow tribunals were seen to be harsher than others was perhaps due to the fact that they simply heard so many cases. Indeed, the City of Glasgow Tribunal heard more cases in the month of July 1916 than the majority of tribunals disposed of in six years during the Second World War.[77] It may also have been the case that political COs were treated more harshly than others, for as *Forward* reported in April 1916, most COs in Glasgow were ILP-ers.[78]

Whatever the outcome, there is little doubt that these public gatherings provided the ILP with an opportunity to carry out some political propaganda:

> In industrial areas, with strong socialist loyalties, an ILP applicant would be accompanied by a vociferous group of supporters. Tribunal members were interrupted and jeered, and it was commonplace for 'The Red Flag' to be sung at the hearing.

The trade union and Labour Party men who sat on the tribunals 'were subjected to special scorn' and were shouted down with cries of 'treachery'. For their part they characterised the political COs as 'renegades'.[79]

In response to their treatment as 'renegades', some attempted to marry the political and moral arguments against conscription. When still a member of the ILP, William Leslie appeared before the Elgin tribunal during July 1916, applying for 'absolute exemption' on conscientious grounds:

> According to his religious and moral beliefs he could take no part in the slaughter of his fellow-creatures. His religion was socialism, and he believed in the law laid down by Christ in the Immortal Sermon on the Mount. He asked for absolute exemption from military service, even non-combatant service, because he would not relieve someone to do what he was not prepared to do himself.

In response to questioning, he stated that 'no righteousness could be gained by armed force', and he admitted to being a member of the ILP and the No-Conscription Fellowship. He was quite willing to undertake work of national importance, he claimed, but not under military discipline. The military representative refused his application, and Leslie was rejected.[80] Leslie appealed the decision in August, and this was conceded on condition that he joined the Friends Ambulance Unit within twenty-one days. He declined the offer and he was later arrested and jailed.[81]

Harvie argues that the ILP was particularly militant on the issue of conscription, but that Scots ILP-ers were 'a more subversive, less principled bunch' who usually 'avoided the martyrdom of prison'.[82] Leslie's admission that he would accept work of national importance, but not under military supervision, was a prime example of this response. Similarly, James Maxton was given an exemption on condition that he obtained himself work of national importance. While he found this difficult, Maxton eventually found employment in a small shipyard, which was not directly involved in war work. Maxton spent some time in prison

for breaches of the Defence of the Realm Act in 1915. Prison attracted
publicity, but as he recollected in his book, *We Did Not Fight* (1935), it
precluded him from socialist agitation:

> I appreciated and understood the attitude of my friends who absolutely
> declined to do anything, and suffered continuous imprisonment over the
> whole war period, but it did not suit my philosophy, which demanded active
> carrying on of the class struggle, nor did it suit my temperament to be cribbed,
> cabined and confined when the urge within me was to be out trying to influ-
> ence my fellows to use the opportunities presented by war conditions for the
> purpose of social revolution.[83]

With war weariness setting in, and more trouble brewing over the issue
of industrial conscription, this pragmatism was soon rewarded. From
1916 onwards, the ILP was increasingly attracting eager listeners. Even
well-known COs were being given a hearing, where before they were cer-
emoniously shouted down, and by early 1917 ILP membership began to
rise.[84] By this point more ILP-ers were being brought before the tribunals
and more cases of exemption on conscientious grounds were being
rejected. Not all were treated harshly, but those who choose prison
accepted that their sentence entailed hard labour.

The mainstream press were all too happy to publish tribunal proceedings, especially when COs were dealt harsh sentences, and particularly if they were being re-arrested and imprisoned for the same offence.
There were several cases where the tribunals and the military authorities acted unlawfully, and one such incident concerned an Edinburgh ILP
member, after a High Court judgment declared he had been illegally
detained and incarcerated for some four months. What surprised
Forward was that the matter was not reported elsewhere.[85] There was a
famous case where thirty-four men, who were deemed to have enlisted
in the Non-Combatant Corps, were to be smuggled into France and
once there 'the sentence of death was read'.[86] Had the NCF not heard
of their plight, those men would have been shot: instead, their sentence
was commuted to ten years' penal servitude.[87] As a result of such cases
and political pressure, after May 1916 it was decreed that the military
had to turn COs over to the civil authorities when they refused to obey
military orders.

As the war progressed, the ILP tended to leave practical CO issues
increasingly to the National Council of the NCF, and *Forward* and the
Labour Leader presented the NCF's underlying philosophical and ethical
stand to a growing readership. Dundee became a leading centre of the
anti-war movement in Scotland, and it was reported in *Forward* in April

1917, that the city was 'fair hotchin' wi conchies'.[88] Aberdeen had a pacifist majority on the Trades Council by May the following year, and *Forward* could report that there was 'certainly more restraint being shown to COs and pacifists' in the city as a result.[89]

But in other locations the clamour for retribution increased and, as was the case with the disturbance at an ILP meeting at Rutherglen, 'some of it was organised'. This was clear in a brutal display of organised violence at a meeting called jointly by the ILP, NCF, the Fellowship of Reconciliation, the Union of Democratic Control, the Society of Friends and the Women's International League, and held in Edinburgh during July 1918. They had gathered to protest against the passing of repeat sentences on COs for the same offence, but an 'organised band' of soldiers and sailors broke up the meeting. They rushed the platform, beat up speakers, destroyed literature and 'confiscated money from one woman's case'. COs were separated out for special treatment, and although the police were called 'little was done on their part'. Victims' pockets were rifled as they lay on the floor and one man's clothes were so ripped that his bare body was exposed to the crowd.[90]

It was all very unsavoury and involved the NSFU who, it later emerged, plied the men with drink and paid men to break up the meeting. Despite being reported as 'a riot', there was no sympathy from the Edinburgh press, who asserted that to hold a pacifist meeting in the city 'was pure madness'. Indeed, the *Edinburgh Evening Dispatch* stated that the promoters of the meeting 'got what they had been asking for', and that the 'riotous demonstration' was simply a 'spontaneous ebullition of National Patriotism'. It was also rumoured that some of the hooligans had been recruited from among dockers at Leith, but George Kibble, secretary of Leith NUDL, stressed that this was not true, and asserted that 'the riot' was not a 'spontaneous demonstration of public feeling', but a careful organised attack. 'On no account would he be party to such hooliganism and neither would the Leith dockers'. 'On the contrary', he argued, 'we value freedom of speech for our own meetings'. There were no hooligans from the docks!'[91]

It was clear that Havelock Wilson was behind the riot at Edinburgh, and when he came to Glasgow in October to speak to a meeting at St Andrew's Hall, chaired by shipowner Sir Thomas Dunlop, it was rumoured that he could expect a rough time for his part in the Edinburgh riot. The hall was full and several hundred more could not get in, and all hell broke loose when the platform party appeared and were met with howls of derision, reported *Forward*. The 'Red Flag' was sung and amidst the *mêlée* Havelock Wilson was heard to shout that 'Bolsheviks were paid 30 shillings to break-up the meeting'. He was shouted down as a 'liar' and the meeting finally had to be abandoned.[92]

But the jewel in the ILP and NCF crown was without doubt Dundee, and its left-radical political reputation continued to build through the war years and beyond, despite the best efforts of the Dundee press. Willie Stewart, after his ILP propaganda campaign around Scotland in February 1918, made a 'special mention' of Dundee in an editorial which appeared in *Forward*:

> The ILP there had stood its ground through the war and the dark days of militaristic oppression. It has its sons in every prison and penal centre set apart for conscientious objectors to militarism. It has steadfastly and fearless fought for liberty and Socialism . . . In the great inevitable political uprising which is destined to place Labour permanently in power, the working class of Dundee will demand a foremost place.[93]

In March 1918 Stewart was to report that the number of ILP branches had risen from 112 to 167 and the membership had swelled from 3,000 to 9,000, confirming his earlier predictions of the ILP's advance in Scotland. During the last days of the war the mood in the ILP camp was even more buoyant and upbeat than usual. Despite the threat of total collapse, the ILP's early unpopularity, its political isolation and its lone stand against the warmongers, the party had won through. It had taken on the 'Official' Labour Party when it 'defected to Militarism', and fought against the 'undermining of democracy', in the wake of the introduction of the Munitions Act, the Defence of the Realm Act, and finally the Conscription Acts 'when the young men of the ILP, along with others . . . had to face a new ordeal'.[94] The ILP was working to spread socialism throughout Scotland, and branches had emerged in Inverurie, Buckie, Keith and Graigelachie; to cap it all, wrote Willie Stewart, 'the ILP is in Banffshire!'[95] The achievement was indeed remarkable, underlined by the simple fact that by 1918 the Scottish ILP accounted for about one-third of the party's total British membership.[96]

CONCLUSIONS

The ILP as a political organisation maintained its anti-war stand throughout the Great War, and in the years after the end of the war continued its fight against British militarism and campaigned to abolish conscription. Within Scotland, the ILP had embarked upon its anti-war mission for political purposes. Where International Socialism failed at the outbreak of war, Scottish war resisters were to provide an alternative tradition to inspire later generations of Scottish socialists.[97] Moreover, there was 'much goodwill' between conscientious objectors and 'conscientious assenters' who had volunteered for armed service in Scotland. One such volunteer wrote from the trenches to a CO in Scotland, just days before he was killed, 'Your situation is worse because you are so misunderstood'.[98]

The ILP quest for international peace had a near-religious quality about it. This was perhaps most eloquently put by one Glasgow minister, quoted in *Forward* in September 1919. He spoke warmly of the ILP's ethical and international outlook during the war, and in particular its stand against conscription and militarism, and he concluded that the ILP in Glasgow was 'the purest Christian institution in the city'.[99]

By the time the war was nearing its end, *Forward* reviewed the progress that the ILP had made over the previous four years. Because of a successful 'Home Front Offensive', the number of branches had risen from ninety-eight to 201 and the membership had increased from 3,000 to over 10,000. In February 1915, there had been fears that the ILP's anti-war message would be 'misunderstood' and that this would adversely affect the party's fortunes. In the event, many thousands of ordinary Scots did listen to the ILP's anti-war message, and by the end of the hostilities *Forward* proudly claimed that 'The ILP in Scotland lives, and in 201 towns and villages bears witness to the vitality of the Socialist Movement'.[100]

NOTES

1. *Forward,* 22 August 1914.
2. *Forward,* 14 February, 22, 29 August, 4 September and 17 October 1914.
3. Hayes, *Conscription Conflict,* pp. 248, 257, 266.
4. *Forward,* 1 March 1919.
5. Harvie, 'Before the Breakthrough', p. 25.
6. Ibid. p. 24.
7. *Daily Record,* 11 August 1914.
8. Harvie, *No Gods and Precious Few Heroes,* pp. 10, 24; Harvie, 'Before the Breakthrough, 1888–1922', p. 21.
9. Dundee *Advertiser,* 8 November 1914.
10. Young, 'Voluntary Recruitment in Scotland, 1914–1916', pp. 11–22.
11. Harvie, 'Before the Breakthrough', pp. 10, 21.
12. *The Glasgow Herald,* 31 August 1914.
13. Harrison, 'The War Emergency Worker's National Committee 1914–1920', p. 219.
14. Milton, *John Maclean,* pp. 76–7.
15. MacDougall, *Militant Miners,* pp. 10–11.

16. *The Glasgow Herald*, 10 August 1914.
17. *Labour Leader*, 13 August 1914.
18. *Forward,* 15 August 1914.
19. *Forward,* 13 February 1915.
20. *Forward,* 5 September 1914.
21. *Forward,* 17 September 1914.
22. *Forward,* 22, 31 October 1914.
23. Hayes, *Conscription Conflict,* p. 150.
24. *The Glasgow Herald,* 8 December 1914.
25. *The Glasgow Herald,* 18 November 1914.
26. *Daily Record,* 1 December 1914.
27. *Forward,* 21 November 1914.
28. *Forward,* 28 November 1914; Milton, *John Maclean,* p. 107.
29. Hayes, *Conscription Conflict,* p. 249.
30. Hayes, *Conscription Conflict,* p. 251.
31. Rae, *Conscience and Politics,* p. 12.
32. Ibid. pp. 83–4.
33. Harvie, 'Before the Breakthrough', p. 23.
34. *Forward,* 2 January 1915.
35. Ibid. 2 January 1915.
36. Marwick, 'Conscientious objection in Scotland in the First World War', pp. 157–60; Brown, '"A Solemn purification by fire"', pp. 82–104.
37. *Forward,* 21 November 1914; Marwick, 'Conscientious objection in Scotland', p. 160.
38. *Forward,* 21 January 1915.
39. Ibid. 21 January and 13 February 1915.
40. *The Glasgow Herald,* 28 May 1915.
41. *People's Journal,* Dundee edition, 16 January 1916.
42. *Forward,* 25 December 1915.
43. MacDougall, *'Hard Work, ye Ken',* p. 28.
44. *People's Journal,* 20 November 1915.
45. *People's Journal,* 22 January 1915.
46. *People's Journal,* 11 March 1916.
47. *People's Journal,* 15 April 1916.
48. Referred to in a later letter in *Forward,* 22 March 1919.
49. *Forward,* 13 February 1915.
50. *Forward,* 13 and 27 March 1915.
51. *Edinburgh Evening Dispatch,* 6 April 1915, and *Sutherland Echo,* 7 April 1915.
52. *Dundee Courier,* and the *Aberdeen Free Press,* 7 April 1915.
53. *Edinburgh Evening News,* 6 April 1915.
54. *Aberdeen Evening Express,* 6 April 1915.
55. *Forward,* 29 May 1915.
56. *Forward,* 21 May to 12 June 1915.

57. Hayes, *Conscription Conflict*, p. 161.
58. Ibid. pp. 218, 224–5.
59. *Forward,* 12 June 1915.
60. Hayes, *Conscription Conflict*, p. 230.
61. *The Glasgow Herald*, 5, 17 January 1916, and *The Scotsman*, 17 January 1916.
62. Hayes, *Conscription Conflict*, p. 233.
63. *Labour Leader*, 25 February and 18 March; *Forward,* 13 March 1915.
64. *Forward,* 18 December 1915.
65. *Forward,* 19 February 1916.
66. *Forward,* 11 March 1916.
67. *Forward,* 15 July 1916.
68. *Forward,* 2 September 1916.
69. *Forward,* 26 February 1916.
70. *Berwickshire News*, 29 February 1916.
71. *Forward,* 4 March 1916.
72. Harvie, 'Before the Breakthrough', p. 23; Marwick, 'Conscientious Objectors', p. 157.
73. *Forward,* 4 March 1916.
74. *Forward,* 1 April 1916.
75. *Forward,* 29 April 1916.
76. *Forward,* 25 March 1916.
77. Rae, *Conscience and Politics*, p. 98.
78. *Forward,* 1 April 1916.
79. Rae, *Conscience and Politics*, p. 99; *The Glasgow Herald*, 16 March 1916.
80. *The Northern Scot, and Moray and Nairn Express*, 8 July 1916.
81. *The Northern Scot, and Moray and Nairn Express*, 2 August 1916, and information from William Leslie's daughter, Mrs Margaret Short, December 1996.
82. Harvie, 'Before the Breakthough', p. 23.
83. Maxton, 'War Resistance By Working Class Struggle', pp. 213–22.
84. Ibid. p. 220.
85. *Forward,* 28 September 1916.
86. Marwick, *The Deluge*, p. 81.
87. Hayes, *Conscription Conflict*, p. 260.
88. *Forward,* 28 April 1917.
89. *Aberdeen Evening Express*, 23 May 1918; *Forward,* 15 June 1918.
90. *Forward,* 27 July 1918.
91. Ibid.
92. *Forward,* 26 October 1918.
93. *Forward,* 23 February 1918.
94. *Forward,* 26 October 1918.
95. Ibid., and see earlier report 19 March 1918: 'ILP gaining ground in Scotland'.

96. Harvie, *'Before the Breakthrough'*, p. 24.
97. Hayes, *Conscription Conflict*, p. 226.
98. Marwick, 'Conscientious objection in Scotland', p. 160.
99. *Forward*, 27 September 1919.
100. *Forward*, 26 October 1918.

7

War and Revolution and the Scottish Working Class

INTRODUCTION

In an article that appeared in the *Sunday Herald* in January 2000, as part of the re-launch of *The Legend of Red Clydeside*, Ian McLean asserted that 'We must free ourselves from the rosy myth of Red Clydeside'. The 'socialism of Glasgow did real harm to the West of Scotland' and that was 'the real legacy of Red Clydeside'.[1] McLean's view not only negates some of the real accomplishments made during this period, but suggests that little of significance occurred beyond Clydeside. There is still much more that can be said regarding 'Red Clyde' than McLean's limited vision and somewhat narrow perspective allows. Indeed, viewed from a broader geographical perspective, and examined from the standpoint of the actions and activities of workers beyond the west of Scotland before, during, and after the war, there is clear evidence to proclaim that Scotland was both 'Radical' and 'Red', and this matter should not simply be measured in relation to the action and activities of the working class of West Scotland.[2] It is also clear that McLean's book is not the last word on the topic. This chapter will demonstrate that other nerve centres of discontent were forming beyond the west, in cities such as Aberdeen, Dundee, Edinburgh and the mining districts of Fife and the east coast. The actions of Scottish war resisters clearly demonstrate that they were politically active across much of Scotland, and that the impact of the Russian Revolution only added an impetus and further momentum in the development of the radical left throughout the country. Scotland's war may have ended in November 1918, but in brokering peace on the 'Home Front' there were still many battles ahead, and there was also some unfinished business to attend to. This chapter begins by completing the story of conscientious objectors in peacetime, and the new problems faced by the NCF and the ILP in Scotland.

CONSCIENTIOUS OBJECTORS IN PEACETIME

Despite the formal end to hostilities in 1918, the political struggle for the ILP, the NCF and *Forward* continued unabated. In the first place they were faced with the task of mobilising opinion to fight for the repeal of the Military Service Act. Moreover, along with the NCF, the ILP was also greatly concerned with the concessions to militarism contained in the Education Act, which allowed local authorities to introduce camps, drills and special military lessons in schools. A letter to *Forward* in January 1919 stated simply: 'Military training had to be driven from the schools'. Meanwhile, by March 1919, a further concern was the continuing plight of the conscientious objectors, whose continued imprisonment remained 'a challenge to whatever sense of justice' still prevailed in Britain.[3]

In that same March 1919 edition of *Forward*, there appeared an upsetting and sad account of yet 'Another Victim' of the government's determination to punish the COs, that had only recently come to light. It was reported first that in February 1918 Charles Yachnies, a Russian Jew, Socialist and ILP member from the Glasgow Gorbals, was taken to Maryhill Barracks after refusing to take up military service. He assured his friends that they could rely on him 'to remain true to the cause of International Socialism', and that 'he would not submit himself to military authority'. He was in perfect physical condition, and regarded by all who knew him as a highly intelligent individual. Nothing more was heard of him until an NCF and ILP member attempted to track him down and, in December 1918, wrote to the prison authorities to enquire into his condition and general health. They learned that Yachnies had been imprisoned in Wormwood Scrubs up until mid-May, at which time he was certified insane, and then transferred on to Colney Hatch Asylum. On his arrival he was described as being 'in an acutely excited condition', and was diagnosed as suffering from jaundice. He died in July of pulmonary tuberculosis. He was described and treated as a 'criminal lunatic – previously unknown'. *Forward* concluded: 'Capitalism took just five months with Army Prison and Asylum to reduce our comrade to insanity, jaundice, consumption, and death'.[4] Perhaps the authorities had read the piece by the good doctor from Morningside in Edinburgh, subsequently reported in the *People's Journal* in March 1916, that there were only two types of COs: lunatics and liars. It was clear that Charles Yachnies had been proclaimed a lunatic, for he evidently died proving he was not a liar. For some there was no justice, particularly when the military became involved. Seventy-one men died in prisons as a result of their experiences of barrack-room justice, and the indignities of the guard-room.⁵ It is not clear whether Charles Yachnies was counted among them.

In March 1919 the campaign to free the COs was stepped up, when *Forward* printed an article, 'The Quiet Safety of Prison', written by W. J. Chamberlain. The article was a response to 'the cruellest slander ever uttered against the COs in prison', and was made by Sir George Cave, the late Home Secretary, who argued that some preferred the 'quiet safety of prison to the more strenuous life of the soldier in the trenches'. For Chamberlain, this was a deliberate attempt to 'mislead the public' as to the true facts of the conscientious objector's case. Sir George Cave knew only too well that the only choice open to the CO was not between prison and the trenches, but between prison and the 'acceptance of work of national importance'. Chamberlain wrote of his own experiences of prison, and noted how the COs and 'soldier prisoners' – those on active duty convicted of serious crimes – were mixed together almost fifty-fifty. For about a week or more, these soldiers thought they were better off than in the trenches. But as the weeks went by, the prison regime began to 'break their resolve', and they petitioned the War Office for 'remission of sentence'; this was nearly always granted 'on condition that the prisoner went back to the front'. Chamberlain concluded that 'every man gladly accepted this condition in order to escape from the horror of the prison regime'.⁶ But for the COs there was no hope of release unless they broke faith with their conscience.

In April it was reported that the government did intend to release 'all COs who had served two years or more' – a move welcomed by the editors of *Forward*, who reminded readers of their duty to these men on their return. They would require 'careful attention, nourishing food, and a good holiday' in order to restore them to good health. To that end a committee was formed comprising the NCF, the ILP and the SLP and others, to raise £4,000 to help returning COs who were expected to be back among them within the course of a fortnight. Ironically, in the following edition, a front-page editorial spoke scathingly of Mr Lloyd George, and his 'party', and their seeming opposition to Churchill's proposed Conscription Bill, which aimed to continue and extend the military conscription in Britain. 'If we are not careful', the editors of *Forward* advised, 'the party that gave us conscription (saladed with trickeries about conscientious objection and attestation) will sweep back into power on a No-Conscription ticket!'⁷

At a meeting at St Andrew's Hall, Glasgow on 11 April 1919, a large crown turned out to hear various speakers at a rally calling for 'Abolition of Conscription and the release of all Conscientious Objectors'. One of the speakers was W. J. Chamberlain, himself only recently released from prison, who reminded his audience:

> That they had been accused of being afraid of their skins, but it was a remark-
> able fact that since the fighting had stopped 240 men had been offered com-
> parative freedom if they would just put on Khaki before demobilisation, and
> not a single man would accept the offer.[8]

Compulsory military conscription was finally abolished in December 1920 just under five years after it was introduced. For those who hoped that it would 'flush out hordes of slackers' it had proved disappointing. In the first six months of conscription, numbers enlisting fell to around 40,000 per month, which was less than half the rate of recruitment under the voluntary system at its lowest.[9] In all there had been around 16,500 conscientious objectors to conscription in Britain, but only 1,500 of these were absolutists, who would not fight the war under any circumstances, and a full five months after the war had ended, some 1,300 were still in prison.[10] As Martin Ceadel argues, although they only accounted for 0.33 per cent of the total of all other conscripts plus volunteers, 'they had a public impact out of proportion to their numbers'.[11]

For those war resisters still in prison, release did eventually come, but many had to serve out their sentence in full before they finally escaped their incarceration. Despite the severity of the sentences, and the desper-ate conditions that many had to endure, they were still victimised even after their release. 'Displaying a conspicuous pique', noted Gerald De Groot, 'Parliament disenfranchised all conscientious objectors for five years (beyond the enactment of the 1918 Representation of the People Act) unless they could prove that they had performed work of national importance'.[12]

FIFE, THE REVOLUTIONARY LEFT AND SOCIALIST POLITICS

In an article that appeared in January 2000, Iain McLean noted his concern that the 'legend of Red Clydeside' was still 'hanging on grimly in modern Scottish life'. Yet it is somewhat ironic that in re-launching his book in 1999, McLean was introducing a whole new generation of readers to the debate on Red Clyde, and at a time when there were clear signs of renewed interest in this area of research within the Scottish his-torical community. Some months later a panel presented 'New Views on Red Clyde' – five fresh perspectives on the Red Clyde debate – at the European Social Science History Conference, Amsterdam, in April 2000. Three held to the usual geographical parameters, but nonetheless demonstrated that the Red Clyde debate still had a resonance in present-day Scotland, while two considered the causes and impact of political change beyond the confines of the west of Scotland.[13]

Concerning events beyond Clydeside, William Kenefick looked into the impact of war and the Russian Revolution on the trade union and labour movement in Aberdeen, and Neil Rafeek considered the 'little Moscows' that were appearing across Scotland, and the role and impact of the Communist Party of Great Britain (CPGB) between 1919 and 1945. Most CPGB members were male and the great majority lived in the west of Scotland, but Rafeek was principally concerned with female membership, and he also explored the growth and development of left-wing radicalism and communism in Fife and Aberdeen. Building on an extensive collection of oral testimony from across Scotland, he examined the role of women in the CPGB, the Young Communist League (YCL) and the Socialist Sunday Schools (SSS), in order to investigate the manner in which young women learned their socialist beliefs when still effectively cut off from the traditional routes into politics during the interwar years. It became clear that, when compared to the female members of the ILP, Communist women had political organisations which generally encouraged equality, rather than pursuing the 'archaic ideology' of the ILP which, Annmarie Hughes argued, promoted traditional gender values based on a well-defined sexual division of labour.[14]

The mining community in Fife was particularly radicalised, and had already formed centres of radical activity before the war, which were to become strongholds for the CPGB in Scotland from the 1920s. Many miners were strongly on the left, staunch supporters and defenders of the Russian Revolution, and active in the Hands Off Russia Campaign. Rafeek also discovered the existence of a Marxist Proletarian Sunday School Movement, which believed that the Socialist Sunday Schools and the Communist Party were not revolutionary enough. They advocated outright class war, and adopted an approach similar to the old Socialist Labour Party (SLP), and their message was unequivocally aimed towards the youth of the country. In Fife, the Proletarian Sunday School Movement used the songbook of the International Workers of the World (IWW), and was organised by the daughter of a French émigré who founded an Anarchist Communist League in Scotland. The CPGB, the YCL and the Socialist and Proletarian Sunday School movements, had a considerable level of support in Fife, and by the 1930s, Communists in Fife accounted for 13 per cent of the total party membership in Scotland.[15]

Like the impact of the socialism of the SDF and BSP, or the syndicalism of the SLP in Edinburgh, it is clear that the roots of militant left-radicalism in Fife were already strongly embedded before the war years. This is indicated in Rafeek's work, and confirmed in the recollections of John McArthur regarding the level of militancy in the mining and working-class districts dotted around Methil and Buckhaven in Fife. He noted the strength and influence of the SDF and later the BSP in this area before 1914, and said that despite the split within the BSP over support of the war, the cause of socialism remained strong in Fife. McArthur noted that militant trade unionists and socialists in Fife had contact with the Clyde Shop Stewards during the later stages of the war, and 'they took a close interest in the Irish Trouble in Fife':

> There was quite a number of Irish Militants in Fife with whom we had a close association because in those days Irishmen were expected to be 'agin the Government' and for the trade union and labour movement. Without exception all of them that I knew were militant left trade unionists and politicians.

They introduced Countess Markiewicz to a 'packed' meeting at the Co-op Hall in Methil, where 'she got a tremendous reception', and they were strongly influenced too by James Connolly and James Larkin. Indeed, because of his close connection with the Irish revolutionary Connolly and other Irish militants, McArthur 'took a close interest in the 1916 Easter Rising in Dublin'.[16]

But it was the impact of the Russian Revolution and the role of John Maclean that was to have 'a profound affect' on politics in Fife; for Maclean was 'a hero among [the] young miners' of Fife, and it was through Maclean's connections with South Wales that the syndicalist-styled Miners' Reform Committee became established. McArthur also noted the role of James MacDougall in raising interest in and awareness of the activities of the Shop Stewards movement in Fife, and attended ILP propaganda meetings to hear Jimmy Maxton and Willie Stewart from Edinburgh (the editor of *Forward*) during the war. Other speakers included Tom Bell and Arthur McManus, Jimmy Clunie and Jimmy Birrell from Dunfermline who were SLP 'Marxian lecturers', and Jack Leckie (of Irish extraction) who was chairman of the Scottish Communist Labour Party (CLP) – which McArthur noted was formed in Glasgow in October 1920 (after absorbing most of the SLP branches). They were also addressed on many occasions by Aberdonian Thomas Kennedy of the SDF (who remained a member of the SDF until its demise in 1941), and who won the by-election in the Kirkcaldy Burgh in Fife in 1921 (he lost it in 1922, regained it in 1923, and retained it until 1931). Led by Jimmy Clunie and Jimmy Birrell of the SLP, a broad socialist group formed the Fife Communist League, which included ILP elements, the BSP and the

Miners' Reform Committee. 'The League was the beginning of a unified political party' in Fife, noted McArthur, and although not initially connected to any national organisation, it was to affiliate to Sylvia Pankhurst's British Section of the Third International after it was formed.[17]

The events that were taking place in Methil and Buckhaven were also the subject of some discussion in Moscow. For example, Tom Bell, on a visit there in August 1921, reported to Lenin on a miners' strike in Methil and Buckhaven, and that a Defence Force of marines had been drafted in to the district to help to 'police' a coal strike. He noted that the marines were openly sympathetic towards the miners, as indeed were the police, and fraternised with them in their off-duty moments. Some of the officers became so concerned about this situation 'that they took away parts of the rifles from some of the soldiers and kept others without ammunition'. He also recounted the case of a strike at Fallin in Stirlingshire, where strikers were angry about the use of scab labour and made attempts to 'clear them out'. As the strikers moved in on the scabs, an officer 'gave the command to fire':

> A soldier shouted to the crowd that they had no ammunition. Another soldier held up a white flag. The officer's command was obviously bluff, and the crowd broke through to the scabs . . . The soldiers were found (later) to be singing and whistling the 'Red Flag' in the streets, and allowed the strikers all kinds of license.

In response to Bell's report, Lenin replied that, 'Perhaps it is the beginning of a real proletarian mass movement in great Britain in the communist sense. Fraternisation between miners and soldiers', he concluded hopefully, 'might prove the beginning of a class war, and everything should be done to develop and strengthen this movement'.[18] Indeed, Communist activity in the mining areas of Fife – like in the city of Dundee – were regularly featured in the Moscow-bound reports to the Politburo in the 1920s and 1930s.

EDINBURGH AND LEITH – THE POLITICS OF LABOUR REFORMED

It is clear that in the general history of the Scottish trade union and labour movement, developments in Edinburgh have been somewhat overshadowed by the narrative of events taking place at Glasgow. The structure of Edinburgh industry and the composition of its workforce was also different from Glasgow, and unlike other industrial regions in Scotland, there was no 'major concentration of its working population in a single industry'.[19] Edinburgh's industry relied largely on artisan labour and, with a much stronger middle-class, was considered a more bourgeois and less proletarian city than Glasgow. Indeed, the city's early socialist pioneers were drawn overwhelmingly from the ranks of the middle and professional classes and the artisan elite. The trade union and labour movement in Edinburgh was similarly influenced by skilled crafts-men, and was viewed as less militant, and it was perhaps for the reason that the Webbs believed there was 'a scarcely concealed rivalry between Edinburgh and Glasgow'.[20]

Over the years there have been several important studies into Edinburgh's trade union and labour movement, but arguably one of the most accomplished for the period it covers is John Holford's *Reshaping Labour: Organisation, Work and Politics – Edinburgh in the Great War and After* (1983). His work is a detailed examination of the industrial and political life of Edinburgh, and considers the impact of the Great War and, to a lesser extent, the Russian Revolution. Despite the fact that the engi-neering sector was much smaller when compared to Glasgow, the engineers nevertheless 'made a substantial contribution to the labour movement' in Edinburgh and during the war were part of a viable shop steward's move-ment. Holford also made special note of the transport workers, and in particular the railwaymen, and their contribution to the developing left-political culture of the city both before and after the war. The railwaymen of the NUR at Edinburgh embraced the theories of syndicalism as they moved ever closer towards realising their goal of creating a mass industrial union.[21] An industrial truce was agreed when hostilities broke out in August 1914, and remained in place throughout the war, but it did not halt industrial conflict. Militant elements within the NUR increasingly 'drew their inspiration and theory from syndicalists and socialists', and in Edinburgh they became highly critical of the leaders of the NUR.[22]

The relationship between the industrial and political wings of the trade union and labour movement in Edinburgh had been growing stronger since the 1880s and 1890s, and resulted in greater cooperation between the Trades Council and the socialist movement on the 'inde-pendent labour' issue. The ILP in particular was useful to the trade unions, for while it was 'explicitly a socialist organisation', its lack of a 'coherent political philosophy' made it more amenable, and thus trade unionists allied themselves to the ILP for electoral purposes. But the war halted this progress. There was a significant anti-war faction operating in Edinburgh during the war, but it was not as well organised or as exten-sive as the movements taking shape in Aberdeen, which by May 1918 had a 'pacifist majority' on the Trades Council.[23] Generally speaking, the war acted to sever the organisational links between the trade unions, the

Edinburgh Trades Council and the ILP. But the ILP's opposition to wartime control, profiteering, military and industrial conscription, and violations of civil liberties, at a time of growing war-weariness found favour among a growing body of workers. Indeed, between 1917 and 1918 the ILP in Edinburgh became 'the largest socialist organisation in the city', and during the last years of the war 'had close informal connections with trade unions'. The BSP did not do so well, but the SLP fared better because of its links with the 'shop stewards and other trade unions movements during the war'.[24]

In fusing industrial and political theory with theories of industrial and political action, those attracted to syndicalism and socialism maintained their political perspective throughout the war, and the October Revolution in Russia in 1917 further strengthened this development. By January 1919, like the Trade Councils across Scotland, the council in Edinburgh set up what was to become a highly influential 'Hands Off Russia' Committee, and in so doing forged closer ties between the trade union and the political movements. It seemed that virtually all sections of the labour movement were fascinated by the workers revolution, so much so that when a speaker such as Willie Gallagher, fresh from Moscow where he was a delegate at the second Congress of the Communist International in the summer of 1920, spoke to packed halls all across Scotland. He appeared at the Usher Hall in Edinburgh, and shared the same platform as the Trades and Labour Council Executive. Many argued that this level of support was primarily due to war weariness in peace-time, but as Holford argued, this factor alone could not have been responsible for the large turnout at such events.[25]

Marxist economic classes, which under the Labour College restarted in 1916, continued with greater purpose between then and 1922. These were already well developed before the war and were made increasingly made by popular lecturers such as John Maclean (SDF and BSP) and the SLP's 'most accomplished propagandist', John S. Clarke. Indeed, when Clarke spoke at public meetings in working-class districts before the war, 'as many as 2,000 people at a time' turned out. Clarke also delivered a series of lectures on syndicalism to the No. 1 branch of the NUR between 1912 and 1913, which led Holford to suggest that 'from the branch's post-war attitude, there is every reason to believe he made some impact'. Thereafter syndicalism 'became the focal point of the railwaymen's revolutionary industrial unionism' in the city.[26]

After the war the railwaymen opened up their Marxian economic classes to other occupations in Edinburgh, while the engineers organised classes with the ILP. In 1920 the Edinburgh District of the Scottish

Labour College (SLC) merged with the Marxian School of Economics to form one single organisation for Marxian education in the city. William McKie noted the expansion of Marxian education by the SLC, and how it was extended from Edinburgh to the 'mining villages', and through the miners reached the agricultural workers. In these districts, classes were held at night in the homes of workers and so the movement spread, while in Edinburgh, noted McKie:

> They had a place, a middle class home [with] about 10 or 20 rooms . . . and a dining room that was used as a lecture hall, and where on Sundays we probably had 70 or 80 people there all day. You had one class from 10 to 12; one from 3 to 5, and somebody else would have a class from 6 to 8 because we used to hold meetings on Sundays nights as well. So that went on for a couple of years . . . We were able to influence a lot of people.[27]

These classes were clearly successful, and from 1919 enrolment levels increased across the country. In Edinburgh they had 120 students in four classes during 1919–20, but this increased to over 600 in eighteen classes by January 1921. By June of that year there were 700 workers in twenty-one classes.[28]

Much of the growth and interest in Marxist education was stimulated by the threat of allied intervention in Russia, and as a result the 'Hands Off Russia' campaign was launched in January 1919. When it looked likely that Britain would intervene on the side of Poland during the Polish-Russian conflict during the summer of 1920, the trade union and labour movement rallied quickly to pressure the government against such actions. The Shop Stewards' Movement in engineering, and the Forth Workers' Committee also encouraged attendance at Marxist education classes, and the railwaymen continued to participate in ever greater numbers. Thus Marxist views flourished among a wide group of workers at Edinburgh and this gained support for the left political parties. After the formation of the Trades and Labour Council in Edinburgh in 1920, however, the Labour Party became the main beneficiary of the transformation of the labour movement in the city.

DUNDEE – THE PRINCIPAL STRONGHOLD OF COMMUNISM IN SCOTLAND

The city of Dundee had been making its own distinctive contribution to the development of the trade union and labour movement in Scotland. Bob Stewart, a Marxist and Prohibitionist, was an active trade unionist and a shipyard shop steward, and on occasions a town councillor. In 1909 he severed his ties with the Scottish Prohibitionist Party and formed the Prohibitionist and Reform Party (PRF). The PRF sought 'complete National Prohibition', 'Socialism', 'Complete Democratic Rule', and 'Internationalism'. Stewart had been involved in the labour unrest in Dundee, and helped to organise the rent strike with the help of the BSP, the ILP and the Dundee Trades Council in 1912. In 1915 he became the local organiser for the Scottish Horse and Motormen's Association, and rejoined the Dundee Trades Council, where he could play his part alongside other like-minded individuals in the fight against the war and conscription. He was also a conscientious objector, and served four separate jail sentences for refusing military service from 1916. He was only finally released from prison in April 1919, and he went immediately back into politics.[29]

Bob Stewart was intimately involved with the 'prohibition' issue, and during the war, because 'it had absorbed many facets of socialism into its policy', the PRF was renamed the Socialist Prohibition Fellowship (SPF). Stuart addressed meetings all over the country on 'Prohibition and Socialism' and because of the SPF's links with the wider prohibition movement, he took his Socialist message to a much greater audience. He actively participated in the 'Hands Off Russia' movement, but as unemployment began to rise at an alarming rate by 1920, he became increasingly occupied with establishing an Unemployed Workers' Committee in Dundee. He was also destined to become a main player in the formation of the CPGB in 1920. After addressing a socialist propaganda meeting in Aberdeen in early 1920, he was approached by Tom Bell and Arthur McManus, and together in April they formed the Communist Unity Group. They held their first conference on 31 July and 1 August 1920, and from this the CPGB came into being. McManus was elected chairman, and Albert Inkpin secretary, and along with Dora Montefiore and four others (including a late convert to communism, the somewhat mysterious Colonel Malone), Stewart was elected onto the executive committee of the party. He was also made Scottish organiser. The party was not yet fully formed, however, for Sylvia Pankhurst's British Section of the Third International and and Jack Leckie's Scottish Communist Labour Party still remained outside the fold. But after the important 'Leeds Conference' in January 1921, all three came together and 'the foundation of the British Communist Party was laid'.

Shortly afterwards Stewart was arrested for sedition for a speech made at a May Day rally in South Wales. After his release in July he stood as the Communist candidate in the Caerphilly by-election in 1921. Helen Crawfurd, Walton Newbold (who was to win Motherwell for the CP in 1922), McManus and Gallagher – among many others – formed his campaign group, but he came last polling nearly 2,600 votes, in a three-cornered contest, which the Labour Party won easily. The next election in which he was involved was in Dundee, where Willie Gallagher was standing for the Communists, against Churchill, in the general election of November 1922. Neither Churchill nor Gallagher was destined to win, but they nonetheless attracted most press and public attention during the election. Churchill had wanted to maintain conscription, and continually attacked Russia and the Communists, which lost him much working-class support in Dundee. Gallagher attracted support from many non-Communists 'because of his powerful personality and forceful campaigning' style.[30] Churchill was relegated to fourth place in a six-horse race, and Edwin Scrymgeour, the Dundee SPP leader and hitherto anti-war activist and anti-conscriptionist, and left-wing pacifist and socialist E. D. Morel of the Labour Party were elected for Dundee's two-seat constituency. Gallagher came last of the six candidates, attracting nearly 6,000 votes (which he pushed up to 10,380 the following year).[31] According to Stewart, 'Willie had no romantic ideas about this election. His main aim was to expose Churchill and contribute to his final defeat and this he did handsomely as the final result showed'. Indeed, in a letter to the Soviet Politiburo after the election, Tom Bell asserted that '75 per cent of the credit for Churchill's defeat' was due to the communists and the good work done by a cadre of seventy active party members at Dundee.[32]

Mary Brooksbank and Jock Thomson were two other well-known Dundee left-radicals and Communists, who were intimately involved with the pacifist movement in the city, staunch supporters of the Russian workers' state, and dedicated activists in the Unemployed Workers' Movement in Dundee. Indeed, in 1922 they were both arrested for breach of the peace for their involvement in an Unemployed Workers' Committee demonstration. Thomson and Brooksbank were found guilty and received sixty and forty days imprisonment respectively, while 'twenty others got fines and lesser sentences'.[33] Immediately upon her release from prison, Brooksbank attended 'a great rally' held at the Caird Hall against 'Bolshevism and Communism', which was 'sponsored by all the religious denominations in the city':

> No sooner did the chairman start to speak than there were interruptions from all over the hall. During the lull, I asked the chairman why the reverend gentlemen had made no protest at the mass slaughter between 1914 and 1918? I was immediately seized and hustled out to a waiting [police] van.[34]

Two other young women were bundled into the police wagon with her, because two plain-clothes policemen overheard them mutter 'Oh! It's

Mary!' as she was whisked past them. In court she pleaded guilty, but protested that the other women had not even been in the hall, and that they were completely innocent. They were released, and she was fined 'three guineas'. But the incident demonstrated 'the bitter hatred of those in authority' towards those on the political left in their efforts to draw attention to the problems of the unemployed.

Brooksbank's great mentor Jock Thomson died in 1923 and as befitted 'a real man of the people', 10,000 people followed his coffin to its final resting place. Thomson was 'a kindly man who felt deeply for the wrongs inflicted on his class' and 'a continual thorn in the side of the authorities', particularly on the unemployment question.[35] Brooksbank and Stewart, and a host of other Dundee radicals and communists, thereafter put much of their time and energy into the Unemployed Workers' Movement, and Marxist education. So much so that by the early 1930s Dundee was considered 'the principal stronghold of communism in Scotland'.[36]

ABERDEEN – 'MORE RED THAN GLASGOW'

In a letter to the Russian Congress in Moscow in 1920, William Leslie, one of Scotland's lesser-known revolutionaries, argued that relative to its population 'Aberdeen was more Red than Glasgow'.[37] But just how accurate was Leslie's political analysis of north-east Scotland and the city of Aberdeen? Unlike Dundee, Edinburgh and Glasgow or the coalfields of Lanarkshire, the Lothians or Fife, Aberdeen was rarely portrayed as a centre of radical industrial working-class activity in the years immediately before the Great War. Apart from a few notable exceptions, there has been very little written about working-class industrial politics in Aberdeen. William Diack's *History of the Trades Council and Trade Union Movement* (1939), Kenneth Buckley's *Trade Unionism in Aberdeen 1887 to 1900* (1955), and C. W. M. Phipps' 'Aberdeen Trades Council and Politics 1900 to 1939' (1980) are the most obvious examples.[38] Indeed, this recently prompted Terry Brotherstone to make a plea for further detailed study into Aberdeen's rich and largely untapped labour history.[39]

With a left-radical history and reputation dating back to the 1880s (and beyond), it is somewhat ironic that Aberdeen seemed so disconnected form the broader Scottish trade union and labour scene before the First World War. It was the Aberdeen Trades Council in 1895 that called for a meeting of all the Scottish Trades Councils which led to the birth of the Scottish Trades Union Congress in 1987. The city adopted Henry Champion to stand as an independent Labour candidate in the early

1890s, and in 1896 the Aberdeen Trades Council adopted Tom Mann to fight Aberdeen North. Indeed, in a straight fight with the Liberal candidate, 'Mann came within a whisker of winning being beaten by a mere 433 votes'.[40] Thomas Kennedy ran as an SDF/Labour candidate at Aberdeen during the general election in 1906, where he polled a respectable 2,000 votes. He also had John Maclean as his election agent, who in assisting Kennedy, had his first taste of parliamentary electioneering.[41]

Yet despite this rich left-radical history and the city's strong political association with the socialism, not discounting the Aberdeen Trades Council's close links with the ILP, the SDF and later the BSP, it seemed that workers in Aberdeen were somewhat apathetic during the labour unrest.[42] Was it therefore the impact of the First World War and the experience of Bolshevism in Russia that transformed and promoted working-class politics in the city? Affiliated membership to the Aberdeen Trades Council did rise considerably during the war. It was just over 5,000 in 1912, had increased to 7,200 by 1914, but had more than doubled to reach 16,684 by 1920. The growing industrial strength of the city's working class paralleled the political developments that were taking place elsewhere, when in 1918 Frank Rose was elected as the city's Labour MP, although his election 'was as much a surprise to local party members as anyone else'.[43] Nevertheless, Rose was one of only seven Labour MPs elected in Scotland in 1918, at a time when Labour could only win one out of fifteen seats in Glasgow.[44] Moreover, in the local elections in November 1919 Aberdeen's labour candidates won six out of eleven seats – including A. Fraser Macintosh who stood as an Independent Socialist and publicly-proclaimed 'Bolshevist'.[45] Thus, according to Phipps:

> The wave of working class militancy which swept Britain in the years after 1918 and was, at least in part, due to the sympathetic response to the Bolshevik Revolution and its aim and principles, was reflected in Aberdeen.[46]

It is clear that the level of industrial militancy in Aberdeen was rising significantly even before the armistice was declared in November 1918. Labour's presence had been growing in Aberdeen for some time, the BSP carried great influence on the Trades Council, and the SLP was also making its presence felt. Aberdeen was also more closely connected with the broader Scottish labour and trade union movement after the war. The Aberdeen Trade Council supported political action, following a resolution from the Clyde District Propaganda Defence Committee, in October 1918, which declared:

> This council views with great indignation the persistent repression of working class liberties in the suppression of free speech and press. We further protest

against the harsh and vindictive sentence passed on John Maclean and demand his immediate and unconditional release.[47]

Other issues included an expansion of educational provision for the study of 'Industrial History and Economics', and in November 1918 the Trades Council agreed that the SLP (which William Leslie was involved with at this time) should conduct these classes. It also approved support for a measure of home rule, separate legislative assemblies for matters of local concern, and that Westminster should be retained as a federal assembly. They also agreed that steps should be taken to 'fight for the establishment of a real People's Party' in the city, and to provide support for the SLP and its fight against the government over closing down its printing and propaganda facilities in Glasgow.[48]

December 1918 saw the Aberdeen council adopt a resolution from the Merthyr Tydfil Trades Council which supported 'non-intervention' and the argued against the use of allied forces in Russia for 'capitalist purposes', and demanded a recall of all British forces 'at once'. In January 1919 the council agreed to assist in 'Co-ordinating the Labour and Socialist Forces in Aberdeen' with a view to running demonstrations in support of the 'Hand Off Russia' campaign, and also agreed to back demands for a general strike in support of the Forty-Hour Movement.[49] After the arrest and incarceration of Shinwell, Gallacher, Kirkwood and others in the aftermath of the 'Battle of George Square', the council agreed to mount a protest against the 'continued imprisonment of the Clyde strikers' and to assist the ILP and the SLP in Aberdeen in organising demonstrations on their behalf.[50]

By the end of 1919 many strikes were being reported among laundry workers, city waitresses, trawlermen, fishermen and engineering apprentices, and all were supported by the Aberdeen Trades Council. The main political concern at this time, however, was 'the immediate establishment of trade relations with Soviet Russia', and in 1920 the Trades Council also asserted its support for the Highland Land League, and protested against the serving of interdicts on Raasay landraiders during the summer of 1920.[51] By 1920 the Trades Council feared the British government was considering sending men, arms and munitions to the aid of Poland, and it issued a resolution that 'Organised labour can and will resort to direct action if this happens', and demanded that Britain immediately end its blockade of Soviet Russia.[52]

The Aberdeen Trades Council was largely responsible for keeping alive the spirit of labour politics in the city. Indeed, the Trades Council held it all together and controlled and influenced not only the industrial wing of the labour movement, but also the political wing (especially after the collapse of the local Labour Party in 1918).[53] The role of the Trades Council in Aberdeen was important in other ways, for as Phipps rightly notes, the left in Britain saw Trades Councils as 'potential soviets for the coming revolution and after 1920 they became prime targets for communist infiltration'. Communists may have been banned from membership of the Labour Party by the early 1920s, but their voices could be heard within local Labour Parties, and when they became delegates on the industrial wing of the Trades Councils.[54]

But what does this tell us of the wider social impact of the First World War and the Russian Revolution in Aberdeen? Even before the establishment of the Aberdeen Communist Group in September 1919, there were regular press reports of 'Bolshevist' activity in and around Aberdeen. A meeting was called as early as December 1918 to form an 'Industrial Council or Soviet', chaired by a mysterious 'stranger' from Glasgow, and the meeting was read a telegram from John Maclean that stated simply: 'Aberdeen workers! Unite!' The meeting discussed 'the necessity for an Industrial Council or Soviet in view of the revolutionary activity on the Continents. The press reported that the action in Aberdeen 'was only part of a movement taking place all over Britain'.[55] But that night a 'provisional committee', or 'Industrial Council', was set up, and among those elected to it was Lewis Grassic Gibbon, essayist and author, then a reporter for an Aberdeen paper. Indeed, he was elected along with another 'cub reporter' who, when asked about the meeting afterwards by their chief reporters, replied that being 'good sovietists . . . they could not report the meeting'.[56]

The Aberdeen Trades Council declined to join the new 'Industrial Council', but this did not prevent it from getting involved in other initiatives and in particular the 'Hands Off Russia' campaign. At a meeting in February 1919, city hairdresser John Paton, Labour member of the Aberdeen School Board, argued for the full withdrawal of troops from Russia, and was seconded by J. C. Allan, the president of the Trades Council. The resolution was also supported by James Gordon, who declared openly 'that he was out for revolution first and foremost and all time . . . by and by they would find different parts of the world thinking and speaking in terms of revolution'. Mr Hay of the discharged Sailors' and Soldiers' Association from Glasgow added his voice: 'The soldiers recognised that their enemy was the same as the workers – the capitalists. Industrial action by all workers was the only way they could get better wages and better housing conditions'.[57] He concluded that the next flag he would fight for would be the Red Flag, for which he received loud applause. After the local elections in November 1919, the growing demand for 'Labour and Housing' became a major issue. This campaign got underway in 1920, and at one meeting in March around 300 people attended to hear 'Red Clydesider' David Kirkwood speak at a daytime meeting. Later that evening 1,500 people attended a meeting addressed by Kirkwood on the topic of the 'Great Betrayal of the Scottish Working Class' and the lack of provision for working-class housing as promised by the government.[58]

The ILP was by then ostensibly forging the political agenda in Aberdeen, but this did not mean that other left-wing groups were being marginalised: indeed, the ILP in Scotland was moving ever closer to the left in any case and was working closely with other socialist and revolutionary parties. Many on the revolutionary side viewed the ILP with a degree of suspicion. Sylvia Pankhurst, for example, when reporting to Moscow on the groups attending the 'Socialist Unity Conference' in January 1920, described the ILP as 'counter-revolutionary in character' although she added that the Scottish ILP had splits within the party.[59] The 'communist nucleus' within the ILP was the concern of Indian communist Shapurgi Saklatvala, who noted at a meeting in Glasgow that every effort was to be made to 'compel true hearted socialists and communists to come together within the ILP'.[60] By May 1920 Walton Newbold was able to confirm that a 'Left Wing Rank and File Group of the ILP' had emerged out of the Glasgow conference. It was an 'unofficial movement', but favoured immediate affiliation to the Third International, and it sought confirmation from Moscow on how it viewed the existing relationship between the ILP and the Labour Party:

> We want to know what your attitude is to our remaining affiliated to the Labour Party, towards the acceptance of the Workers' Committee or Soviet principle, towards participation in parliamentary and municipal elections and policy if elected, towards arming the proletariat and disarming the bourgeoisie ... The Left Wing of the ILP is now organising with a view of securing a majority for affiliation to the Third International at the ensuing Special Party Conference.

Newbold stressed that the stated aim of the Left Wing Group was to make the ILP a Communist Party, and to join with the BSP and any other parties to form One Communist Party. He concluded that the group would stand by any ruling from Moscow on these or other matters.[61] Indeed, Newbold, and later Helen Crawfurd (who was to stand as a Communist candidate in Aberdeen in the 1930s), confirmed not only the

ILP's commitment to the Third International, but also the setting-up of 'Soviet Councils' and the 'Dictatorship of the Proletariat'. Newbold stressed that the 'communist group within the ILP were committed to converting the ILP machine towards socialism.[62] Helen Crawfurd later reported that the Scottish ILP had agreed by 158 votes to twenty-eight to affiliate to the Third International.[63]

In the meantime the ILP in Aberdeen organised a large 'Hands Off Germany' rally in the city in the aftermath of the failed Sparticist revolution. The objective was to encourage support for the 'party of true socialists' who were 'demanding the execution of Herr Noske for the murder of Karl Liebkneckt and Rosa Luxemburg'. It was their duty 'to give support to the Sparticists in their revolution . . . acting on the same part in Germany as the bolshevists had done in Russia under Lenin and Trotsky'.[64] In an interesting, report to Moscow in March 1920, marked 'secret', J. T. Murphy, leader of the Sheffield shop stewards and a leading member of the CPGB, identified 'Macintyre of Aberdeen' as one of the main leaders 'of the Scottish left wing' who, with John Maclean, was one of the 'cleverest minds' on the political scene in Scotland.[65] It is likely that Murphy was in fact describing A. Fraser Macintosh, a well-known socialist and self-proclaimed Bolshevik, for there are no references to any Macintyre of that political stature in Aberdeen. It is nonetheless a further indicator of the high esteem in which the radical left in Aberdeen was held among leading Communist Party members by 1920.

The arrangements for the May Day rally in 1920 illustrate that the political left and the industrial wings of the Labour movement in Aberdeen were working closely together. The procession was led by Aberdeen's most famous Bolshevik, A. Fraser Macintosh, and the Painters Union, which was the most 'communist' of all the unions in the city. The Aberdeen Communist Group was in attendance with a banner urging 'Workers [to] Follow Bolshevik Russia', while representatives of the Co-operative Movement proclaimed 'Vive La International'. The Aberdeen Branch of the Scottish Labour Housing Committee (SLHC) stood behind a banner proclaiming 'Socialism – The Hope of the Workers', and the National Union of Ex-Servicemen stood behind one that read 'Promises of the Government to Ex-Servicemen – Died 11th November 1918'.[66] The Aberdeen SLHC was also very active and vigorously backed a resolution for the Glasgow branch to organise 'rent strikes' across Scotland. Fraser Macintosh disrupted a meeting of the Aberdeen Town Council during July over the government's intention to raise rents, and, 'in an incident without parallel in the municipal history of Aberdeen', the press reported that

Councillor Macintosh was removed from his seat and escorted out of the council chamber.[67]

Macintosh thereafter conducted his campaign through a series of street meetings in working-class areas around the city, and it was reported that he regularly attracted crowds of 200 people and more. By the end of July 1920 around 9,000 Aberdonians had signed a covenant to the effect that they would initiate rent strikes should there be any increase in rents.[68] In the nineteenth and early twentieth centuries the issue of housing in Scotland 'became a battleground for class struggles'. Indeed, it was felt by many that there was 'a greater likelihood that housing would generate class-consciousness than periodic bouts of industrial conflict', particularly when unemployment began to rise from the mid-1920 onwards. McCrone and Elliot correctly point out that, although during the war the 'Clydeside rent strikes were perhaps the best known', but that strikes occurred in other parts of the country including Aberdeen, Dundee and Edinburgh.[69] Rent increases were being called for at a time when the 'Scottish industrial economy slipped from boom conditions to the sharp and sustained depression', so it was an issue that had broad appeal across Scotland, and one in which the ILP was to take the leading role.[70]

As for William Leslie, the *Northern Scot* newspaper first reported on Leslie's trip to Russia, and his intention to speak to the people of Aberdeen on that subject upon his return. It was reported that his journey was far from trouble-free, and that when returning he had been arrested by the police in Norway.[71] He was released after going on hunger strike and arrested by Scotland Yard detectives at Newcastle, before being allowed to travel onto Aberdeen. The *Northern Scot* concluded that it was unclear whether Leslie 'achieved the dream of his life – the privilege of shaking Lenin by the hand', noting that Leslie was to speak at Aberdeen's 'Picturedrome' on Sunday 7 November.[72] All the Aberdeen newspapers reported on this meeting, and the *Aberdeen Daily Journal* published the story under the banner headline 'REVOLUTION OPENLY ADVOCATED IN ABERDEEN', and commented tersely on the 'communist wild talk of Mr Leslie'. It was noted that Leslie 'urged his hearers to follow the lead of the Russian working-classes, and take matters into their own hands'. He stressed that he did not believe in the last war, which was a purely capitalist war, but that 'he was a soldier of the revolution and when the time came he was prepared to die for the cause'. The report noted that Leslie's concluding remarks were met with loud applause.[73]

The Aberdeen Communist Group became increasingly focused on the issues of unemployment and housing, and within the ILP Newbold felt that the issue was ideal for promoting revolution. In March 1920, he reported accordingly to Moscow:

> The situation in Britain grows more and more hopeful. Prices of coal and other necessaries are going up fast. House rents are to go up thirty percent and the dearth of houses is already unprecedented . . . send us all you can about industrial, social and political organisation in Russia and we will do what we can.[74]

By the early 1920s serious splits appeared within the Labour ranks within the left in Scotland, but it is far from clear whether Aberdeen was similarly affected. Frank Rose certainly had his problems with the left, and more particularly the Communist Group in his North Aberdeen constituency. He complained vehemently to the Trades Council in August 1920, because of its actions in helping set up the 'Council of Action' with a 'view to provisioning the City in the event of a General Strike', should the government intervene against Russia to supply Poland. He argued that the Council of Action was controlled 'by the buglemen of syndicalism' who sought only to promote 'direct action'. He became a target of the left thereafter.[75] Indeed, during February 1922 a series of public meetings organised on behalf of Rose were thoroughly disrupted by persistent heckling and interruption from what was reported to be a 'large representation of the extreme wing of the city'. The *Aberdeen Daily Journal* suggested that this was typical of the insidious tactics of the 'Reds in North Aberdeen', and that this 'coterie of communists' simply wished to convert the meeting 'into a Russian wilderness'. The report stated that members of this 'extreme wing' were known collectively as the 'Comrades of the Red Dawn'.[76]

CONCLUSION

In surveying much of the historical literature on this topic, the modern reader might be forgiven for thinking that such concerns and reports of discontent were largely confined to the west of Scotland. Nerve-centres of discontent were clearly forming beyond the west in cities such as Aberdeen, Dundee and Edinburgh and the mining districts of the Lothians and Fife. The war both helped and hindered the left radicals, socialist and revolutionaries alike, but by the later stages of war they were gaining ever greater currency within the Scottish trade union and labour movement. The effects of war weariness continued well into the armistice, and clearly played their part, but it was the example of the workers' revolution in Russia that imbued the political left and the socialist and revolutionary movement with renewed zest and political purpose. The 'Hands Off Russia' campaign drew together the industrial and political wings of the trade union and labour movement in Scotland. Indeed, as John Holford argued, in Edinburgh elements of labour movement 'were predisposed to see revolution in industrial terms by their background in syndicalism or industrial unionism' before the war, while at the same time the Russian Revolution actively 'brought Marxist socialists together to pursue common objectives' after the war had ended. By 1920 the workers' revolution in Russia had become an 'object of fascination and solidarity from virtually all sections of the labour movement'.[77]

Dundee became a leading centre of the anti-war movement in Scotland and it was here that the NCF and the ILP doggedly stood their ground 'through the war and the dark days of militaristic oppression'.[78] The example of Aberdeen shows a high degree of support and approbation for the ideology and aims of revolutionary Russia revolutionaries, but the war had also helped to radicalise the city's working class, so much so that by May 1918 there was a 'pacifist majority' on the Aberdeen Trades Council.[79] In Edinburgh and the coalfields of east Scotland there was a substantial anti-war minority, but it was less well-organised and articulate than movements in Aberdeen and Dundee. Support for the war had split the BSP and this was reflected in the mining districts of Fife, but the propaganda of the radical left and revolutionary parties remained strong, and revolution in Russia quickly unified the movement after the war was over. As with Aberdeen and Dundee, the coalfields of Fife were to become strongholds of communism in the 1920s.

William Leslie not only argued that 'Aberdeen was more Red than Glasgow', but that it could provide the perfect base from which to 'rouse the spirit of the Scottish Highlanders'. And there is some evidence to suggest that the Leslie was at least partly correct in his analysis. In April 1918, reporting on a series of land raids. *Forward* proclaimed that 'Bolshevik tactics' were being pursued in the Highlands. In Kyleakin in Skye, for example, twenty men had taken over possession of vacant land; on Raasay twenty-four land-raiders seized land and put it under cultivation; in Tiree eight men put over fifty acres, incorporating 300 farms, under pasture; on Coll forty-four families took possession of an acre of land for each family unit; and landless men of Barra and Uist declared squatters' rights. Crofters in Helsmdale gave notice to the Duke of Sutherland that they would take possession of vacant land if he did not voluntarily make it available to them.[80] Perhaps Aberdeen would have been the right ideological base for Leslie in his quest to revolutionise Scottish Highlanders, but whether they were ready to be converted to a revolutionary ideology is quite another matter. It is also entirely possible that the nascent socialist movement in Inverness might well have had something to say about this.

Willie Gallagher asserted that the Clyde was different because it was 'never completely submerged in the wave of patriotic enthusiasm which drowned the rest of the country'. And this was why it was the centre of the anti-war movement in Scotland.[81] In an order of magnitude, the Clyde was clearly the principal centre of industrial and political unrest in Scotland, but that does not mean it was necessarily the most radically transformed. Being an 'original Red Clydesider,' and the author of *Revolt on the Clyde*, it is perhaps inevitable that Gallagher would see the Clyde as the leading centre of the revolutionary movement, and it should come as no great surprise that he held this view. Ironically, in his efforts to refute much of what Gallagher had written, and the cult of Red Clyde that grew following the publication of Gallagher's book in 1936, Iain McLean maintained the same geographical perspective as Gallagher. The die it seemed was cast, and the theme of the 'Red Clyde' was indelibly printed on the collective mind of a nation. Yet this demonstrates a clear disregard of the actions and activities of workers in other important locations across Scotland. As early as January 1918 Willie Stewart of the ILP seemed equally dismayed that the working class across Scotland expected revolutionary developments and leadership to emerge from the excitement on the Clyde. But for him the revolution was as likely 'to start on Tayside or the North East Coast as on the banks of the Clyde'. Stewart clearly saw the bigger picture: it was not simply about the Clyde, it was about the country as a whole. Given the evidence that the trade union and labour movement across much of the country became more radicalised and class-conscious between 1910 and 1922, the discussion should focus on 'Red Scotland' rather than simply the myth, or otherwise, of revolutionary Clydeside.

NOTES

1. 'We must free ourselves from the rosy myth of Red Clydeside', *Herald on Sunday*, 30 January 2000.
2. Gall, *The Political Economy of Scotland*, p. 6.
3. *Forward*, 22 March 1919.
4. *Forward*, 1 March 1919.
5. Hayes, *Conscription Conflict*, p. 260.
6. *Forward*, 1 March 1919.
7. *Forward*, 19 April 1919.

8. *Forward,* 12 April 1919.
9. John Stevenson, *British Society*, pp. 64–5; Taylor, *English History*, pp. 54–5.
10. *Forward,* 12 April 1919.
11. Ceadel, 'Attitudes to War: Pacifism and Collective Security', p. 223.
12. De Groot, *Blighty,* pp. 312–13.
13. European Social Science History Conference (ESSHC), Vrije University, Amsterdam, 12–15 April 2000: *Red Clyde . . . Red Scotland?: New Perspectives on Capital and Labour in Scotland, c. 1889 to 1939;* panel contributors, Ronald Johnston, Annmarie Hughes, William Kenefick, Arthur McIvor and Neil Rafeek.
14. Annemarie Hughes, 'Red Skirts on Clydeside 1919–1936' (unpublished paper presented to the ESSHC), April 2000.
15. Neil Rafeek, 'Radicalism Continued 1919–1945: Where did Women in the Communist Party Learn their Socialist Politics? An Oral History' (unpublished paper presented to the ESSHC), April 2000.
16. MacDougall, *Militant Miners*, p. 18.
17. Ibid, pp. 21–4: see also CPGB online – www.cpgb.org.uk/ourhistory/index/.html.
18. Bell, *Pioneering Days*, p. 223: see also Stuart Macintyre, *Little Moscows.* Macintyre identified the mining community of Lumphinnins in Fife as one of Scotland's 'little Moscows'.
19. Holford, *Reshaping Labour*, pp. 17–18, 63.
20. Quoted in Knox, *Industrial Nation*, p. 158.
21. Bagwell, *The Railwaymen*, pp. 309–44.
22. Holford, *Reshaping Labour*, pp. 82–3; Holton, *British Syndicalism*, pp. 97–9, 108–9, 164–7.
23. *Aberdeen Evening Express*, 23 May 1918; *Forward,* 15 June 1918.
24. Holford, *Reshaping Labour*, pp. 157–63.
25. Ibid. pp. 169–71; Edinburgh Trades and Labour Council minutes, 17 August 1920, pp. 179–81; and Gallagher's own account of his visit to Moscow, *Revolt on the Clyde*, pp. 250–4.
26. Holford, *Reshaping Labour*, pp. 150, 181.
27. The McKie Papers, Nat Ganley Collection, Archives of Labour and Urban Affairs, Wayne State University; Box 33, Folder 17, pp. 1–2 – occasional papers.
28. MacDougall, *Militant Miners*, p. 12; Holford, *Reshaping Labour*, p. 185.
29. Stewart, *Breaking The Fetters,* see chapters 7 to 12.
30. Ibid. pp. 126–30.
31. Ibid. pp. 85–99, 100, 115–19.
32. RTsKhIDNI, f. 495, op. 100, d. 55 ('Note of contest at Dundee' – report by Tom Bell to Politburo, Moscow, November 1922); and op. 100, d. 62 (report by James Gardner, Communist Party election agent for Dundee, November 1922).
33. Brooksbank, *No Sae Lang Syne*, p. 29.

34. Ibid. *No Sae Lang Syne*, p. 30.

35. Ibid. *No Sae Lang Syne*, p. 21.

36. Lewis Grassic Gibbon and Hugh MacDiarmid, *Scottish Scene or The Intelligent Man's Guide to Albyn* (London, 1934), pp. 158–63.

37. The first of a series of letters deposited in the Russian Centre for the Preservation and Study of Documents of Recent History (RTsKhIDNI), f. 495, op. 100, d. 17, ll. 86–99 (Leslie to Sub-Committee of the Third International, Moscow, 29 July 1920). This letter was written by Leslie while he was in Finland *en route* to Moscow. He set out on 10 July 1920, without passport or papers, as a stowaway from London to Finland, eventually arriving in Petrograd and proceeding to Moscow.

38. Phipps, 'Aberdeen Trades Council and Politics 1900–1939'.

39. Brotherstone and Witherington, *The City and its Worlds*; see introduction and chapter 13 by Brotherstone.

40. For James Leatham, see Duncan, 'Leatham, James' (1865–1945) *Oxford Dictionary of National Biography*; and Dey, 'For the Rights of Labour' pp. 12–13.

41. Milton, *John Maclean*, pp. 33–4.

42. Phipps, 'Aberdeen Trades Council and Politics 1900–1939', p. 85.

43. Ibid. pp. 92–3.

44. Harvie, *No Gods and Precious Few Heroes*, pp. 28–9.

45. *Aberdeen Weekly Journal*, 7 November 1919.

46. Phipps, 'Aberdeen Trades Council', p. 195.

47. Aberdeen Trades and Labour Council Records (hereafter ATLCR), Aberdeen University Library Special Collections (M.S. 3130), minute of meeting, 9 October 1918.

48. ATLCR, minutes of meetings, 27 October and 6 November 1918.

49. ATLCR, minutes of meetings, 18 December 1918 and 8, 29 January 1919.

50. ATLCR, minute of meeting, 4 June 1919, and Special Executive Council Meeting, 5 June 1919.

51. ATLCR, minute of meeting, 12 May 1920: see also Cameron, *Land Fit For the People*, pp. 182–3.

52. ATLCR, minute of meeting, 11 November 1920.

53. Phipps, 'Aberdeen Trades Council', pp. 99–104: by July 1918 the Aberdeen Trades Council functioned as a dual -purpose body – industrial and political.

54. Phipps, 'Aberdeen Trades Council', pp. 113, 155.

55. *Aberdeen Weekly Journal*, 27 December 1918.

56. Gibbon and MacDiarmid, *Scottish Scene*, pp. 199–210; see also Manson, 'Grassic Gibbon's Glasgow', pp. 12–13.

57. *Aberdeen Weekly Journal*, 7 February 1920.

58. *Aberdeen Weekly Journal*, 5 March 1920.

59. RTsKhIDNI, f. 495, op. 100, d. 10 (Sylvia Pankhurst to Sub-Committee of the Third International, Moscow, 31 January 1920).

60. RTsKhIDNI, f. 495, op. 100, d. 10 (Shapurgi Saklatvala, in London, to Sub-

Committee of the Third International, March 1920).

61. RTsKhIDNI, f. 495, op. 100, d. 10 (Walton Newbold to Sub-Committee of the Third International, 5 March 1920).

62. RTsKhIDNI, f. 495, op. 100, d. 10 (Walton Newbold, in Moscow, to Sub-Committee of the Third International, 6 June 1920).

63. RTsKhIDNI, f. 495, op. 100, d. 10 (correspondence of Helen Crawfurd, written in Moscow, August 1920. Crawfurd met Leslie there).

64. *Aberdeen Weekly Journal*, 26 March 1920.

65. RTsKhIDNI, f. 495, op. 100, d. 9 ('Notes on the Observations of the Working Class Movement in Great Britain', marked 'not for publication', by J. T. Murphy, 28 March 1920).

66. *Aberdeen Weekly Journal*, 7 May 1920.

67. *Aberdeen Weekly Journal*, 9 July 1920.

68. *Aberdeen Weekly Journal*, 30 July 1920.

69. McCrone and Elliot, 'The Decline of Landlordism', p. 225.

70. Melling, 'Clydeside Rent Struggles', pp. 72–83.

71. Leslie's arrest in Norway was the subject of a report to the Immigration Police in Bergen and appeared in the Norwegian Police Gazette – *Polititidende* – later published on Friday, 12 November 1920. It noted that that he was a British Communist from Elgin and it included a photograph of Leslie. Arkivverket, Statsarkivet I Bergen (Regional State Archives, Bergen, Norway), 'Espionage Reports, Closed Files 1/11–31/12–1920. I would like to acknowledge the help and assistance of Nik Brandel, First Executive Officer of the Bergen Regional State Archives.

72. *Northern Scot*, 6 November 1920.

73. *Aberdeen Daily Journal*, 8 November 1920.

74. RTsKhIDNI, f. 495, op. 100, d. 10 (Walton Newbold to Comintern, Moscow, 5 March 1920).

75. Phipps, 'Aberdeen Trades Council', p. 196.

76. *Aberdeen Daily Journal*, 3 February 1922.

77. Holford, *Reshaping Labour*, pp. 168–86.

78. *Forward*, 23 February 1918.

79. *Aberdeen Evening News*, 23 May, 1918; *Forward*, 16 June 1918.

80. *Forward*, 6 April 1918.

81. Quoted in Broom, *John Maclean*, p. 52.

8

The Fall of the Radical Left, c. 1920 to 1932

INTRODUCTION

As the portent of revolution faded, the ILP emerged as the strongest and most important of the left political parties by the 1920s, and finally achieved its big breakthrough in the general election in 1922. The ILP was in every sense a movement of 'thriving community politics', and it was the ILP's grass-roots approach, and its rejection of the 'democratic centralism' associated with the growing Labour Party, that brought it success in Scotland. The ILP formed a party within a party, the intellectual wing and conscience of the Labour Party, and this often brought it into conflict with Labour over ideology and how best to achieve Socialism. But it played its part in helping Labour form a minority government in 1924, and five years later Labour formed a second administration between 1929 and 1931. But Labour's period in office coincided with a world economic slump, and disagreements over how to deal with the problem of massive unemployment and how to reduce public expenditure split the party. The administration collapsed in August 1931, and the former Labour premier, Ramsey MacDonald, formed a national government. In October Labour's vote crashed, as the National Coalition swept the board. In the meantime, ideological differences between Labour and the ILP had intensified, and finally came to a head in the summer in 1932, when the ILP disaffiliated from Labour.

The remainder of this chapter fills in some of the important detail of the development of both Labour and the trade union movement between 1918 and 1932. It considers briefly the unprecedented growth and impact of trade unionism and its political impact on labour, and the relationship between the ILP and the extreme left-wing political parties, and specifically the Communist Party after 1920. This chapter begins, however, by examining the decline in industrial militancy during the early 1920s, what this meant for the workers such as the dockers and the railwaymen, and the impact of unemployment and falling membership in what was to prove a troublesome and difficult decade for the trade unions. This is the closing chapter of this book and it will conclude by considering the impact of the ILP's decision to leave the Labour Party. Importantly, it will raise the question: 'To what extent did the 1930s mark the decline and disintegration of the radical left in Scotland?'

THE RED DAWN

By 1919 the revolutionary tide, such as it was, was clearly on the ebb 'even before the abortive forty-hour strike got underway'. With the fairly rapid demobilisation of soldiers and sailors, and with unemployment beginning to rise sharply, the economic circumstance's of the early 1920s 'weakened the self-confidence of workers who had successfully engaged in spontaneous mass struggle' up until then. Nonetheless, the labour movement in Scotland was still strong, much more radical, and 'outward-looking'. The desire for political self-determination and Home Rule was also very much in evidence, and the experience of war and the growth of left-radicalism had further encouraged this impulse. Indeed, a month before the war ended, the Aberdeen Trades and Labour Council approved a resolution 'for a measure of Home Rule all round' and 'separate legislative assemblies for matters of local concern'. Westminster was to be retained as a 'Federal Assembly'.[1]

Trotsky attacked Scottish socialists, however, for 'threatening to set up a Scottish Parliament for which they had, in his view, 'absolutely no need.' In Britain, Theodore Rothstein robustly promoted the view that the Scots should not be encouraged to 'establish independent institutions'. He could accept that the Scottish working class might well be considered more militant than workers elsewhere in Britain, and could provide 'the spark that would alight the rest of Britain', but Scotland was not to be treated 'in isolation from the rest of the British workers movement'.[2] John Maclean disagreed with this view, for he clearly believed that as Scotland was more radical than the rest of Britain, it should have its own Communist Party to fight for a Scottish Workers' Republic. In the end the founding members of the Communist Party of Great Britain, the great majority of whom were Scottish and, like Bob Stewart, close associates of Maclean, embraced the viewpoint of Rothstein and Trotsky. Maclean's vision of how socialism would take root and develop in Scotland would thus never materialise.

But a 'growing number of Scottish militants', and even some close to the Communist party, asserted that the pursuit of Scottish political

self-determination would result in a Scottish parliament dominated by
socialists, and from this perspective Home Rule was not considered
'incompatible with international socialism'.[3] The year following the
great election result in 1922, the chairman of the Scottish Conference of
the Labour Party (SCLP) argued that if Scotland had had Home Rule the
year before, 'a Labour Government would have been in power north of
the Tweed'. Moreover, that such progress had been made in such a short
period of time, was mainly down to the ILP for it had 'undertaken the
spadework . . . and provided funds for most of the elections'. 'Had it not
been for the ILP', he concluded, 'most of the branches would never have
been contested'.[4] There was also an important development in the
'growth of a strong and wide sense of working-class solidarity or consciousness' in the years after the war. And while this did not perhaps
point to 'the formation of an equally powerful socialist consciousness',
Labour in Scotland was more clearly working-class after 1918, and much
of this was due to the upsurge in trade union membership.[5] For example,
across Britain trade union membership swelled from 2.6 million people
in 1910 to reach 8.3 million by 1920, and the war and its aftermath 'witnessed a tremendous increase in the number of union members in
Scotland'. Affiliated membership to the Scottish Trades Councils in 1909
stood at just under 135,500, by 1914 it was around 225,000, and,
according to an STUC survey of 1924 'around a third, or 536,432 Scots
. . . were members of a trade union, of which 14.6 per cent were female'.[6]
The union upsurge was disproportionately higher among lesser skilled
workers between 1910 and 1920. Everything pointed to electoral breakthrough, for there was 'some correlation between high unionisation and
Labour voting strength'.[7] Scottish Labour was on the threshold of a
political breakthrough.

DIRECT ACTION, 'BLACK FRIDAY' AND THE FAILURE OF THE TRIPLE ALLIANCE

The Scottish dockers, who were composed almost equally of Irish and
Scottish dockers by early 1920, warmly endorsed the ILP's campaign for
Home Rule.[8] Like Maclean and many others, they believed that there
was a lack of militancy among English trade unionists, and that English
influence on Scottish affairs had generally stifled a more radical pattern
of development within the trade union and labour movement in
Scotland, where the rank and file were more favourably disposed to the
syndicalist-style tactics of direct action. The historic decision of the
Triple Industrial Alliance not to support the miners in April 1921, made

by the English trade unionists who largely directed its activities, was cited by the dockers as a prime example. The STUC Conference at Aberdeen in April 1921 heard an SUDL delegate declare that 'there would have been no Triple Alliance failures north of the Tweed if the Scottish workers had been free to decide for themselves' rather than suffer under the diktat of the '"great" people of London', and whose inactivity resulted in 'disastrous consequences'. The debate ended with an agreement to call upon workers throughout Scotland to show their support for the miners and call a general strike.[9]

The miners' strike of 1921 was an important watershed in the history of the British trade union movement, but for the Scottish dockers it was to have dire and, indeed, 'disastrous consequences'. The dispute initially arose over the threat of wage reduction and government de-control of the mining industry in 1920. As a reward for calling off industrial action during October that year, the miners secured a guarantee from the government that it would negotiate with the mine-owners to establish a national wages board by the end of March 1921. The government reneged on this assurance, and the miners struck on 1 April 1921. They immediately requested the support of the Triple Industrial Alliance and it was agreed they would call a 'General Strike' on 15 April. The action was quickly called off, however, and the episode became known as 'Black Friday'. This marked the end of the Triple Alliance as an effective industrial weapon and the beginning of a major attack on wages. Indeed, key sections of the trade union movement sustained heavy defeats in the conflicts that followed.[10]

Robert Williams, who led the NTWF, dockers leaders Ernest Bevin and James Sexton, and NUR leader James Thomas all refused to support the miners. Indeed, Williams was expelled from the Communist Party 'because of the part he played in destroying the triple industrial alliance of miners, railwaymen and transport workers'.[11] The decision not to invoke the Triple Industrial Alliance enraged and angered many of the rank and file among the railwaymen, and in particular the Scottish dockers. During 1919 and 1920 the railwaymen moved 'into the vanguard of industrial struggle' as they 'mobilised in national strikes'. Indeed, their victory in the dispute of October 1919, 'was seen as a vindication industrial unionism', and brought them to view such forms of 'solidarity action . . . as a realistic strategy for revolution'. Lloyd George labelled the strike 'a anarchist conspiracy', but in reality Thomas, the NUR leader, marginalised the militants in his midst by ignoring his executive's instructions to call out the Triple Alliance. Thereafter, the militant Edinburgh rank-and-file members of the NUR became deeply distrustful of Thomas 'and his political clap-trap'. They passionately believed that the Triple Alliance, if invoked nationally, had revolutionary potential, and, denied their opportunity in October 1919, they looked forward to the expected miners' general strike the following year. It finally took place in April 1921, but when the NUR refused to back the miners, Thomas was singled out by the Edinburgh NUR 'for his wrecking tactics'.[12]

The failure of the Triple Industrial Alliance disheartened the members of the NUR across Scotland, but it more or less confirmed the growing belief among a growing group of workers that direct action had gained few 'real achievements for labour and socialism'. After the full formation of the Communist Party in January 1921, the conversion of the old SLP elements to parliamentary action, and the commitment to work with the Labour Party in the field of electoral politics, it seemed that the constitutional path to achieving socialism was the way forward. After Labour and the ILP's stunning electoral success in Scotland in 1922, and again in 1923, it seemed that this was the route to success. But it more or less marked a more wide spread rightward drift among the membership of the NUR, and away from the policy of direct action. It seemed a similar trend was taking place within the ranks of the ILP, for in February 1921, they failed to respond to John MacLean's request 'for support in calling a general strike' over falling wage levels and rising unemployment. Later in June, the ILP moved 'no action' to an appeal from the CPGB 'for financial and political backing in the face of attacks by the government'. In January the year before, the Scottish ILP had been preparing to join the Third (Communist) International, but by the summer of 1921, an ideological chasm had opened up between it and Communist Party in Scotland, and this chasm widened as the 1920s progressed.[13]

For the Scottish dockers, who did strike in solidarity with the miners in May 1921, the failure of direct action was quite literally catastrophic. Their strike ended in defeat, with the SUDL on the point of financial collapse and the rank and file left demoralised and dejected. The minutes of the Executive Council of the SUDL show that it was in full support of the proposed strike action by the Triple Alliance, and had made detailed strike plans for the eagerly awaited general strike. The SUDL set up an Emergency Committee to oversee the strike, and made arrangements with the Scottish Co-operative Wholesale Society to arrange for food supplies in lieu of cash 'in the event of cash being commandeered by the Government'. Meetings were organised all around the important port of Glasgow and across Scotland, to inform all members of the arrangements for the strike. On 17 April, however, Joe Houghton, the leader of the

SUDL, was informed by the NTWF that the strike had been called off. It was agreed that imports of foreign coal were not to be handled, but beyond that no sympathetic action was to be taken unless officially sanctioned by the NTWF.[14]

The SUDL had clearly planned for the strike and the rank and file overwhelmingly approved of the proposed sympathy action with the miners, but it is not entirely clear why the union decided to go it alone. It may well have been rank-and-file inspired, for after the whole of Rothesay Dock in Glasgow 'knocked off' on 6 May 1921, the remaining Glasgow dockers then downed tools, and shortly after they were joined by Ardrossan, Ayr, Bo'ness and Dundee, and sometime later most other branches followed their lead.[15] Beyond the dock labour force, however, there was little support for industrial action, although the railwaymen refused to transport 'blackleg' coal from Glasgow harbour.[16] Indeed, the NTWF embargo on all incoming foreign coal, which the SUDL thought wholly inadequate in any case, was being disregarded by the NUDL on the eastern seaboard of Scotland. Despite rank-and-file support for sympathy action, James Sexton, leader of the NUDL, 'ordered striking dockers at Leith to go back to work on Belgian coal', and declared emphatically that NUDL members were to play no further part in the strike. Shortly thereafter, the SUDL executive advised the men return to work, and in June the strike ended.[17]

In the aftermath of the dock strike the SUDL rapidly disintegrated, and ever suspicious of the type of 'corporate' trade unionism symbolised by the English-dominated NTWF, the dockers were already in retreat. In September the Glasgow Trades Council declared that it intended to offer 'every possible assistance' to the dockers 'in order to bring about the solidarity they had known at Glasgow prior to the strike'.[18] But by then it was already too late. Before the strike the SUDL's financial balance was £20,330 8s 2d: six months later and its balance stood at £1,894 1s 9d.[19] The SUDL also owed £4,000 to the NUR, which was looking for repayment of that 'loan' by January 1922.[20] Around this time the SUDL was approached again to consider amalgamation with the proposed Transport and General Workers' Union (TGWU), but for a third time, and despite rising debt, the membership rejected the proposal.[21] In November 1922 Ernest Bevin notified the SUDL that if the membership transferred to the TGWU it would honour all debts and all legal liabilities.[22] The SUDL was hardly in any position to refuse and early in 1923 it was officially closed down.[23]

During the amalgamation discussion it was stressed to TGWU officials that there was a strong minority in Glasgow who might legally challenge the transfer procedure.[24] John Veitch, the area secretary of the TGWU, dismissed such reports, and he felt sure that this minority would come over to the TGWU and thus 'bring unity where unity was so much desired'.[25] Unity, however, was the last thing that this strong and influential minority wanted, and unity was something that the TGWU would ultimately fail to achieve at Glasgow. The dockers' confidence and their faith in the trade union movement had been dealt a seriously blow in 1921, and this was further compounded by Bevin's part in influencing the TUC to end the General Strike, after only nine days, in 1926. In January 1932, the same year as the ILP was to disaffiliate from the Labour Party, the Glasgow dockers seceded from the TGWU. The series of events that led inexorably towards secession lay in the failure of key sections of the British labour movement to back the miners in 1921. In every respect 'Black Friday' was to prove a historical watershed for dock unionism in Scotland.[26]

THE GROWTH OF SCOTTISH LABOUR AND THE FIRST LABOUR GOVERNMENT

In terms of forming branches and encouraging the growth in membership, the advance of the ILP in Scotland during the war years and beyond was nothing short of spectacular.[27] To put this in some perspective, the ILP had a membership of around 1,250 members in twenty-two branches in Scotland in 1900. Ten years later there were around 5,000 members in 125 branches.[28] This fell for a time during the war, but by October 1918, just weeks before the armistice, the ILP could boast 201 branches and a combined membership of well over 10,000.[29]

Such a rapid rise pointed to the first clear indication that the key political casualty of the outcome of the war would be the Liberal Party. Indeed, between 1918 and 1924, the fortunes of the Liberal Party declined swiftly as Scottish Labour continued its rapid rise to political and electoral prominence. In a very real sense the political map of Scotland had been redrawn by 1924, for the Liberal Party had dominated the Scottish political scene since 1832, and its rapid decline as a political power signalled a new era in Scottish politics.[30] Labour's rise was truly meteoric. In 1906, for example, Labour managed to return only two MPs in Scotland (Dundee and Glasgow Blackfriars), it returned three in 1910 (Dundee, Glasgow Gorbals and West Fife), and despite the extension of the franchise through the Reform Act in February 1918 (which 'expanded the electorate from 7.7 million in 1910 to 21.4 million in 1918'), Labour only managed to return seven MPs in the 1918 election. In England and Wales

Labour won fifty-two seats. Dundee and West Fife were retained in 1918, however, and there were gains in Aberdeen, Govan, Edinburgh Central and two mining seats in South Ayrshire and Hamilton. Labour later 'captured Kirkcaldy and Bothwell at by-elections'.[31]

It was hardly the result that Scottish Labour had expected, given the growth in membership and branches. To be sure, the turnout in the 1918 was fairly low and many ex-servicemen had yet to be demobilised, but had Labour acted more quickly to mobilise and register its support, it could reasonably have expected to do better. But it was the 1922 election that provided the breakthrough. Labour won 142 seats across Britain, and returned twenty-nine Labour MPs in Scotland (plus the prohibitionist and pacifist Edwin Scrymgeour at Dundee, and J. Walton Newbold for the Communists at Motherwell). Of the forty-three candidates run by Labour in 1922, forty were sponsored by the ILP. Little wonder then that many people believed that the ILP was the Labour Party in Scotland.[32] Indeed, throughout the 1920s, and up until the ILP's disaffiliation from the Labour Party in 1932, the ILP dominated the political scene in Scotland. According to Arthur Woodburn: 'There was practically no Labour Party in Scotland . . . the real drive was the Independent Labour Party', and the 'vast majority' of Scottish MPs were ILP members.[33]

Labour further increased its seats in Scotland to thirty-four in 1923, and with 191 seats overall, Labour became the main party of opposition at Westminster. Indeed, in January 1924, following the resignation of Stanley Baldwin's Conservative administration, Labour, with Liberal support in Parliament, was able to form a minority administration with Ramsey MacDonald as premier. It was the Red Clydesiders who were largely responsible for electing Ramsey MacDonald as Labour leader, and perhaps unsurprisingly Scots were to make up a quarter of MacDonald's cabinet. Indeed, it was Scottish political initiatives, and in the main John Wheatley's Housing Act, which provided the administration with its most outstanding political success.[34] Within nine months, however, the Labour administration found itself caught up in a 'Red Scare' and largely 'spurious' allegations of disreputable ties with Moscow, at a time when the Labour administration was attempting to establish a trading agreement with Russia. Bob Stewart, well-known Dundee Communist and Scottish organiser for the CPGB, remembered that foreign policy was the big talking point during the early days of the Labour government, and specifically 'the *de jure* recognition of the Soviet Union'. A majority of Labour MPs wanted to establish normal and diplomatic relations with Russia, and in April 1924 negotiations began when a Soviet delegation met with Sir Arthur Ponsonby at the Ministry of Foreign Affairs. The discussions were protracted, but by August all but the matter of compensation had been agreed (compensation for British business and capital nationalised by the Russian government after the revolution). Shortly afterwards, however, the negotiations broke down, and the 'Tories were jubilant', noted Stewart, for this demonstrated that 'it was impossible to do business with [the] Bolsheviks':

> In this situation, when it was obvious that the future of the Labour Government was in jeopardy, a number of Labour MPs went into action. One of them who played a leading part . . . was Edmund Morel, MP for Dundee . . . Morel was secretary of the Union of Democratic Control, a champion of the colonial people and founder of the Congo Reform Association in 1904.

There was a successful last-ditch attempt to restart the negotiation after a compromise was reached over the wording relating to the claim for compensation. The British wanted 'valid claims' inserted in the joint agreement; the Russian insisted upon 'valid and approved by both Governments'. They finally settled on 'agreed claims'. But the treaty never came into effect, because the Conservatives, with Liberal support, voted against the agreement, and the Labour government were defeated, and the Labour administration resigned.[35]

The Conservative Party and the Liberals, supported by a vigorous press campaign, continually asserted that the Labour Party seemed 'obsessed with Russia', and that until Britain was dealing with a democratically elected government, they would never concede to any trade agreement with Russia.[36] The ILP was in full agreement with the Labour's determination to trade with Russia, and importantly the granting of a £30 million loan to help Russia recover its former trading position:

> We stand by the Russian Treaties because they will help bring Russia within the comity of nations, because a settlement with Russia [was] necessary to the peace in Europe, because they will do something to right the wrongs of British military intervention, and because they will stimulate industry at home and brighten the lives of thousands of our unemployed.[37]

Right-wing political opinion welcomed the proposed loan of £40 million to Germany, as agreed under the Dawes plan, for this was in the interests of 'European peace and the restoration of normal economic activities'. But to 'throw away' money on 'Socialist Russia' was quite another matter. It was an outrage![38]

While there was genuine and widespread supported for the 'Russian Treaties', within the leadership of the Labour Party, a great many of the rank and file, particularly among the centre-right trade unionists, were determined that the Labour Party distance itself from the Communist Party. On the afternoon of Tuesday, 7 October 1924, on the opening day of the Labour Party Conference, the decision was made to ban Communists from affiliating to the Labour Party, or to hold any position within the party. Despite protests against the 'Labour Split' from those on the left, and assertions that both the Communists and Labour should be 'working and fighting' together to defend working-class interests, the vote for the ban was emphatic. Several days later an editorial in *The Times* reported that 'the struggle which began on Tuesday is certainly not finished', and that it would be interesting to watch how this struggle developed over the coming months and years.[39]

In the meantime, there was an election to fight, and the Labour campaign in 1924 was to open at Glasgow. Labour tried to concentrate on issues such as trade, unemployment and housing, but Labour's political opponents, and the establishment press, were determined to focus on 'Labour and the Russian Loan'. In the last week of the election, however, the anti-Communist lobby received a significant boost when the 'infamous' Zinoviev letter was made public. It was alleged that this letter provided proof of a plot to 'overthrow' political institutions in Britain. With banner headlines such as 'Soviets Intervene in British Elections', 'Revolution Urged by Zinoviev', and 'Red Hands on Britain's Throat', the British press had a field day, and leading Conservative and Liberal politicians took to their political platforms over the final days before the election with renewed vigour. Winston Churchill arguably summed up this mood well when proclaiming at a meeting in Dundee that 'The issue of the election was whether we were to be governed by Britons or "Bolshies," and whether we were to remain under the Union Jack or the Red Flag'.[40]

There is little doubt that the general 'Red Scare', the persistent allegations that support for the Russian loan was foisted upon Labour by 'Bolshevik sympathisers' within the Labour Party, not discounting the 'Zinoviev Incident', had a cumulative impact on the election results. The press asserted that Labour might be the party in office, but it was the Communists who were the party in power. Thus, according to Bob Stewart, the British electorate went to the polls believing the Zinoviev letter 'was a genuine document and not a forgery', and the 'greatest hoax ever perpetrated in British political history had paid off'. The Conservative Party won with a landslide victory, and increased their number of seats from 258 to 419. Labour seats fell from 191 to 151, a loss of forty, and in Scotland Labour lost eight seats. But this was not the collapse the Conservatives, Liberals and the press had predicated and, as the following

Table 8.1   Total Votes Cast in General Elections in England and Scotland, 1918–1924; Showing ILP Vote as a Percentage of Total Votes.

	ENGLAND				SCOTLAND		
Year	Total Votes	ILP Vote	%	Year	Total Votes	ILP Vote	%
1918	16,050,943	194,794	1.21	1918	2,232,666	112,836	5.05
1922	17,052,907	341,599	2.00	1922	2,264,801	256,749	11.34
1923	17,126,505	454,166	2.65	1923	2,277,873	278,742	12.15
1924	17,518,505	592,605	3.38	1924	2,299,368	372,090	16.18

Table 8.2   Labour Party and ILP Votes in General Elections in England and Scotland, 1918–1924; Showing ILP Vote as a Percentage of Labour Vote.

	ENGLAND				SCOTLAND		
Year	Labour Vote	ILP Vote	%	Year	Labour Vote	ILP Vote	%
1918	1,485,124	194,794	13.12	1918	182,361	112,836	61.89
1922	3,383,045	341,599	10.10	1922	501,224	256,749	51.22
1923	3,552,951	454,166	12.78	1923	532,463	278,742	51.97
1924	4,499,101	592,605	13.17	1924	708,784	372,090	52.50

Source: Derived from calculations made by the Rev. James Barr, contained in the Brody Collection, Glasgow University Library Special Collections.[41]

tables demonstrate, despite Labour's 'real or supposed' Communist connections, the party actually increased its share of the vote in 1924.[42]

With a big majority in parliament the government and the Tory Party set out on their offensive against the working class. Workers wanted increases in wages; Stanley Baldwin declared that 'all wages must come down'. In June 1925 the mine-owners terminated all existing national and district trade union agreements, and made clear their intention to cut wages and impose longer hours. The Miners' Federation called on the TUC for support, and met with the government to request it stop the wage cuts, but Baldwin refused, stating that the 'government was fully supporting the coal-owners'. The TUC convened another meeting, and the miners' leaders passed a resolution on industrial action, and it was agreed that the transport unions were not to move any coal by road or rail once the action was underway. The government gave way, 'and instituted legislation giving the coal-owners a subsidy for nine-months to maintain the wages and hours of labour of the miners'. The *Daily Herald* called this 'Red Friday' – a day of trade union victory – to distinguish it from Black Friday in 1921, 'when the Triple Industrial Alliance was burst asunder'. There was 'much euphoria' among trade unionists, but others were less convinced and viewed the deal merely as a palliative, and Herbert Smith, president of the Miners' Federation, asserted 'the main battle was still to be fought and won'.[43]

In the meantime, the ILP continued to expand in Scotland during the first half of the 1920s, and by 1925 'could claim 307 branches out of a total of 1,028 in the British Isles'.[44] But this was to prove the peak period for the ILP, and while the party remained the main Labour organisation in Scotland until disaffiliation from Labour in 1932, the period was to prove a difficult one. In essence, and as Bob Stewart had predicted, after the landslide victory for the Conservative Party in 1924, the road was 'open for a direct attack on the British working class'.[45] The election also marked the end of the Liberal party as an effective electoral organisation, and while Labour were to win the following election in 1929, by then 'inadequacies of organisation' and various setbacks 'had taken their toll' – not least in relation to the failure of the General Strike in 1926, and the impact of the Trades Disputes Act in 1927.[46] Life was about to get much more difficult for the trade union and labour movement in Scotland.

THE COMMUNISTS AND THE LABOUR AND TRADE UNION MOVEMENT

As was the case before the Great War, one of the problems facing the trade union and labour movement immediately after the war was the extent to which a real and lasting labour or socialist unity could be built, which would embrace a much wider section of the movement as whole. After 1918, the trade union movement fully supported Labour and the ILP in Scotland, but for a time some trade unions, or sections within them, flirted with more extreme political organisations. They included the Communist and Bolshevik inspired leadership of the Aberdeen Painters' Union, the engineers and boilermakers of the SLP-led Clyde Workers' Committees, the Edinburgh branches of the NUR which were heavily influenced for a time by the SLP, and the Communist-enthused miners of Lanarkshire and Fife.

Partly, this 'flirtation' with left radicalism and revolutionary politics developed out of the federal structure of the Scottish trade union movement, which enabled rank-and-file advocates of direct action to develop within smaller independent trade unions such as the Aberdeen Painters, and the even larger Scottish dockers' union. The early close relationship between the ILP and the Communists in Scotland was also arguably an important factor, and for a time workers perceived little difference between the two in their defence of the working-class interest. But this did not continue for long. When the CPGB was formed in 1920, the ILP was 'faced with a rival invested with the political authority of the Russian Revolution'. The ILP did have a 'brief flirtation with Bolshevism', but in 1921 this came to end when it withdrew its support for the Third (Communist) International.[47] Some elements of the ILP had a fairly close relationship with Moscow and the Communist Party even after 1920, but few among them ever considered leaving the Labour Party. After 1921, the ILP's political focus shifted firmly back to reform politics and its role as the intellectual wing of the Labour Party. The ILP clearly stated its ideological position *vis-à-vis* the Communist Party in August 1922, when James Maxton and Patrick Dollan rejected outright the Communist way to socialism, and asserted that 'the ILP did not advocate the use of force as means to Socialism . . . It is evolutionary rather than cataclysmic. It keeps an open mind and is not bound by iron dogma'. According to Bob Morris, the terms 'revolutionary' and 'reformist' were 'no longer overlapping but were mutually exclusive', and this proved to be the ILP's decisive ideological break with the Communists.[48]

The difference between the ILP and the Communists, and their counter-attack on what they viewed 'the middle-class ideology' of the ILP, caused some confusion among the electorate and 'alienated as many Labour voters' as the Communist Party had won over. In effect, there had been something of an awkward compromise between the ILP and the forces of the political left even before the full establishment of the Communist Party in January 1921. Indeed, in many locations, the previous close ties between elements of the ILP and the Communists continued in an 'ad hoc' fashion, even after Labour banned Communists from affiliating to the party between 1924 and 1925.[49] There were close links between Labour and the Communists in and around the Fife coalfields, and in 1926 five divisional ILP parties within Glasgow were identified 'as cases of unacceptable Communist influence'.[50] The process of mass union amalgamation from 1922 onward had also acted to break local trade unionists' links with what was increasingly viewed as an overt and unwelcome political extremism. The growth of corporate-style trade unions mirrored the expansion of the British Labour Party and its emergence as a popular mass political party, and both gradually marginalised the more extreme elements of the left within the labour movement – and in particular the Communists.

During the election of October 1924 the Labour leadership publicly set in motion the campaign to purge all communist influence from the party. In the aftermath of the Conservative Party's stunning electoral success in

1924, the Labour leadership and its trade union allies were even more determined to eradicate Communist influence within the party, and to demonstrate to the public that they – and not the communists – controlled Labour. Labour was aided in its quest when during October 1925 twelve executive members of the CPGB were arrested, charged and later found guilty of 'Uttering and publishing seditious libel, conspiring to incite soldiers to mutiny, and receiving Moscow gold'. Bob Stewart became acting General Secretary of the party, and in January 1926 he called a special executive meeting of the party to which he invited left-radicals and trade unionists to come together in defence of working-class interests, and in preparation for the coming industrial struggle. And he specifically targeted Labour:

> We must change the leadership of the labour movement. We cannot leave MacDonald, Thomas and the Labour right wingers to use the movement for the benefit of the capitalists. We must build a definite left wing in the labour movement. This cannot be all Communist, but if it does not contain the Communists it ceases to be left. There can be nothing of a revolutionary victory in this country unless we build a mass Communists Party.[51]

His plea was destined to fall on deaf ears, and from there on the relationship between Labour, the ILP and the trade unions went from bad to worse.

As the Miners' Federation and the Communists predicted, the 'great struggle' between the government and the miners began after the coal subsidy, negotiated on 'Red Friday', 31 July 1925, came to an end, and between 3 and 12 May 1926 Britain was on General Strike. There was every indication from the very beginning that the trade union leadership had little stomach for the fight. The government had been preparing for this dispute since the industrial successes of the railwaymen in 1919, and the miners in 1920, and by the time of the strike it had contingency plans in place for the 'Preservation of Public Order'. Bob Stewart believed that apart from the influential, Communist-led (and Moscow-funded) National Minority Movement, which was launched in 1924 on the platform of a 'United Front with the trade-union movement', and initiatives by closely organised, activist-led movements around the country, particularly in the mining districts, the trade union movement in Scotland (and Britain as a whole) was just not adequately prepared for the struggle. The CPGB may have predicted the dispute, but their role in the strike was thought to be 'patchy and short-lived'. Indeed, as Stewart noted, the membership of the CBGP trebled during the strike, but afterwards it was more or less back to normal levels.[52]

This is not to suggest that the 1926 strike did not have an impact, for there are many well-documented demonstrations of working-class solidarity in certain areas. Two million workers came out on strike, about half the number that could have been called out by the TUC, and while there was 'a great spirit of unity among those involved in the action', poor organisation and a general confusion about who should actually be on strike acted to undermine the dispute. Press and public propaganda, government use of intelligence – gathered by the Economic League and passed on to the employers – not discounting the use of middle-class volunteers and troops to fill the places of strikers clearly had an adverse impact of the strike. The strike was called off after just nine days and, as occurred after Black Friday in 1921, the miners were left to fight alone. They were 'virtually starved into submission' six months later, and many strikers were 'sacked, demoted, or otherwise victimised' as a result of the strike.[53]

The period after the General Strike also marked a decisive shift to the right for the trade union movement. Membership levels began to fall, and this brought trade unions into competition with each other as they attempted to sign up new recruits. For example, the NUR was actively attempting to recruit railway carters across Scotland in the 1920s and 1930s, and this brought the union into direct conflict with the Scottish Horse and Motormen, and the formidable Hugh Lyons. The matter was referred to the Joint Industrial Council for the transport industry, and the NUR was roundly condemned for its actions in this case. Clearly, the NUR had moved significantly from the militancy of direct action that characterised the union's activities in the immediate post-war years, and the leadership was working hard to rehabilitate the trade union movement generally and to regain public confidence. As a result, the NUR decided to exclude Communists, or those affiliated to parties 'proscribed by the Labour Party', from leading positions within the executive of the union. It was not entirely successful in this endeavour, and many NUR members remained close to the Communist Party, but the decision demonstrated how far to the right NUR had lurched since the great victory for direct action in the strike of October 1919.[54]

The carters in Scotland were reasonably well organised in to two main carters' unions after the war, but like the seaman and the dockers they fell on opposing sides over the question of direct action and the political strike. Peter Gillespie's North of Scotland Horse and Motormen's Association (NSHMA) was a founder member union of the TGWU in 1922, along with the smaller Associated Horsemen's Union of Greenock, which also affiliated in that year. But Hugh Lyons's Scottish Horse and Motormen refused to consider amalgamation, and it was their organisation which was set to dominate the road haulage industry in Scotland. Lyons increasingly adopted a non-partisan political approach to industrial relations, and after 1923, when his union's selection for Labour candidate at St Rollox was over turned in favour of an ILP candidate (a month after the official closing-date for candidates' submission), he pulled back from party politics, and from any dealings with the Socialists, Communists or left-radicalism. Lyons also refused to become involved in the 'Forty-Hour' strike in 1919 and the General Strike in 1926. Indeed, in his desire to keep party politics and trade unionism separate, he was more reminiscent of the non-partisan Samuel Gompers of the American Federation of Labour than the trade unionist of the TUC.[55]

The National Sailors and Firemen is Union (NSFU), under the leadership of Havelock Wilson, never advocated direct action during the war or its aftermath, nor did its members seem to desire it. The membership of the Amalgamated Marine Workers' Union (AMWU) – formed through the amalgamation of the British Seafarers' Union and the National Union of Ships' Stewards, Cooks, Butchers and Bakers in 1922 – was a much more militant organisation. The NSFU emerged from the war, however, as the strongest of the maritime unions, and this was in large part due to its joint cooperation with the Shipping Federation in forming the National Maritime Board in 1917. Both organisations extended the Board's remit in 1922, which in effect meant that the NSFU and the Shipping Federation jointly controlled employment in the shipping industry. This infuriated many in the trade union movement, and in the AMWU in particular, and the NSFU's reputation was further tarnished when it refused outright to take part in the General Strike in 1926. The NSFU changed its name to the National Union of Seamen (NUS) in 1926, and by this time the AMWU had collapsed. The TGWU formed a seafarers' section to accommodate the old AMWU members, but this led to yet another inter-union dispute over recruitment. The NUS had few friends in the trade union movement at this time, however, and the TUC was further dismayed and angered by Wilson's decision to provide a loan of £10,000 to the recently-formed Miners Industrial Union – or the Miners' Non-Political Fund – during September 1927.[56] The NUS was subsequently embroiled in a legal action, brought by the TUC, on the grounds that the NUS had acted 'unconstitutionally' in providing a loan to the Miners' Non-Political Fund. The NUS was expelled from the TUC a year later in September 1928. The NUS also seceded from the NTWF in 1927, and the subsequent loss of membership meant that it could no longer function in any meaningful sense. The NTWF had proved at times an effective weapon against the might of the Shipping Federation, but with its demise, and with the compliance of the NUS, the shipping employers exerted total control over the industry.[57] Wilson died in April 1929, and shortly after, with its inter-union squabble with the TGWU – and the rift between the NUS and the TUC – amicably settled, the NUS was allowed back into the TUC. The NUS remained the principal sea-farers' union and a corporate closed shop.[58]

THE SECOND LABOUR GOVERNMENT AND ILP DECLINE

From the end of the General Strike and the early 1930s, the relationship between Labour and the ILP went from bad to worse. Labour leader Ramsey MacDonald saw defeat in the General Strike as a victory for 'parliamentarianism over direct action'. James Maxton saw the miners' defeat as the direct result of repressive state action, and believed that rather than signalling the end of mass working class action, it 'made rev-olution inevitable'. When Maxton collaborated with miners' leader A. J. Cook to publish the Cook-Maxton Manifesto in 1928, it was a reaffir-mation of the policies outlined in 'Socialism in Our Time'. Indeed, it was thought that workers' radicalism would become re-energised by state repression.

But in truth few in the labour and trade union movement, other than the miners, or indeed, the left of the ILP itself, were in any mood to engage in the type of class war against capital that Maxton believed was inevitable. James McNair attempted to explain Maxton's position, when he wrote an 'Appreciation of Maxton' following his death in 1946: 'A series of huge meetings was held all over the country but the British workers had not recovered from the disillusionment of the General Strike and the response did not correspond with the hopes raised'. He suggested that the campaign 'kept alive the spirit of militancy in some sections of the working class and was the only fitful gleam of working-class solidarity during that dark period'. The last nail in the coffin of Labour unity was finally driven home after the failure of the second Labour administration between 1929 and 1931, 'for not taking a bold socialist line' in the defence of working-class interests against those of the capitalist system.[59]

For John McNair, the Labour government fell because it was 'reduced to lowering the standard of life of the working class', by supporting cuts in wages and cuts in unemployment benefits, to maintain the capitalist system and imperialism. Cuts in unemployment benefits and wages were made to the tune of £70 million and, to add insult to injury, means testing was introduced for those on benefits. Ramsey MacDonald formed a National Government in August 1931, and twice Conservative premier

Stanley Baldwin was invited to join the Cabinet. During October 1931, noted Bob Stewart, Baldwin went round the country explaining why workers and the unemployed had to accept cuts in benefits and wages. At the same time, however, his ordinary share returns for that year – from Baldwin Limited (a large steel company) – advanced by '£650,000 in value'. Stewart was in Perth prison when the Labour split came in August 1931. He was jailed for thirty days after his arrest at an anti-means test demonstration at Dundee, where he was again standing for the Communist Party in the coming election scheduled for October.[60] He outlined parts of MacDonald's radio broadcast, made on the evening of 26 August; on the day MacDonald received royal approval to form the National Government he said

> I speak to-night in unusual and, to me, rather sorrowful circumstances. I have given my life to building up a political party. I was present at its birth; I was a nurse when it emerged from infancy and it attained to adult years. At this moment I have changed none of my beliefs and none of my ideals. I see that it is said that I have no Labour credentials for what I am doing. That is true. I do not claim to have them, though I am certain that in the interest of the working-class I ought to have them. Be that as it may, I have credentials from even a higher authority. My credentials are those of national duty as I have conceived it, and I obey them irrespective of consequences.

MacDonald then made commented on the need to defend the pound and to maintain it its current value:

> Thus commerce and the well-being, not only of the nation, but a large part of the civilised world, have been built up and rest upon the confidence in the pound sterling, and if that confidence be destroyed it means dislocation of the world trade, on which everyone and most of all the working people of this country will suffer. Further, if the value of the pound were to fall suddenly and catastrophically, not by plan as some people suggest, but without plan, by the force of economic circumstances, without control – should that happen, prices would rise much faster than wages and incomes could be adjusted, even if adjustment were possible.

This was reported in *The Scotsman* on 27 August 1931. *The Times* reported likewise, but chose to leave out reference to the 'political party' that MacDonald had nursed from infancy: the same party 'he sold out to the capitalist just the same', noted Bob Stewart.

Stewart predictably came last out of the five candidates contesting Dundee's two parliamentary seats in October 1931, although with 10,262 votes he increased considerably the Communist Party's share of the vote. Labour was to lose a seat that it had held since 1906, and the prohibitionists lost one they had held since 1922 (their only Parliamentary seat in Britain), when Dingle Foot of the National Liberals, and Florence Horsburgh of the National Conservatives (the first 'Tory' to be returned for Dundee since the nineteenth century and the city's first female MP) won both seats. Stewart was one of eight Communist candidates standing in that election, and along with Willie Gallagher in West Fife, Manny Shinwell in the Gorbals, and Helen Crawfurd in Aberdeen North, attracted over 35,000 votes, marginally increasing their share of the vote in Scotland. Gallagher managed a creditable 6,829 votes in West Fife, but Stewart's tally accounted for nearly 30 per cent of the Communist vote and was far and away the party's best performance.

Labour's losses on the other hand were quite staggering. They had won 288 seats in the 1929 General Election, but this fell to fifty-one in October 1931. Scottish Labour took half of Scotland's seventy-four Parliamentary seats in 1929, but only held onto seven in October 1931. The 1931 election was considered an 'unmitigated disaster' for Scottish Labour when National Government candidates captured sixty-four Scottish seats. But Labour still attracted a third of the popular vote in Scotland, and this was perhaps some consolation, for it clearly had a sizeable constituency of support.[61]

Bob Stewart 'profoundly believed' that when Ramsey MacDonald made his radio address to the nation on the day the National Government was formed in August 1931, MacDonald actually imagined that 'he was presiding over the death of the Labour Party and the British working class movement' – for his 'ego was that big'.[62] In the aftermath of the 1931 General Election, and with Labour teetering on the precipice of an electoral abyss, many could well have believed that Labour's demise was not far off. Few would have thought that it would be the ILP which would suffer, however, and not as a direct result of the election defeat in 1931, but rather its disaffiliation from the Labour Party in July 1932. The ideological difficulties, which had dogged relations between the ILP and Labour since the mid-1920s, had finally came to a head, and in the long-term it did precipitate ILP's political demise. The ILP had dominated Scottish Labour from the late nineteenth century, and more so since the end of the war in 1918, but as a result it had held back the Labour Party's own organisational development in Scotland. The ILP was the Labour Party in Scotland. The disaffiliation mean that ILP was no longer 'a party within a party', and in effect would compete with Labour in the electoral arena, and for Labour to rival the ILP it would have to strengthen and build up the party apparatus. This meant 'the virtual remaking of the Labour Party in Scotland in terms of its organisation, ethos and ideology', in order to fill the 'cultural' vacuum left by the ILP, and this would need to be accompanied by a subsequent shift in trade union support from the ILP to Labour.[63]

The ILP was more than a political party, however, for it played a cultural, social and educational role within the trade union and labour movement in Scotland. Indeed, it was arguably the beating heart of a community-based political movement, with overlapping involvement in the Socialist Sundays Schools, Clarion Clubs, Socialist music and dramatic societies, and Socialist study groups, and it had a long and close association with the Co-operative movement and the Trades Councils in Scotland. It also played an important propaganda role and regularly organised meetings across the country, both large and small, on almost any topic that could be imagined, and in *Forward* it had a socialist newspaper, which Bruce Glasier described during the First World War, as 'courageous and brilliant Red Flag Propaganda'.[64]

This role would be difficult to fill because, for the Labour Party in Scotland, it meant 'mobilising working-class aspirations on a variety of levels beyond simple parliamentarianism'. It proved a forlorn task and it ditched this approach 'in favour of electoral mobilisation'.[65] The democratic centralism of the Labour Party had triumphed over the 'diffused community-based authority' championed by the ILP.[66] The 1930s would prove to be a difficult time for the Scottish working classes, and the demise of the ILP, its brand of community-based activism, the infectious enthusiasm for socialism, and a genuine desire to improve the conditions of the working class could not have come at a worse time. The ILP was to fall into political decline and, as its influence waned, grass-roots activism diminished, and membership of Scottish Labour fell away. Indeed, it presaged the decline of a radical left and socialist tradition that could trace its roots to the closing decades of the nineteenth century.

NOTES

1. ATLCR, minutes of meetings, 9 October 1918.
2. Thatcher, 'Representation of Scotland', p. 157.
3. Young, *The Rousing*, pp. 196–7, 200–1; Trotsky, *Where is Britain Going?*, pp. 44–5.
4. Wood, 'Labour in Scotland in the 1920s', pp. 36, 38.
5. Hutchison, *Political History of Scotland*, pp. 285–7.
6. Smyth, *Labour in Glasgow*, pp. 28–9; Knox, *Industrial Nation*, pp. 220–1. For trade union affiliations to the Scottish Trades Councils, see Chapter 1, Table 1.1 of this book.

7. Hutchison, *Political History of Scotland,* pp. 258–9.
8. Kenefick, *Rebellious and Contrary,* p. 112.
9. Scottish Trades Union Congress, Aberdeen, 20–3 April 1921: 'The Call-Off of the Triple Industrial Alliance General Strike'; see also Young, *The Rousing,* p. 201.
10. Hinton, *Labour and Socialism,* pp. 113–15.
11. Stewart, 'Breaking the Fetters', p. 195.
12. Holford, *Reorganisation of Labour,* pp. 183–4.
13. Hutchison, *Political History of Scotland,* p. 299.
14. SUDL Executive Council (EC), Emergency Committee, 11 and 17 April 1921.
15. SUDL (EC), Emergency Committee 6, 9, 2 May; Special Executive Committee Meeting, 14, 18 May.
16. Glasgow Trades Council Minutes, 14 May 1921.
17. EC Emergency meeting, 23 May 1921; reluctance of men to return to work noted in SUDL Executive Minutes, 6 June 1921.
18. Glasgow Trades and Labour Council Industrial Committee Minutes, 5 September 1921.
19. SUDL Executive Minutes, 25 December 1920 and 2 November 1921.
20. SUDL (EC) Emergency Committee Meeting, 19 January 1922.
21. SUDL Executive Minutes, 4 January 1922.
22. SUDL Executive Minutes, 18 and 25 November 1922.
23. SNA, FS 8/18, Registrar of Friendly Societies in Scotland.
24. SUDL Executive Minutes, 24 May 1923.
25. Executive Meeting of the Scottish Union of Dock Labourers and Transport Workers, 19 December 1922. Typed minute signed by John Veitch, area secretary of the Transport and General Workers' Union, on accepting the transference of the liabilities and membership of the SUDL.
26. Kenefick, *Rebellious and Contrary,* pp. 233–41.
27. Harvie, 'Before the Breakthrough', p. 24.
28. Ibid. pp. 13, 16.
29. *Forward,* 26 October 1918; Harvie, 'Before the Breakthrough', p. 24.
30. Hutchison, *Political History of Scotland,* pp. 321–8.
31. Ibid. p. 276; Harvie, 'Before the Breakthrough', pp. 7, 27; see also Harvie, *No Gods and Precious Few Heroes,* pp. 28–9.
32. Wood, 'Labour in Scotland in the 1920s', pp. 37–8.
33. Smyth, *Labour in Glasgow,* pp. 98–9.
34. Harvie, *No Gods and Precious Few Heroes,* Table 4.1, pp. 90, 92.
35. Stewart, *Breaking the Fetters,* p. 156: also widely reported in the establishment and socialist press.
36. *The Times,* 4 October 1924.
37. Issued by the National Council of the ILP, reported widely in the press on, 6 October 1924.
38. *The Times,* Editorial Leader, 7 October 1924.

39. Labour Party Annual Conference, Queen's Hall, London, 7 October 1924; and *The Times,* 9 October 1924.
40. Reported variously in the press, 12 October 1924.
41. The Brody Collection has a catalogue of printed published materials, held at Glasgow University Library Special Collections, relating to the Labour Party for the first half of the twentieth century. This reference is to uncatalogued manuscript material for the Rev. James Barr previously the Brody Collection, Acc. 3721; Box 16/41.
42. Wood, 'Labour in Scotland in the 1920s', p. 43.
43. Laybourn, *British Trade Unionism*, pp. 131–2.
44. Wood, 'Labour in Scotland in the 1920s', p. 38.
45. Stewart, *Breaking the Fetters*, pp. 162–3
46. Harvie, *No Gods and Precious Few Heroes*, p. 92.
47. Knox, *Industrial Nation*, p. 234.
48. Morris, 'Introduction', *The ILP on Clydeside*, p. 6; Hutchison, *A Political History*, pp. 299–300.
49. Wood, 'Labour in Scotland in the 1920s', pp. 41, 43.
50. MacDougall, *Militant* Miners, pp. 138–43; Wood, 'Labour in Scotland in the 1920s', pp. 41–3.
51. Stewart, *Breaking the Fetters*, pp. 166–70.
52. Laybourn, *British Trade Unionism*, p. 138; Stewart, *Breaking the Fetters*, p. 172.
53. Stewart, *Breaking the Fetters*, pp. 171–2; Harvie, *No Gods and Precious Few Heroes*, pp. 93–4; MacDougall, *Voices from Home and Work*; Laybourn, *British Trade Unionism*, pp. 133–9.
54. *The Scotsman*, 29 March 1930.
55. Kenefick, 'Transport Unions in Scotland from the Nineteenth Century to the Present'.
56. *The Times*, 24 September 1927.
57. *The Times*, 4 November 1927.
58. Coates and Topham, *The Making of the TGWU*, pp. 857, 859, 863, 865; Fraser, *British Trade Unionism*, pp. 162–3; Kenefick, 'Transport Unions in Scotland'.
59. McKinlay and Smyth, 'The end of "the Agitator Workman"', p. 177: Knox, *Industrial Nation*, p. 238; *James Maxton 1885–1946: An Appreciation with a Number of Tributes*, p. 10.
60. McNair, *James Maxton*, p. 11; Stewart, *Breaking the Fetters*, p. 183.
61. Donnachie, 'Scottish Labour in the Depression', pp. 51–4.
62. Stewart, *Breaking the Fetters*, p. 184.
63. Knox, *Industrial Nation*, pp. 239–40.
64. *Forward*, 2 January 1915.
65. Knox, *Industrial Nation*, pp. 239–40.
66. Morris, 'The ILP, 1893–1932, Introduction, pp. 14–15.

Epilogue

On Radicalism –
and Exporting Scottish Left Radicalism

The roots of the modern European socialist movement were regarded to lie in France, and on the occasion of the first general assembly of the 'Association Internationale des Travailleurs' in Paris, April 1870, the *Pall Mall Gazette* reported on a proclamation by 'Citizen Valin':

> That freeing of working men should be the labour of working men. We should no longer put faith in those men who . . . soothed us with vain promises in order to obtain our votes, and who on obtaining power, have deserted and betrayed us.[1]

After those 'bold and violent men' of the Paris Commune 'usurped power' during March 1871, it seemed to many in France and across much of Europe that the middle classes had good reason to be fearful of 'Socialism' for they were viewed as 'an inpregnable bulwark against socialism'.[2] In September the editors of *The Scotsman* considered a report by the *Saturday Review* linking the strike by engineers at Newcastle and 'the same class of operative at Brussels':

> The leaders of the union have gradually been expanding under the genial illumination of the *International Association*. They have learned to despise mere narrow trade disputes, except as a means to an end, and to aim at greater things.

The report clearly saw a link between industrial action and politics, and concluded that our 'own demagogues of the pavement' have discovered 'the strength of the unions for political purposes'.[3]

The press was often guilty of sensationalism, but when reporting on the Edinburgh Workmen's campaign to abolish the Master and Servants' Act in September 1873, there was general agreement that they were gathered 'for political purposes'. The *Economist* was to report:

> The working men of Edinburgh . . . have raised a question which, so far as we know, has never been formally raised yet . . . They require, and intend that

their members should require, that the whole of the law of breach of contract as between master and servant should be abolished.

In an echo of the works of 'Citizen Valin', in Paris three years before, it was reported that the principal speakers at Edinburgh 'urged their adherents to vote only for members who would promise to comply with their demands', and even suggested that Mr M'Laren (the sitting MP, and darling of the Edinburgh middle classes), 'should be supplanted as member for Edinburgh by a working man'. The report concluded that the workmen of Edinburgh viewed the Master and Servants' Act as 'class legislation'.[4] In the same year 'working men of the city of Aberdeen and the North of Scotland' produced the *Working-Man's* newspaper. It was owned and controlled by workmen, 'was independent in its politics', and was clear that the state of the 'labourer or workman was at present, in a state of transition'.

In January 1880, in a lecture presented at the Statistical Society in London on 'The Strikes of the Last Ten Years', it was stated there had been some 2,352 strikes across Britain, and that 473 strikes took place in Scotland. Indeed, Glasgow topped the league of the 'Top-Ten Strike Towns' in Britain, with Edinburgh/Leith and Dundee in fourth and eighth position respectively. The report stated that wage demands were 'in ninety percent of cases' the major source of dispute, but that north of the border other forces were at work:

> Scotland had an extraordinary preponderance in strikes, and especially in her collieries and mines: and this seemed to be due to the constant spirit of opposition fostered in them by those claiming to be their leaders. [5]

The report gave no detail as to the cause of this 'spirit of opposition', but at this time the craft and mining unions were considered to be 'strongly conciliationist'. The evidence presented above suggests something different and that the industrial pacifism commonly associated with Scottish workers was 'more a chimera than a reality'.[6] Indeed, this is further evidence of 'a willingness' on the part of Scottish workers 'to campaign on wider political issues rather than just economic ones', and in this they were as radical, if not more so, than workers elsewhere in Britain.[7]

In December 1880, *The Scotsman* reported on a discussion on the state of 'Scotch Socialism' prompted by a correspondence by one Henry Coleridge of Greenock, 'a sympathiser with Monsieur Felix Pyat's views as to the right of regicide', and which appeared in the French Republican *La Marseillaise* on 9 December 1880.[8] *The Scotsman* was to run with the story for several days, and Mr Coleridge's thoughts on socialism were

closely analysed. Mr Coleridge stressed that Scotland was at that juncture some way from forming a Socialist movement, but that he wished
to form 'a Socialist group' in Greenock, and provide active support for
the principles of 'liberty, equality and fraternity'. M. Pyat dedicated two
articles to the subject of 'Scotch Socialism' in *La Marseillaise*, in which
he asserted 'by reason of its race and history, Scotland [was] more
extreme and democratic than England', and that 'a mighty moral and
political force [was] destined to transform Scotland'. But who was Henry
Coleridge? It is enough to know 'that he is the mouthpiece of Scottish
Socialism, and that M. Pyat is its priest and interpreter'. But to suggest
that 'Scotland was more ripe for revolution' than even the Scottish
Socialists themselves thought possible, concluded the report in *The
Scotsman*, was a clear testament to the 'remarkable proof of that won-
derful French gift of generalisation'.[9]

And this was not the last word on the subject, for in late December
The Scotsman printed a reply from the Provost of Greenock, to a letter
sent by M. Felix Pyat, looking for information on Mr Coleridge. The
Provost replied that he found neither trace of Henry Coleridge nor the
Socialist group he claimed to represent: 'If any such group exists it certainly lacks visibility', and he stated that he did not think the letter was
written by a Scotchman, 'unless it was written as a joke'. He was
unaware of any local affinity with Socialism, but wrote that he had
'decided sympathy with the French people and the French Republic', and
in concluding added: 'That the Scotch people detest Imperialism'.[10] The
mysterious Mr Coleridge was somewhat ahead of his time, although *The
Scotsman* confirmed that there were 'Scottish Socialists' around at this
time, while Provost Campbell of Greenock was clearly happy to make
public his anti-imperialist credentials.

The socialist movement may not have manifested itself until the early
1880s, but since the days of the Paris Commune the topic had been
earnestly and widely discussed, and it was part of the curriculum at
Edinburgh University, so perhaps this level of debate was having an affect
on people? As was the case with political action, Scotland seemed to be
ahead of the game in many respects, and this was certainly noted by those
from outside the country. William McKie, from Carlisle, grew up in the
Methodist religion, and asserted that although they had a 'Socialist
Party' in England in the 1880s, it actually 'had no conception of what
socialism was like'. And neither did McKie, until, that is, he came to
Edinburgh in the early 1890s. 'Somebody must have discussed socialism
as developed by Marx', McKie noted, but in his young days he 'never
came across anything until [he] was in Edinburgh'.[11] His great mentor

was John Leslie, the uncle of James Connolly, and through him he became very familiar with Marx, and met William Morris, Keir Hardie, Cunninghame Graham, and many others. He also addressed the question of workers' militancy:

> The militant working class [are] those people who are independent in spirit and mind, who see further than their wages, who see liberation of mind and thought and also the question of their economic position being in their hands instead of someone else's power.

He learned this while in Edinburgh, where he lived for over thirty-five years, and when he left for America in the mid-1920s he was fully paid up member of the CPGB. He eventually settled in Detroit where he joined the Ford motor plant, and the American Communist Party. Together with Phil Bonoski, he founded the United Auto Workers of America, and in 1935, on a Communist ticket and at sixty years of age, he went into public office as councillor. According to Phil Bronski, 'Bill' McKie 'became a forerunner of AFL-CIO policy of running Labor candidates for public office'.[12]

McKie was not Scottish, but his brand of socialism was, for it was acquired from thirty-five years of active involvement with the trade union and socialist Labour movement in Scotland. When he emigrated, his radicalism went with him – just as the Irish brought their radicalism with them when they settled in nineteenth-century Scotland; as did Jewish and Lithuanian revolutionary socialists in the twentieth century. Scotland exported people and ideas, and there has been considerable research of late on the relationship between the Scots and the British Empire. But such studies tends to ignore the experience of working-class Scots abroad. Emigration increased significantly from the 1880s and in the years preceding the Great War. In the 1920s, over 400,000 Scots left their homeland and, as was the case of 'Bill' McKie, some of the country's most experienced and politically active workers went with them, and this perhaps helps explain in part the decline of Scottish left radicalism in Scotland in the 1920s.

The same was the case before the war, and was evident in February 1914, when nine deported South African trade union and labour movement activists arrived in Britain. They were deported by the South African authorities because of the leading part they played in the great syndicalist-style strike wave which was felt across the Rand in 1913 and early 1914. Six of the deportees were Scots, and they included Dundee-born James Thompson Bain and Glasgow-born Archie Crawford.[13] Indeed, Crawford was inspired to establish the socialist and syndicalist

Johannesburg *Voice of Labour*, after James Keir Hardie's visit to South Africa some years earlier.[14] There were also Scottish hands at work in the foundation of the South African Labour Party's *Eastern Record*, for the driving force behind the venture was Glasgow-born Christina Barnet (secretary of the Benoni Women's Labour League) and her husband Robert.[15] Scots were pioneers in the promotion of wide-ranging and intensive political debate through the socialist press both at home and abroad, and *Forward* was read widely in Australia, Canada and South Africa. For example, the Lanarkshire miners involved in the Vancouver Island Miners' strike placed an article in *Forward*, in February 1914, urging miners in the 'old country' *not* to emigrate to Canada, because they were being unwittingly recruited as scab labour.[16] John MacLean travelled across Scotland and Britain proclaiming the socialist message; James Keir Hardie traversed the globe disseminating his radical critique of capitalism and British imperialism; and a host of Scottish political emigrés circulated the message throughout the Empire. And where they went, so too did the socialist press. The Scots exported social divisions and 'class-identified politics' and one example of this was the ideological division that was apparent between left-wing and colonial establishment Scots.

The radical and socialist press was the conduit for an intra-regional, national and international exchange of ideas, and thus an examination of the Scots abroad becomes relevant and compatible to what is essentially a study of left radicalism in Scotland. For example, Andrew Fisher, a former Ayrshire miner and associate of Keir Hardie, became prime minister in the first Labour Administration in Australia in 1910, and the aforementioned James Thompson Bain is accredited as the father of the South African Labour Movement and arguably the single most influential figure in that movement up until his death in 1922. After the Great War, and given the heavy involvement of Scots in the Communist Party of Great Britain – such as Arthur McManus, Willie Gallagher and Dundee's 'own' Bob Stewart, to name only a few – it was speculated that there was a virtual 'human bridge' between Scotland and Moscow during the interwar years. But this also extended across the Atlantic where another Scot, J. B. McLachlan, proved the driving force behind the formation of the Canadian Communist Party during the politically turbulent interwar years and the Canadian Red Scare period. Another group of Scots were heavily influential in establishing the Workers' Education Association in Toronto in 1919. Thereafter it quickly expanded across Ontario and Canada and became affectionately known as the 'Scotch Club'.[17] Indeed, the Scots were significant in promoting international socialism, syndicalism, communism and anti-imperialism across the globe, both before and after the Great War.

This is clearly a matter for further investigation and examination with a view to writing the history of the working-class Scot abroad. Indeed, in the final analysis, some of the more important aspects of Scottish political radicalism may be better revealed in the context of how well left-radical ideas were received by the imperial working class.

NOTES

1. *The Scotsman*, 22 April 1870.
2. *The Scotsman*, 30 June 1870.
3. *The Scotsman*, 18 September 1870.
4. *The Scotsman*, 1 September 1873.
5. 'A Decade of Strikes': lecture presented to the Statistical Society, King's College, London, by Mr G. Phillips Bevan, *The Times*, 22 January 1880.
6. Knox, *Industrial Nation*, p. 118; Kirk, *Comrades and* Cousins, p. 10.
7. Gall, *The Political Economy of Scotland*.
8. *The Scotsman*, 13 December 1880. *La Marseillaise* was only recently resurrected in Paris in November 1880 when Felix Pyat took over the editorship. This was reported variously in the British Press: see 'Letter From Paris', *The Scotsman*, 9 November 1880. Felix Pyat fled Paris shortly after writing the 'Scotch Socialism', to escape prosecution and imprisonment by the French authorities.
9. *The Scotsman*, 14 December 1880.
10. *The Scotsman*, 27 December 1880. The reply was signed D. Campbell, Provost of Greenock.
11. The McKie interviews are transcribed and held in the Nat Ganley Collection, Archives of Labour and Urban Affairs, Wayne State University, Detroit, Michigan, USA; Box 33, Folder 26.
12. Bonoski, *Brother 'Bill' McKie*; see also N. Lichtenstein, *The Most Dangerous Man in Detroit*.
13. J. Hyslop, *The Notorious Syndicalist J.T. Bain: A Scottish Rebel in Colonial South Africa* (Johannesburg, 2004).
14. D. Ticktin, 'The Origins of the South African Labour Party, 1888–1910' (PhD Thesis, University of Cape Town, South Africa, 1976), p. 4.
15. W. Kenefick, 'The Scots and the South African Labour Movement', (paper presented to the European Social Science History Conference, Berlin March 2003): see also Hyslop, 'Cape Town Highlanders, Transvaal Scottish', p. 267, and *The Notorious Syndicalist*.
16. *Forward*, 8 February 1914.
17. Inventory of the Workers' Education Association Papers, Archives of Ontario; F1217-MU3990, series A, Box 1. I would also like to acknowledge the help of Prof. Joan Sangster, Trent University, Ontario, Canada.

Bibliography

BOOKS AND ARTICLES

Alcock, G., *Fifty Years of Railway Trade Unionism* (London, 1922).

Bagwell, P. S., *Railwaymen: The History of The National Union of Railwaymen* (London, 1963).

Bell, A., 'A Glorious Lesson in Solidarity?: The Dundee Carters' Strike 1911' (unpublished dissertation, University of Dundee, 1999).

Bell, A., 'New Sources in Labour History', *Labour History*, 83, November 2002.

Bell, J., *We Did Not Fight* (London, 1935).

Bell, T., *Pioneering Days* (London, 1941).

Benson, J., *The Working Class in Britain, 1850–1939* (London, 1989).

Bonoski, B., *Brother Bill McKie, Building the Union at Ford* (New York, reissued 2000)

Brooksbank, M., *No Sae Lang Syne: A Tale of This City* (Dundee, 1968).

Broom, J., *John Maclean* (Loanhead, 1973).

Brotherstone, T., 'Does Red Clydeside Really Matter Anymore?', in R. Duncan and A. McIvor (eds), *Militant Workers: Labour and Class Conflict on the Clyde 1900–1950* (Edinburgh, 1992).

Brotherstone, T. and Witherington, D. J. (eds), *The City and Its Worlds: Aspects of Aberdeen's History since 1794* (Glasgow, 1996).

Brown, C., 'Religion and the Development of an Urban Society, Glasgow 1780 to 1914' (unpublished PhD thesis, University of Glasgow, 1981).

Brown, C., *The People and the Pew: Religion and Society in Scotland since 1780* (Dundee, 1993).

Brown, S. J., '"A Solemn Purification by Fire": Responses to the Great War in the Scottish Presbyterian Churches 1914–19', *Journal of Ecclesiastical History*, xlv (1994).

Buckley, K., *Trade Unionism in Aberdeen, 1878–1900* (Edinburgh, 1955).

Bull, P., *Land, Politics and Nationalism: A Study of the Irish Land Question* (Dublin, 1996).

Burgess, K., *The Challenge of Labour Shaping British Society, 1850–1930* (London, 1980).

Cage R. A. (ed.), *The Working Class in Glasgow, 1750–1914* (Glasgow, 1987).

Cameron, E., *Land Fit for People?: The British Government and the Scottish Highlands c. 1880–1914* (East Linton, 1996).

Campbell, R., *Scotland Since 1707: The Rise of an Industrial Society* (Edinburgh, 1992).

Cavanach, S. (ed), *Pumpherston. The Story of a Shale Oil Village* (Edinburgh, 2002).

Ceadel, M., 'Attitudes to War: Pacifism and Collective Security', in Paul Johnson (ed.), *20th Century Britain: Economic, Social and Cultural Change* (London, 1994).

Cesarani, D. and Romain, G. (eds), *Jews and Port Cities 1590–1990: Commerce, Community and Cosmopolitanism*, 'Special Issue' *Journal of Jewish Culture and History*, vol. 7, nos. 1–2, Summer/Autumn 2004.

Challinor, R., *The Origins of British Bolshevism* (London, 1977).

Charlesworth, A. (et al.), *An Atlas of Industrial Protest in Britain 1750–1990* (Basingstoke, 1996).

Church, R., 'Edwardian Labour Unrest and Coalfield Militancy, 1890–1914', *Historical Journal*, 30, 4 (1987).

Clegg, H., *A History of British Trade Unionism*, vol. II, *1911–1933* (London, 1985).

Coates, K. and Topham, T., *The Making of the Transport and General Workers' Union 1870–1922*, vols I and II (Oxford, 1991).

Cole, G. D. H., *The World of Labour* (London, 1913).

Cornwall, M. and Frame, M. (eds), *Scotland and the Slavs: Cultures in Contact 1500–2000* (Newtonville, MA and Sankt-Peterburg, 2001).

Cronin, J. E. and Schneer, J. (eds), *Social Conflict and the Political Order in Modern Britain* (London, 1982).

Dangerfield, G., *The Strange Death of Liberal England* (London, 1997 edition, with *Foreword* by Peter Stansky [first published in New York, 1935]).

De Groot, G., *Blighty: Briitish Society in the Era of the Great War* (London and New York, 1996).

Devine T. M. (ed), *Irish Immigrants and Scottish Society in the Nineteenth and Twentieth Centuries* (Edinburgh, 1991).

Devine, T. M., *The Scottish Nation 1700–2000* (London, 1999).

Dewey, C., 'Celtic Agrarian Legislation and the Celtic Revival: Historicist Implications of Gladstone's Irish and Scottish Land Acts, 1870–1886, *Past and Present*, 64, 1974.

Dey, M., 'For the Rights of Labour; The Story of Aberdeen Trades Council', *Scottish Labour History Review*, 9, Winter 1995/Spring 1996.

Donnachie, I., 'Scottish Labour in the Depression: the 1930s', in Donnachie, I. (et al.), *Forward! Labour Politics in Scotland 1888–1999* (Edinburgh, 1989).

Donnachie, I., Harvie, C. and Woods, I. S (eds), *Forward! Labour Politics in Scotland 1888–1999* (Edinburgh, 1989).

Duffy, A. E. P., 'The Eight-Hour Day Movement in Britain, 1886–1893', *Manchester School of Economic Studies*, XXXVI, 1968.

Duncan, R., *James Leatham, 1865–1945: Portrait of a Socialist Pioneer* (Aberdeen, 1978).

Duncan, R. and McIvor, A. (eds), *Militant Workers: Labour and Class Conflict on the Clyde 1900–1950* (Edinburgh, 1992).

Duncan, R., 'Motherwell for Moscow: Walton Newbold, Revolutionary Politics and the Labour Movement in a Lanarkshire Constituency 1918–1922', *Scottish Labour History Society*, 28, 1993.

Duncan, R., *The Mine Workers* (Edinburgh, 2005).

Finlay, R., *Modern Scotland, 1914–2000* (London, 2004).

Foster, J., 'Red Clyde, Red Scotland', in I. Donnachie and C. Whatley (eds), *The Manufacture of Scottish History* (Edinburgh, 1992).

Fraser, W. H., 'Trade Councils in the Labour Movement in Nineteenth Century Scotland', in I. MacDougall (ed.), *Essays in Scottish Labour History* (Edinburgh, 1978).

Fraser, W. H., *Trade Unions and Society: The Struggle for Acceptance, 1850–1880* (Aldershot, 1993).

Fraser, W. H., *A History of British Trade Unionism* (Basingstoke, 1999).

Fraser, W. H., *Scottish Popular Politics: From Radicalism to Labour* (Edinburgh, 2000).

Fraser, W. H. and Morris, R. J. (eds), *People and Society in Scotland,* vol. II, 1830–1914 (Edinburgh, 1990).

Gall, G., *The Political Economy of Scotland: Red Scotland? Radical Scotland?* (Cardiff, 2005).

Gallagher, T., 'The Catholic Irish in Scotland: In Search of Identity', in T. M. Devine (ed.) *Irish Immigrants and Scottish Society in the Nineteenth and Twentieth Centuries* (Edinburgh, 1991).

Gallagher, W., *Revolt on the Clyde* (London, 1936).

Gilbert, D., 'Industrial Protest: 1900–39', in A. Charlesworth (et al.), *An Atlas of Industrial Protest in Britain 1750–1990* (London, 1996).

Glasgow Labour History Workshop, *The Singer Strike Clydebank, 1911* (Glasgow, 1989).

Gore, V., 'Rank-and-File Dissent', in C. J. Wrigley (ed.), *A History of British Industrial Relations, 1875–1914* (Brighton, 1982).

Grassic Gibbon, L. and MacDiarmid, H., *Scottish Scene or The Intelligent Man's Guide to Albyn* (London, 1934).

Gray, J., *City in Revolt, James Larkin and the Belfast Dock Strike of 1907* (Dublin, 1985).

Harrison, R., 'The War Emergency Worker's National Committee 1914–1920', in A. Briggs and J. Saville (eds), *Essays in Labour History 1886–1923* (London, 1971).

Harvie, C., 'Before the Breakthrough, 1888–1922', in Donnachie, I. (et al.), *Forward! Labour Politics in Scotland 1888–1999* (Edinburgh, 1989).

Harvie, C., *Few Gods and Precious Few Heroes* (Edinburgh, 1993).

Hayes, D., *Conscription Conflict: The Conflict of Ideas in the Struggle for and against Military Conscription in Britain Between 1901 and 1939* (London, 1949).

Haynes, M., 'The British Working Class in Revolt, 1910–14', *International Socialism*, no. 22 (winter 1984).

Hinton, J., *Labour and Socialism* (London, 1983).

Hobsbawm, E., *Labouring Men* (London, 1968).

Holford, J., *Reshaping Labour: Organisation, Work and Politics – Edinburgh in the Great War and After* (London, 1988).

Holton, R. J., *British Syndicalism 1900–1914* (London, 1976).

Hughes, A. M., 'The Politics of the Kitchen and Dissenting Domestics, The ILP, Labour Women and the Female "Citizens" of Inter-war Clydeside', *Scottish Labour History*, 34, 1999.

Hunt, E. H., *Regional Wage Variations in Britain, 1850–1914* (London, 1973).

Hunt, E. H., *British Labour History* (London, 1981).

Hutchison, I. G. C., 'Scottish Politics', in C. M. M. MacDonald and E. McFarland (eds), *Scotland and the Great War* (East Linton, 1999).

Hyslop, J., 'Cape Town Highlanders, Transvaal Scottish: Military "Scottishness" and Social Power in Nineteenth and Twentieth Century South Africa', *South African Journal*, 47, November 2002, pp. 97–8.

Hyslop, J., *The Notorious Syndicalist J. T. Bain: A Scottish Rebel in Colonial South Africa* (Johannesburg, 2004).

Johnson, G., *Social Democratic Politics in Britain 1881–1911* (London, 2002).

Johnson, R., *Clydeside Capital 1870–1920: A Social History of Employers* (East Linton, 2000).

Kenefick, W., *The Key To the Clyde: With Particular Reference to the Ardrossan Dock Strike, 1912–1913* (Irvine, 1993).

Kenefick, W., 'A Struggle for Control: the Importance of the Great Unrest at Glasgow Harbour, 1911 to 1912', in W. Kenefick and A. McIvor (eds), *Roots of Red Clydeside 1910–1914: Labour Unrest and Industrial Relations in West Scotland* (Edinburgh, 1996).

Kenefick, W., 'Irish Dockers and Trade Unionism on Clydeside', *Irish Studies Review*, 19, 1997.

Kenefick, W., 'Vliianie Rossiiskoi revoliutsii 1917 goda na Aberdin I severnuiu Shotlandiiu', in V. I. Goldin (ed.), *Rossiia, 1917: vzgliad skvoz' gody*, (Arkhangel'sk, 1998). ['The Impact of the Russian Revolution in Aberdeen and the North of Scotland, in *Russian 1917: A View of that Year.*]

Kenefick, W., 'War Resisters and Anti-Conscription in Scotland: an ILP Perspective', in C. M. M. MacDonald and E. McFarland (eds), *Scotland and the Great War* (East Linton, 1999).

Kenefick, W., *Rebellious and Contrary: The Glasgow Dockers, 1853–1932* (East Linton, 2000).

Kenefick, W., ' "Aberdeen was More Red than Glasgow", The Impact of the First World War and the Russian Revolution beyond Red Clydeside', in M. Cornwall and M. Frame (eds), *Scotland and the Slavs: Cultures in Contact 1500–2000* (Newtonville, MA and Sangt-Peterburg, 2000).

Kenefick, W., 'Technological Change and Glasgow's Dock Labour Force, c

1860–1914', *International Journal of Maritime History*, Vol. XIII No. 2, December 2001.

Kenefick, W., 'Jewish and Catholic Irish Relations: The Glasgow Waterfront c. 1880–1914', in D. Cesarani and G. Romain (eds) *Jews and Port Cities 1590–1990: Commerce, Community and Cosmopolitanism*, 'Special Issue', *Journal of Jewish Culture and History*, vol. 7, nos. 1–2, Summer/Autumn 2004.

Kenefick, W., 'Transport Unions in Scotland from the Nineteenth Century to the Present', in Christopher Harvie and K. Veitch (eds), *Scottish Life and Society. A Compendium of Scottish Ethnology*, Vol. 8: Transport and Communications (Edinburgh, c. 2007).

Kenefick, W., 'Scottish Dock Trade Unionism, 1850 to present', in M. A. Mulhern, (ed.), *Scottish Life and Society, A Compendium of Scottish Ethnology*, vol. 7; Craft and Service: The Working Life of the Scots (Edinburgh, c. 2007).

Kenefick, W. and McIvor, A. (eds), *Roots of Red Clydeside 1910–1914: Labour Unrest and Industrial Relations in West Scotland* (Edinburgh, 1996).

Kirk, N., *Comrades and Cousins: Globalization, Workers, and Labour Movements in Britain, the USA, and Australia from the 1880s to 1914* (London, 2003).

Knox, W., 'The Politics and Workplace Culture of The Scottish Working Class, 1832–1914', in W. H. Fraser and R. J. Morris (eds), *People and Society in Scotland*, Vol. II, 1830–1914 (Edinburgh, 1990).

Knox, W., *Industrial Nation: Work, Culture and Society in Scotland, 1800–Present* (Edinburgh, 1999).

Laybourn, K., *A History of British Trade Unionism* (Stroud, 1997).

Lee, H. W. and Archbold, E., *Social-Democracy in Britain: Fifty Years of the Socialist Movement* (London, 1935).

Leng, P. J., *The Welsh Dockers* (Ormskirk, 1981).

Lichtenstein, N., *The Most Dangerous Man in Detroit: Walter Reuther and the Fate of American Labor* (New York, 1995).

Lovell, J., *Stevedores and Dockers* (London, 1969).

Lovell, J., 'Sail, Steam and Emergent Dockers' Unionism in Britain, 1850–1914', *IRSH*, xxxii, 3, 1987.

Lowe, D., *Souvenirs of Scottish Labour* (Glasgow, 1919).

Lynch, M., *Scotland: A New History* (London, 1991).

Lyon, H., *The History of the Scottish Horse and Motormen's Association* (Glasgow, 1919).

McCrone, D. and Elliot, B., 'The Decline of Landlordism', in R. Rodger (ed.), *Scottish Housing in the Twentieth Century* (Leicester, 1989).

MacDonald, C. M. M., *The Radical Thread: Political Change in Scotland. Paisley Politics, 1885–1924* (East Linton, 2000).

MacDonald, C. M. M. and McFarland, E. (eds), *Scotland and the Great War* (East Linton, 1999).

MacDougall, I. (ed.), *Essays in Scottish Labour History* (Edinburgh, 1978).

MacDougall, I., *A Catalogue of some Labour Records in Scotland* (Edinburgh, 1978).

MacDougall, I., *Militant Miners: Recollections of John McArthur, Buckhaven; and Letters, 1924–1926, of David Proudfoot, Methil to G. Allen Hunt* (Edinburgh, East Linton, 1981).

MacDougall, I., *'Hard Work, Ye Ken': Midlothian Women Farmworkers* (East Linton, 1993).

MacDougall, I., *Voices from Home and Work* (Edinburgh, 2000).

MacDougall, I. (ed.), *Mid and East Lothian Miners' Association Minutes, 1894–1918* (Edinburgh, 2003).

MacIntyre, S., *Little Moscows: Communism and Working-Class Militancy in Inter-War Britain* (London, 1980).

McIvor, A., 'Were Clydeside Employers More Autocratic?: Labour Management and the "Labour Unrest", c. 1910–1914', in W. Kenefick and A. McIvor, *Roots of Red Clydeside 1910–1914: Labour Unrest and Industrial Relations in West Scotland* (Edinburgh, 1996).

McIvor, A., 'The Rise of the British Labour Movement, c1850–1939', in W. B. Wurthmann (ed.), *Britain, 1850–1979, Politics and Social Change* (Glasgow, 1995).

McIvor, A., 'Red Dawn Fades', in Scotland on Sunday, *The History of a Nation: 300 Years of a Scottish Nation*, Part 5, War and Upheaval 1914–1945 (Edinburgh, 1999).

McKay, J. H., 'A Social History of the Scottish Shale Mining Community' (unpublished PhD thesis, Open University, 1984).

McKinlay, A., 'Philosophers in Overalls? Craft and Class on Clydeside, c. 1900–1914', in W. Kenefick and A. McIvor, *Roots of Red Clydeside, Labour Unrest and Industrial Relations in West Scotland* (Edinburgh, 1996).

McKinlay, A., and Smyth, J. J., 'The End of "the Agitator Workman": 1926–1932', in A. McKinlay and R. J Morris (eds), *The ILP on Clydeside 1893–1932: from Foundation to Disintegration* (Manchester, 1991).

McLean, I., *The Legend of Red Clydeside* (Edinburgh, 1999).

McNair, John, *James Maxton 1885–1946: An Appreciation with a Number of Tributes* (London, 1946).

Manson, J., 'Grassic Gibbon's Glasgow, *Scottish Labour History Review*, 10, Winter 1996/Spring 1997.

Manton, K., 'The Fellowship of the New Life: English Ethical Socialism Reconsidered', *History of Political Thought*, vol. XXIV, 2, Summer 2003.

Marwick, A., *The Deluge: British Society and the First World War* (Basingstoke, 1991).

Marwick, W. H., 'Early Trade Unionism in Scotland', *Economic History Review*, 2, 1935.

Marwick, W. H., *A Short History of Trade Unionism in Scotland* (Edinburgh, 1967).

Marwick, W. H., 'Conscientious Objection in Scotland in the First World War', *Scottish Journal of Science* I (June 1972).

Mavor, J., *The Scottish Railway Strike 1891, A History and Criticism* (Edinburgh, 1891).

Mavor, J., *My Window on the Street of the World*, vol. 1 (London, 1923).

Maxton, J., 'War Resistance By Working Class Struggle', in Julian Bell (ed.) *We Did Not Fight* (London, 1935).

Melling, J., 'Clydeside Rent Struggles and the Making of Labour Politics in Scotland, 1900–39', in R. Rodger (ed.), *Scottish Housing in the Twentieth Century* (Leicester, 1989).

Milton, N., *John Maclean* (London, 1973).

Morris, R. J., 'The ILP, 1893–1932', in A. McKinlay and R. J. Morris (eds), *The ILP on Clydeside 1893–1932: From Foundation to Disintegration* (Manchester, 1991).

Morris, R. J. (et al.), *Atlas of Industrialising Britain, 1780–1914* (London, 1986).

Mortimer, J., 'The Formation of the Labour Party – Lessons for Today', *Socialist History Society*, Socialist History Occasional Papers Series, no. 10, 2000.

O'Day, A., *The Edwardian Age: Conflict and Stability, 1900–1914* (London, 1979).

Pelling, H., *A History of British Trade Unionism* (London, 1992).

Petrie, A., 'The 1915 Dundee Rent Strike' (unpublished dissertation, University of Dundee, 1999).

Phipps, C. W. M., 'Aberdeen Trades Council and Politics 1900–1939': The Development of the Local Labour Party in Aberdeen' (unpublished Master of Letters dissertation, University of Aberdeen, 1890).

Powell, L. H., *The Shipping Federation: The First Sixty Years 1890–1950* (London, 1950).

Price, R., *Masters, Unions and Men* (London, 1980).

Price, R., *Labour in British Society* (London, 1986).

Quelch, H., *Trade Unionism, Co-operation and Social Democracy* (London, 1892).

Rae, J., *Conscience and Politics: The British Government and the Conscientious Objectors to Military Service, 1916–1919* (Oxford, 1970).

Rafeek, N., 'Radicalism Continued 1919–1945: Where did Women in the Communist Party Learn their Socialist Politics? An Oral History', (unpublished PhD thesis, University of Strathclyde, 1998).

Rodgers, M., 'The Glasgow Jewry', in B. Kay (ed.), *The Complete Odyssey: Voices From Scotland's Recent Past* (Edinburgh, 1996).

Rodgers, M., 'The Lanarkshire Lithuanians', in B. Kay (ed.), *The Complete Odyssey: Voices from Scotland's Recent Past* (Edinburgh, 1996).

Rodgers, R., 'Crisis and Confrontation in Scottish Housing, 1880–1914', in R. Rodgers (ed.) *Scottish Housing in the Twentieth Century* (Leicester, 1989).

Rodgers, R. (ed.), *Scottish Housing in the Twentieth Century* (Leicester, 1989).

Saunders, D., 'The 1905 Revolution on Tyneside', in A. Heywood and J. Smele (eds), *The Russian Revolution of 1905: Centenary Perspectives* (London, 2005).

Saunders, D., 'A Russian Babel Revisited: The Individuality of Heinrich Matthaus Fischer (1871–1935)', *Slavonic and East European Review*, 2004, 82, (3).

Smout, T. C., *A Century of the Scottish People, 1830–1950* (London, 1986).

Smyth, J. J., *Labour in Glasgow 1896–1936: Socialism, Suffrage, Sectarianism* (East Linton, 2000).

Southall, H., 'The Revolt of the Field, 1872–74', and 'The Nine-hours Movement of 1871', in A. Charlesworth (et al.), *An Atlas of Industrial Protest in Britain 1750–1990* (Basingstoke, 1996).

Stevenson, J., *British Society 1914–45* (Harmondsworth, 1990).

Stewart, B., *Breaking The Fetters: The Memoirs of Bob Stewart* (London, 1967).

Taplin, E., *The Dockers Union: A Study of the National Union of Dock Labourers* (Leicester, 1986).

Taylor, A. J. P., *English History, 1914 to 1945* (London, 1981).

Thatcher, I., 'Representations of Scotland in Nache Slova during the First World War', in M. Cornwall and M. Frame (eds), *Scotland and the Slavs: Cultures in Contact 1500–2000* (Newtonville, MA and Sangt-Petersburg, 2000).

Thomas, C., 'How the Labour Party was Formed', *Socialism Today*, 45, February 2000 (online edn).

Ticktin, D., 'The Origins of the South African Labour Party, 1888–1910' (unpublished PhD thesis, University of Cape Town, South Africa, 1976).

Treble, H., 'Unemployment in Glasgow: Anatomy of a Crisis', *Scottish Labour History Society Journal* 29, 1990.

Trotsky, L., *Where is Britain Going?* (London, 1926).

Tuckett, A., *The Scottish Carter: History of the Scottish Horse and Motormen*, (London, 1967).

Wallace, M., *Single or Return: the History of the Transport Salaried Staff Association* (London, 1996).

Webb, S. and Webb, B., *Industrial Democracy* (London, 1897).

White, J., '1910–1914 Reconsidered', in J. E. Cronin and J. Schneer (eds), *Social Conflict and the Political Order in Modern Britain* (London, 1982).

Wood, I. S., 'Hope Deferred: Labour in Scotland in the 1920s', in I. Donnachie (et al.), *Forward! Labour Politics in Scotland 1888–1999* (Edinburgh, 1989).

Young, D. R., 'Voluntary Recruitment in Scotland, 1914–1916' (unpublished PhD thesis, Glasgow University, 2001).

Young, J. D., *The Rousing of the Scottish Working Class* (London, 1979).

Young, J. D., *John Maclean: Educator of the Working Class* (Glasgow, 1988).

ARCHIVES, REPORTS, PARLIAMENTARY PAPERS AND WEBSITES

Railway Servants Hours of labour: Report from the Select Committee; Proceedings, minutes of evidence, appendix and index, 1891 (1890–91), vols xiv–xvi, p. 681 [Sessional Papers no. 342].

Royal Commission on Labour on Labour, 2nd Report, 1892, Group B, Minutes of Evidence ii, William Hannay Raeburn Q. 13,417 [C. 6795-II, 1892, xxxvi, pt III].
Aberdeen Trades Council, Minutes, 1890–1932.
Glasgow Trades Council, *Annual Reports*, 1889–1914.
Edinburgh Trades and Labour Council, Minutes, 1920.

Board of Trade, *Report on Trade Unions in 1899 with Comparative Statistics for 1892–1898 (British Parliamentary Papers (BPP))*, Cd. 422.

McKie Papers, Nat Ganley Collection, Archives of Labour and Urban Affairs, Wayne State University: Box 33.

Jute and Flax Workers' Committee, Minutes, Dundee City Archives; GD/JF/1/7.

Scottish Trades Union Congress, *Annual Report of Proceedings*; delegates list and societies and numbers represented – 1900 to 1914.

The Voice of Radicalism: Socialism 1850–1900; Historic Collections – DISS – University of Aberdeen [www.abdn.ac.uk/radicalism/socialism1850/].

CPGB online – www.cpgb.org.uk/ourhistory/index/.html

Russian Centre for the Preservation and Study of Documents of Recent History (RTsKhIDNI), f. 495, op. 100.
RTsKhIDNI, f .495, op. 100, d. 10 – Sylvia Pankhurst to Sub-Committee of the Third International, Moscow, 31 January 1920.
RTsKhIDNI, f. 495, op. 100, d. 10 – Walton Newbold to Sub-Committee of the Third International, 5 March 1920.
RTsKhIDNI, f. 495, op. 100, d. 10 – Walton Newbold to Comintern, Moscow, 5 March 1920.
RTsKhIDNI, f. 495, op. 100, d. 10 – Shapurgi Saklatvala, in London, to Sub-Committee of the Third International, March 1920.
RTsKhIDNI, f. 495, op. 100, d. 9 – 'Notes on the Observations of the Working Class Movement in Great Britain' [Marked 'Not for publication'], by J. T. Murphy, 28 March 1920.
RTsKhIDNI, f. 495, op. 100, d. 10 – Walton Newbold, in Moscow, to Sub-Committee of the Third International, 6 June 1920.
RTsKhIDNI), f. 495, op. 100, d. 17 – Letter from William Leslie to Sub-

Committee of the Third International, Moscow, 29 July 1920.

RTsKhIDNI, f. 495, op. 100, d. 10 (correspondence of Helen Crawfurd written in Moscow, August 1920.

RTsKhIDNI, f. 495, op. 100, d. 55 – 'Note of contest at Dundee', report by Tom Bell to Politburo, Moscow, November 1922.

RTsKhIDNI, f. 495, op. 100, d. 62 – Report by James Gardner, Communist Party election agent for Dundee, November 1922.

Arkivverket, Statsarkivet I Bergen (Regional State Archives, Bergen, Norway), 'Espionage Reports, Closed Files 1/11–31/12–1920.

NEWSPAPERS AND PERIODICALS

The Aberdeen Daily Journal
Aberdeen Evening Express
Aberdeen Free Press
Aberdeen Weekly Journal
Berwickshire News
Dundee Courier
Daily Record
Forward
Edinburgh Evening Dispatch
Edinburgh Evening News
The Engineer
The Glasgow Herald
Labour Leader
Leven Advertiser and Wemyss Gazette
North British Daily Mail
The Northern Scot, and Moray and Nairn Express
The Scotsman
Sutherland Echo

Index